Snapshot Prediction Using
Yogini Dasha

V.P. Goel

Published by:

Sagar Publications
72, Janpath, Ved Mansion
New Delhi-110001
Tel.: 23320648, 23328245
E-mail: s.sagarpublications@gmail.com
Website: www.sagarpublications.com

First edition, 2013
Second revised edition, 2016
Reprint, 2019

© V.P. Goel
E-mail: vinodpgoel@rediffmail.com

Published and Printed by:
Saurabh Sagar for **Sagar Publications** New Delhi-110001

Printed at:
The Artwaves, New Delhi-110019, Telfax.: 41609709;
E-mail: theartwaves@gmail.com

Dedication

This book is dedicated to
my father late shri M.L. Goel and
my mother late smt. Prabha Goel

Preface

Dasha system of hindu astrology is a unique system for timing of events. Yogini dasha is a prime dasha having universal application. It is not commonly used as the correct method of interpretation is hot known. This is now presented in this book.

Interpretation of dasha results is normally a complex process and needs years of experience. A snapshot method has been explained and the results are seen quickly even by a beginner of astrology.

My thanks to Mr. Narender Sagar for constantly pursuing me for writing this book.

Ram Navmi
19 Apr., 2013

V.P. Goel
E-mail: vinodpgoel@rediffmail.com

Contents

Chapter 1

Classic

Sage Parashar states that "Now I explain Yogini dasha as enunciated by Lord Mahadeva". Such is the importance of Yogini dasha.

Yogini dasha has universal application and is applicable on all horoscopes.

The total period of one cycle of Yogini is of thirty six years and there are eight yoginis in one cycle. Compared to Vimshottari dasha having 120 years in one cycle, Yogini is more condensed and gives timing of shorter duration. Small errors in the longitude of Moon will not make much difference in yogini dasha balance.

Yogini dasha is a planetary dasha and is based on the Nakshatra occupied by Moon in the birth chart.

The yogini dasha comprises of eight yoginis dasha periods. These are Mangla, Pingla, Dhanya, Bhramari, Bhadrika, Ulka, Siddha and Sankata. These dasha periods are lorded by eight planets which are Moon, Sun, Jupiter, Mars, Mercury, Saturn, Venus and Rahu respectively. Ketu is not taken into consideration. Normally while reading Sankata we can take the Rahu/Ketu axis. The dasha period of each yogini is from one year to eight years. Starting from Mangla with one year and increasing by one year for the next yogini. These yoginis repeat in the same sequence and is now tabulated in table 1.

Table 1

S. No.	Name of Yogini	Lord	Dasha\ Period Years
1	Mangla	Moon	One
2	Pingla	Sun	Two
3	Dhanya	Jupiter	Three
4	Bhramari	Mars	Four
5	Bhadrika	Mercury	Five
6	Ulka	Saturn	Six
7	Siddha	Venus	Seven
8	Sankata	Rahu	Eight

The dasha period of benefic planets totals to 16 years and of malefics planets is 20 years. This is the ratio of good and bad Dasha granted naturally by the creator.

Calculation of Birth Nakshatra

Zodiac is divided in 27 Nakshatra having equal span (excluding Abhijit which do not figure in yogini calculations). Each Nakshatra span is 13° - 20′ or 800 minutes. One Nakshatra contribute one yogini dasha. It is, therefore, necessary to know the birth Nakshatra occupied by Moon.

1. Convert the longitude of Moon into minutes (including sign).

2. Divide this by 800.

3. The quotient is the number of Nakshatra already covered by Moon. The remainder is the portion of Nakshatra covered in the Nakshatra occupied.

4. Add one to the quotient to get the Nakshatra occupied by Moon.

Example:

Moon is placed in Scorpio 10° − 48′ in the birth horoscope. Date of birth is 22 December, 1973.

1.   The longitude converted into minutes is 13248.

2.   After dividing by 800 we get 16.56.

3.   Sixteen Nakshatra have passed. Moon has covered 0.56 of the seventeenth Nakshatra.

4.   Moon is placed in 17th Nakshatra i.e. Anuradha.

Yogini Dasha at birth

To get the Yogini Dasha at birth, follow the method given.

1.   Work out the number of Nakshatra occupied by Moon at birth. Ashwani Is 1 and Revati is 27.

2.   Add 3 in the Nakshatra number.

3.   Expunge multiplies of 8 from the sum so arrived till the remainder is 8 or less than 8.

4.   The remainder is the number of Yogini Dasha at birth (Table 1). The corresponding Yogini is the Yogini Dasha at birth. The first Yogini Dasha Mangla belongs to Ardra Nakshatra and as such three is added to the Nakshatra number.

Example:

We had worked the birth Nakshatra 17th i.e. Anuradha.

1.   Add 3 to 17 to get 20

2.   Expunge multiplies of 8 i.e. 16 and we get remainder as 4.

3.   The fourth Yogini Dasha is of Bhramari and is the Dasha at birth.

Dasha balance at birth

Each Yogini Dasha is of one Nakshatra. Therefore, the balance of Yogini Dasha is proportional to the balance of the Nakshatra yet to be covered by Moon at birth.

While working to find the Nakshatra at birth, we divided the longitude of Moon (in minutes) by 800. We got the Nakshatra covered by Moon and some fraction. This fraction or the part after decimal is the portion of the Nakshatra covered. Deduct this fraction from 1 to get the portion of Nakshatra yet to be covered.

We have worked out the Yogini Dasha at birth. So the portion yet to be covered is the proportional part of the Yogini Dasha. Multiply this portion by the full dasha period of Yogini at birth to get the Dasha balance at birth.

Example:

We had worked the birth Nakshatra 17th i.e. Anuradha.

1. After dividing by 800 we got 16.56. The Nakshatra at birth is 17th.

2. The 0.56 part of 17th Nakshatra is already covered.

3. Deduct 0.56 from 1 and we get 0.44 as the balance of Nakshatra of Moon.

4. The Yogini Dasha is of Bhramari at birth. Bhramari full dasha is of 4 years. Multiply 0.44 by 4 to get the balance of Bhramari dasha at birth. It works out to 1.76 years or 1 year 9 months 4 days.

A ready table for balance of Yogini Dasha based on Longitude of Moon is given.

Table 2

Long. Moon	Dasha Balance	Long. Moon	Dasha Balance
Deg. Min.	Yr. Mo. Day	Deg. Min.	Yr. Mo. Day
Aries 00 – 00	Bhramari 04 – 00 – 00	Taurus 00 – 00	Ulka 04 – 06 – 00
00 – 40	03 – 09 – 18	00 – 40	04 – 02 – 12
01 – 20	03 – 07 – 06	01 – 20	03 – 10 – 24
02 – 00	03 – 04 – 24	02 – 00	03 – 07 – 06
02 – 40	03 – 02 – 12	02 – 40	03 – 03 – 18
03 – 20	03 – 00 – 00	03 – 20	03 – 00 – 00
04 – 00	02 – 09 – 18	04 – 00	02 – 08 – 12
04 – 40	02 – 07 – 06	04 – 40	02 – 04 – 24
05 – 20	02 – 04 – 24	05 – 20	02 – 01 – 06

06 – 00	02 – 02 – 12	06 – 00	01 – 09 – 18
06 – 40	02 – 00 – 00	06 – 40	01 – 06 – 00
07 – 20	01 – 09 – 18	07 – 20	01 – 02 – 12
08 – 00	01 – 07 – 06	08 – 00	00 – 10 – 24
08 – 40	01 – 04 – 24	08 – 40	00 – 07 – 06
09 – 20	01 – 02 – 12	09 – 20	00 – 03 – 18
10 – 00	01 – 00 – 00	10 – 00	Siddha 07 – 00 – 00
10 – 40	00 – 09 – 18	10 – 40	06 – 07 – 24
11 – 20	00 – 07 – 06	11 – 20	06 – 03 – 18
12 – 00	00 – 04 – 24	12 – 00	05 – 11 – 12
12 – 40	00 – 02 – 12	12 – 40	05 – 07 – 06
13 – 20	Bhadrika 05 – 00 – 00	13 – 20	05 – 03 – 00
14 – 00	04 – 09 – 00	14 – 00	04 – 10 – 24
14 – 40	04 – 06 – 00	14 – 40	04 – 06 – 18
15 – 20	04 – 03 – 00	15 – 20	04 – 02 – 12
16 – 00	04 – 00 – 00	16 – 00	03 – 10 – 06
16 – 40	03 – 09 – 00	16 – 40	03 – 06 – 00
17 – 20	03 – 06 – 00	17 – 20	03 – 01 – 24
18 – 00	03 – 03 – 00	18 – 00	02 – 09 – 18
18 – 40	03 – 00 – 00	18 – 40	02 – 05 – 12
19 – 20	02 – 09 – 00	19 – 20	02 – 01 – 06
20 – 00	02 – 06 – 00	20 – 00	01 – 09 – 00
20 – 40	02 – 03 – 00	20 – 40	01 – 04 – 24
21 – 20	02 – 00 – 00	21 – 20	01 – 01 – 18
22 – 00	01 – 09 – 00	22 – 00	00 – 08 – 12
22 – 40	01 – 06 – 00	22 – 40	00 – 04 – 06
23 – 20	01 – 03 – 00	23 – 20	Sankata 08 – 00 – 00
24 – 00	01 – 00 – 00	24 – 00	07 – 07 – 06

24 – 40	00 – 09 – 00	24 – 40	07 – 02 – 12
25 – 20	00 – 06 – 00	25 – 20	06 – 09 – 18
26 – 00	00 – 03 – 00	26 – 00	06 – 04 – 24
26 – 40	Ulka 06 – 00 – 00	26 – 40	06 – 00 – 00
27 – 20	05 – 08 – 12	27 – 20	05 – 07 – 06
28 – 00	05 – 04 – 24	28 – 00	05 – 02 – 12
28 – 40	05 – 01 – 06	28 – 40	04 – 09 – 18
29 – 20	04 – 09 – 18	29 – 20	04 – 04 – 24
Gemini 00 – 00	Sankata 04 – 00 – 00	Cancer 00 – 00	Pingla 00 – 06 – 00
00 – 40	03 – 07 – 06	00 – 40	00 – 04 – 24
01 – 20	03 – 02 – 12	01 – 20	00 – 03 – 18
02 – 00	02 – 09 – 18	02 – 00	00 – 02 – 12
02 – 40	02 – 04 – 24	02 – 40	00 – 01 – 06
03 – 20	02 – 00 – 00	03 – 20	Dhanya 03 – 00 – 00
04 – 00	01 – 07 – 06	04 – 00	02 – 10 – 06
04 – 40	01 – 02 – 12	04 – 40	02 – 08 – 12
05 – 20	00 – 09 – 18	05 – 20	02 – 06 – 18
06 – 00	00 – 04 – 24	06 – 00	02 – 04 – 24
06 – 40	Mangla 01 – 00 – 00	06 – 40	02 – 03 – 00
07 – 20	00 – 11 – 12	07 – 20	02 – 01 – 06
08 – 00	00 – 10 – 24	08 – 00	01 – 11 – 12
08 – 40	00 – 10 – 06	08 – 40	01 – 09 – 18
09 – 20	00 – 09 – 18	09 – 20	01 – 07 – 24
10 – 00	00 – 09 – 00	10 – 00	01 – 06 – 00
10 – 40	00 – 08 – 12	10 – 40	01 – 04 – 06
11 – 20	00 – 07 – 24	11 – 20	01 – 02 – 12
12 – 00	00 – 07 – 06	12 – 00	01 – 00 – 18

12 – 40	00 – 06 – 18	12 – 40	00 – 10 – 24
13 – 20	00 – 06 – 00	13 – 20	00 – 09 – 00
14 – 00	00 – 05 – 12	14 – 00	00 – 07 – 06
14 – 40	00 – 04 – 24	14 – 40	00 – 05 – 12
15 – 20	00 – 04 – 06	15 – 20	00 – 03 – 18
16 – 00	00 – 03 – 18	16 – 00	00 – 01 – 24
16 – 40	00 – 03 – 00	16 – 40	Bharamari 04 – 00 – 00
17 – 20	00 – 02 – 12	17 – 20	03 – 09 – 18
18 – 00	00 – 01 – 24	18 – 00	03 – 07 – 06
18 – 40	00 – 01 – 06	18 – 40	03 – 04 – 24
19 – 20	00 – 00 – 18	19 – 20	03 – 02 – 12
20 – 00	Pingla 02 – 00 – 00	20 – 00	03 – 00 – 00
20 – 40	01 – 10 – 24	20 – 40	02 – 09 – 18
21 – 20	01 – 09 – 18	21 – 20	02 – 07 – 06
22 – 00	01 – 08 – 12	22 – 00	02 – 04 – 24
22 – 40	01 – 07 – 06	22 – 40	02 – 02 – 12
23 – 20	01 – 06 – 00	23 – 20	02 – 00 – 00
24 – 00	01 – 04 – 24	24 – 00	01 – 09 – 18
24 – 40	01 – 03 – 18	24 – 40	01 – 07 – 06
25 – 20	01 – 02 – 12	25 – 20	01 – 04 – 24
26 – 00	01 – 01 – 06	26 – 00	01 – 02 – 12
26 – 40	01 – 00 – 00	26 – 40	01 – 00 – 00
27 – 20	00 – 10 – 24	27 – 20	00 – 09 – 18
28 – 00	00 – 09 – 18	28 – 00	00 – 07 – 06
28 – 40	00 – 08 – 12	28 – 40	00 – 04 – 24
29 – 20	00 – 07 – 06	29 – 20	00 – 02 – 12
Leo 00 – 00	Bhadrika 05 – 00 – 00	Virgo 00 – 00	Siddha 05 – 03 – 00
00 – 40	04 – 09 – 00	00 – 40	04 – 10 – 24

01 – 20	04 – 06 – 00	01 – 20	04 – 06 – 18
02 – 00	04 – 03 – 00	02 – 00	04 – 02 – 12
02 – 40	04 – 00 – 00	02 – 40	03 – 10 – 06
03 – 20	03 – 09 – 00	03 – 20	03 – 06 – 00
04 – 00	03 – 06 – 00	04 – 00	03 – 01 – 24
04 – 40	03 – 03 – 00	04 – 40	02 – 09 – 18
05 – 20	03 – 00 – 00	05 – 20	02 – 05 – 12
06 – 00	02 – 09 – 00	06 – 00	02 – 01 – 06
06 – 40	02 – 06 – 00	06 – 40	01 – 09 – 00
07 – 20	02 – 03 – 00	07 – 20	01 – 04 – 24
08 – 00	02 – 00 – 00	08 – 00	01 – 01 – 18
08 – 40	01 – 09 – 00	08 – 40	00 – 08 – 12
09 – 20	01 – 06 – 00	09 – 20	00 – 04 – 06
10 – 00	01 – 03 – 00	10 – 00	Sankata 08 – 00 – 00
10 – 40	01 – 00 – 00	10 – 40	07 – 07 – 06
11 – 20	00 – 09 – 00	11 – 20	07 – 02 – 12
12 – 00	00 – 06 – 00	12 – 00	06 – 09 – 18
12 – 40	00 – 03 – 00	12 – 40	06 – 04 – 24
13 – 20	Ulka 06 – 00 – 00	13 – 20	06 – 00 – 00
14 – 00	05 – 08 – 12	14 – 00	05 – 07 – 06
14 – 40	05 – 04 – 24	14 – 40	05 – 02 – 12
15 – 20	05 – 01 – 06	15 – 20	04 – 09 – 18
16 – 00	04 – 09 – 18	16 – 00	04 – 04 – 24
16 – 40	04 – 06 – 00	16 – 40	04 – 00 – 00
17 – 20	04 – 02 – 12	17 – 20	03 – 07 – 06
18 – 00	03 – 10 – 24	18 – 00	03 – 02 – 12
18 – 40	03 – 07 – 06	18 – 40	02 – 09 – 18
19 – 20	03 – 03 – 18	19 – 20	02 – 04 – 24
20 – 00	03 – 00 – 00	20 – 00	02 – 00 – 00

20 – 40	02 – 08 – 12	20 – 40	01 – 07 – 06
21 – 20	02 – 04 – 24	21 – 20	01 – 02 – 12
22 – 00	02 – 01 – 06	22 – 00	00 – 09 – 18
22 – 40	01 – 09 – 18	22 – 40	00 – 04 – 24
23 – 20	01 – 06 – 00	23 – 20	Mangla 01 – 00 – 00
24 – 00	01 – 02 – 12	24 – 00	00 – 11 – 12
24 – 40	00 – 10 – 24	24 – 40	00 – 10 – 24
25 – 20	00 – 07 – 06	25 – 20	00 – 10 – 06
26 – 00	00 – 03 – 18	26 – 00	00 – 09 – 18
26 – 40	Siddha 07 – 00 – 00	26 – 40	00 – 09 – 00
27 – 20	06 – 07 – 24	27 – 20	00 – 08 – 12
28 – 00	06 – 03 – 18	28 – 00	00 – 07 – 24
28 – 40	05 – 11 – 12	28 – 40	00 – 07 – 06
29 – 20	05 – 07 – 06	29 – 20	00 – 06 – 18
Libra 00 – 00	Mangla 00 – 06 – 00	Scorpio 00 – 00	Dhanya 00 – 09 – 00
00 – 40	00 – 05 – 12	00 – 40	00 – 07 – 06
01 – 20	00 – 04 – 24	01 – 20	00 – 05 – 12
02 – 00	00 – 04 – 06	02 – 00	00 – 03 – 18
02 – 40	00 – 03 – 18	02 – 40	00 – 01 – 24
03 – 20	00 – 03 – 00	03 – 20	Bharamari 04 – 00 – 00
04 – 00	00 – 02 – 12	04 – 00	03 – 09 – 18
04 – 40	00 – 01 – 24	04 – 40	03 – 07 – 06
05 – 20	00 – 01 – 06	05 – 20	03 – 04 – 24
06 – 00	00 – 00 – 18	06 – 00	03 – 02 – 12
06 – 40	Pingla 02 – 00 – 00	06 – 40	03 – 00 – 00
07 – 20	01 – 10 – 24	07 – 20	02 – 09 – 18

08 – 00	01 – 09 – 18	08 – 00	02 – 07 – 06
08 – 40	01 – 08 – 12	08 – 40	02 – 04 – 24
09 – 20	01 – 07 – 06	09 – 20	02 – 02 – 12
10 – 00	01 – 06 – 00	10 – 00	02 – 00 – 00
10 – 40	01 – 04 – 24	10 – 40	01 – 09 – 18
11 – 20	01 – 03 – 18	11 – 20	01 – 07 – 06
12 – 00	01 – 02 – 12	12 – 00	01 – 04 – 24
12 – 40	01 – 01 – 06	12 – 40	01 – 02 – 12
13 – 20	01 – 00 – 00	13 – 20	01 – 00 – 00
14 – 00	00 – 10 – 24	14 – 00	00 – 09 – 18
14 – 40	00 – 09 – 18	14 – 40	00 – 07 – 06
15 – 20	00 – 08 – 12	15 – 20	00 – 04 – 24
16 – 00	00 – 07 – 06	16 – 00	00 – 02 – 12
16 – 40	00 – 06 – 00	16 – 40	Bhadrika 05 – 00 – 00
17 – 20	00 – 04 – 24	17 – 20	04 – 09 – 00
18 – 00	00 – 03 – 18	18 – 00	04 – 06 – 00
18 – 40	00 – 02 – 12	18 – 40	04 – 03 – 00
19 – 20	00 – 01 – 06	19 – 20	04 – 00 – 00
20 – 00	Dhanya 03 – 00 – 00	20 – 00	03 – 09 – 00
20 – 40	02 – 10 – 06	20 – 40	03 – 06 – 00
21 – 20	02 – 08 – 12	21 – 20	03 – 03 – 00
22 – 00	02 – 06 – 18	22 – 00	03 – 00 – 00
22 – 40	02 – 04 – 24	22 – 40	02 – 09 – 00
23 – 20	02 – 03 – 00	23 – 20	02 – 06 – 00
24 – 00	02 – 01 – 06	24 – 00	02 – 03 – 00
24 – 40	01 – 11 – 12	24 – 40	02 – 00 – 00
25 – 20	01 – 09 – 18	25 – 20	01 – 09 – 00
26 – 00	01 – 07 – 24	26 – 00	01 – 06 – 00
26 – 40	01 – 06 – 00	26 – 40	01 – 03 – 00

27 – 20	01 – 04 – 06	27 – 20	01 – 00 – 00
28 – 00	01 – 02 – 12	28 – 00	00 – 09 – 00
28 – 40	01 – 00 – 18	28 – 40	00 – 06 – 00
29 – 20	00 – 10 – 24	29 – 20	00 – 03 – 00
Sagittarius 00 – 00	Ulka 06 – 00 – 00	Capricorn 00 – 00	Sankata 06 – 00 – 00
00 – 40	05 – 08 – 12	00 – 40	05 – 07 – 06
01 – 20	05 – 04 – 24	01 – 20	05 – 02 – 12
02 – 00	05 – 01 – 06	02 – 00	04 – 09 – 18
02 – 40	04 – 09 – 18	02 – 40	04 – 04 – 24
03 – 20	04 – 06 – 00	03 – 20	04 – 00 – 00
04 – 00	04 – 02 – 12	04 – 00	03 – 07 – 06
04 – 40	03 – 10 – 24	04 – 40	03 – 02 – 12
05 – 20	03 – 07 – 06	05 – 20	02 – 09 – 18
06 – 00	03 – 03 – 18	06 – 00	02 – 04 – 24
06 – 40	03 – 00 – 00	06 – 40	02 – 00 – 00
07 – 20	02 – 08 – 12	07 – 20	01 – 07 – 06
08 – 00	02 – 04 – 24	08 – 00	01 – 02 – 12
08 – 40	02 – 01 – 06	08 – 40	00 – 09 – 18
09 – 20	01 – 09 – 18	09 – 20	00 – 04 – 24
10 – 00	01 – 06 – 00	10 – 00	Mangla 01 – 00 – 00
10 – 40	01 – 02 – 12	10 – 40	00 – 11 – 12
11 – 20	00 – 10 – 24	11 – 20	00 – 10 – 24
12 – 00	00 – 07 – 06	12 – 00	00 – 10 – 06
12 – 40	00 – 03 – 18	12 – 40	00 – 09 – 18
13 – 20	Siddha 07 – 00 – 00	13 – 20	00 – 09 – 00
14 – 00	06 – 07 – 24	14 – 00	00 – 08 – 12
14 – 40	06 – 03 – 18	14 – 40	00 – 07 – 24
15 – 20	05 – 11 – 12	15 – 20	00 – 07 – 06

16 – 00	05 – 07 – 06	16 – 00	00 – 06 – 18
16 – 40	05 – 03 – 00	16 – 40	00 – 06 – 00
17 – 20	04 – 10 – 24	17 – 20	00 – 05 – 12
18 – 00	04 – 06 – 18	18 – 00	00 – 04 – 24
18 – 40	04 – 02 – 12	18 – 40	00 – 04 – 06
19 – 20	03 – 10 – 06	19 – 20	00 – 03 – 18
20 – 00	03 – 06 – 00	20 – 00	00 – 03 – 00
20 – 40	03 – 01 – 24	20 – 40	00 – 02 – 12
21 – 20	02 – 09 – 18	21 – 20	00 – 01 – 24
22 – 00	02 – 05 – 12	22 – 00	00 – 01 – 06
22 – 40	02 – 01 – 06	22 – 40	00 – 00 – 18
23 – 20	01 – 09 – 00	23 – 20	Pingla 02 – 00 – 00
24 – 00	01 – 04 – 24	24 – 00	01 – 10 – 24
24 – 40	01 – 01 – 18	24 – 40	01 – 09 – 18
25 – 20	00 – 08 – 12	25 – 20	01 – 08 – 12
26 – 00	00 – 04 – 06	26 – 00	01 – 07 – 06
26 – 40	Sankata 08 – 00 – 00	26 – 40	01 – 06 – 00
27 – 20	07 – 07 – 06	27 – 20	01 – 04 – 24
28 – 00	07 – 02 – 12	28 – 00	01 – 03 – 18
28 – 40	06 – 09 – 18	28 – 40	01 – 02 – 12
29 – 20	06 – 04 – 24	29 – 20	01 – 01 – 06
Aquarius 00 – 00	Pingla 01 – 00 – 00	Pisces 00 – 00	Bhramari 01 – 00 – 00
00 – 40	00 – 10 – 24	00 – 40	00 – 09 – 18
01 – 20	00 – 09 – 18	01 – 20	00 – 07 – 06
02 – 00	00 – 08 – 12	02 – 00	00 – 04 – 24
02 – 40	00 – 07 – 06	02 – 40	00 – 02 – 12
03 – 20	00 – 06 – 00	03 – 20	Bhadrika 05 – 00 – 00

04 – 00	00 – 04 – 24	04 – 00	04 – 09 – 00
04 – 40	00 – 03 – 18	04 – 40	04 – 06 – 00
05 – 20	00 – 02 – 12	05 – 20	04 – 03 – 00
06 – 00	00 – 01 – 06	06 – 00	04 – 00 – 00
06 – 40	Dhanya 03 – 00 – 00	06 – 40	03 – 09 – 00
07 – 20	02 – 10 – 06	07 – 20	03 – 06 – 00
08 – 00	02 – 08 – 12	08 – 00	03 – 03 – 00
08 – 40	02 – 06 – 18	08 – 40	03 – 00 – 00
09 – 20	02 – 04 – 24	09 – 20	02 – 09 – 00
10 – 00	02 – 03 – 00	10 – 00	02 – 06 – 00
10 – 40	02 – 01 – 06	10 – 40	02 – 03 – 00
11 – 20	01 – 11 – 12	11 – 20	02 – 00 – 00
12 – 00	01 – 09 – 18	12 – 00	01 – 09 – 00
12 – 40	01 – 07 – 24	12 – 40	01 – 06 – 00
13 – 20	01 – 06 – 00	13 – 20	01 – 03 – 00
14 – 00	01 – 04 – 06	14 – 00	01 – 00 – 00
14 – 40	01 – 02 – 12	14 – 40	00 – 09 – 00
15 – 20	01 – 00 – 18	15 – 20	00 – 06 – 00
16 – 00	00 – 10 – 24	16 – 00	00 – 03 – 00
16 – 40	00 – 09 – 00	16 – 40	Ulka 06 – 00 – 00
17 – 20	00 – 07 – 06	17 – 20	05 – 08 – 12
18 – 00	00 – 05 – 12	18 – 00	05 – 04 – 24
18 – 40	00 – 03 – 18	18 – 40	05 – 01 – 06
19 – 20	00 – 01 – 24	19 – 20	04 – 09 – 18
20 – 00	Bhramari 04 – 00 – 00	20 – 00	04 – 06 – 00
20 – 40	03 – 09 – 18	20 – 40	04 – 02 – 12
21 – 20	03 – 07 – 06	21 – 20	03 – 10 – 24
22 – 00	03 – 04 – 24	22 – 00	03 – 07 – 06

22 – 40	03 – 02 – 12	22 – 40	03 – 03 – 18
23 – 20	03 – 00 – 00	23 – 20	03 – 00 – 00
24 – 00	02 – 09 – 18	24 – 00	02 – 08 – 12
24 – 40	02 – 07 – 06	24 – 40	02 – 04 – 24
25 – 20	02 – 04 – 24	25 – 20	02 – 01 – 06
26 – 00	02 – 02 – 12	26 – 00	01 – 09 – 18
26 – 40	02 – 00 – 00	26 – 40	01 – 06 – 00
27 – 20	01 – 09 – 18	27 – 20	01 – 02 – 12
28 – 00	01 – 07 – 06	28 – 00	00 – 10 – 24
28 – 40	01 – 04 – 24	28 – 40	00 – 07 – 06
29 – 20	01 – 02 – 12	29 – 20	00 – 03 – 18

Table 3: Proportional Parts

Long of Moon Minutes	Mangla		Pingla		Dhanya		Bhra-mari		Bhad-rika		Ulka		Siddha		Sankata	
	M	D	M	D	M	D	M	D	M	D	M	D	M	D	M	D
1	00 – 00		00 – 01		00 – 01		00 – 02		00 – 02		00 – 03		00 – 03		00 – 04	
2	00 – 01		00 – 02		00 – 03		00 – 04		00 – 05		00 – 05		00 – 06		00 – 07	
3	00 – 01		00 – 03		00 – 04		00 – 05		00 – 07		00 – 08		00 – 09		00 – 11	
4	00 – 02		00 – 04		00 – 05		00 – 07		00 – 09		00 – 11		00 – 13		00 – 14	
5	00 – 02		00 – 04		00 – 07		00 – 09		00 – 11		00 – 13		00 – 16		00 – 18	
6	00 – 03		00 – 05		00 – 08		00 – 11		00 – 13		00 – 16		00 – 19		00 – 22	
7	00 – 03		00 – 06		00 – 09		00 – 13		00 – 16		00 – 19		00 – 22		00 – 25	
8	00 – 04		00 – 07		00 – 11		00 – 14		00 – 18		00 – 22		00 – 25		00 – 29	
9	00 – 04		00 – 08		00 – 12		00 – 16		00 – 20		00 – 24		00 – 28		01 – 02	
10	00 – 04		00 – 09		00 – 13		00 – 18		00 – 22		00 – 27		01 – 01		01 – 06	
11	00 – 05		00 – 10		00 – 15		00 – 20		00 – 25		00 – 30		01 – 05		01 – 10	
12	00 – 05		00 – 11		00 – 16		00 – 22		00 – 27		01 – 02		01 – 08		01 – 13	
13	00 – 06		00 – 12		00 – 18		00 – 23		00 – 29		01 – 05		01 – 11		01 – 17	
14	00 – 06		00 – 13		00 – 19		00 – 25		01 – 01		01 – 08		01 – 14		01 – 20	
15	00 – 07		00 – 13		00 – 20		00 – 27		01 – 04		01 – 10		01 – 17		01 – 24	
16	00 – 07		00 – 14		00 – 22		00 – 29		01 – 06		01 – 13		01 – 20		01 – 28	
17	00 – 08		00 – 15		00 – 23		01 – 01		01 – 08		01 – 16		01 – 24		02 – 01	
18	00 – 08		00 – 16		00 – 24		01 – 02		01 – 10		01 – 19		01 – 27		02 – 05	
19	00 – 09		00 – 17		00 – 26		01 – 04		01 – 13		01 – 21		02 – 00		02 – 08	
20	00 – 09		00 – 18		00 – 27		01 – 06		01 – 15		01 – 24		02 – 03		02 – 12	

Dasha Sequence of Major Period (Maha Dasha)

We have worked that the dasha balance at birth is 1 year 9.months 4 days for the example. The date of birth is 22 Dec., 1973. The Yogini Dasha follows the sequence as given in the table 1 above. This sequence is repeated after 36 years in the same order. We will now write the major dasha periods for the example.

D	M	Y
22	12	1973
4	9	1 Bhramari
26	9	1975
		5 Bhadrika
26	9	1980
		6 Ulka
26	9	1986
		7 Siddha
26	9	1993
		8 Sankata
26	9	2001
		1 Mangla
26	9	2002
		2 Pingla
26	9	2004
		3 Dhanya
26	9	2007
		4 Bhramari
26	9	2011
		5 Bhadrika
26	9	2016

Sub Periods

Each major period of Yogini Dasha is further divided into eight parts called sub periods or Antar dasha. The duration of each major period is shared by all eight Yoginis in proportion of their major period. Each major period Yogini keeps the first sub period to herself and the others follow in the sequence.

The total of major periods of eight Yoginis in one cycle is 36 years. Thus each major period is shared by the eight Yoginis whose total periods are 36 years. Each major period is therefore broken into 36 parts. Each sub period lord takes its period according to its share in 36 years. We can write it as

$$\textbf{Sub Period} = \frac{\textbf{Major Period x Sub Period YEAR}}{\textbf{36}}$$

To simplify we multiply it by 360.

The result is sub period = Major period x sub period x 10 days.

The quick rule to find sub period of a Yogini Say A in the major period of a Yogini Say B is A in years x B in years x 10 days.

For example: we find sub period of Ulka in Siddha. We multiply their Dasha period and again multiply by 10 i.e. 6 x 7 x 10 = 420 days.

Sub Period rule states that the major period Yogini keeps the first sub period to itself. Therefore to work the sub period at birth, we must start the sub periods from beginning of birth major period. The start can be known by deducting the full dasha period of Yogini Dasha at birth from the ending date of birth dasha Yogini. In the example the Yogini Dasha at birth is Bhramari which ends on 26th September, 1975. The full dasha period of Bhramari is 4 years. Deducting 4 years from ending date we get 26th September, 1971 as the start date of Bhramari.

Sub Period of Bhramari major dasha

D	M	Y	
26	9	1971	
10	5	0	Bhramari 4 x 4 x 10
6	3	1972	
20	6	0	Bhramari 4 x 5 x 10
26	9	1972	
0	8	0	Ulka 4 x 6 x 10
26	5	1973	
10	9		Siddha 4 x 7 x 10

Since date of birth is 22 December 1973 which falls in Siddha Sub period, the sub period at birth is Siddha in Bhramari major.

We now calculate the sub period in Sankata major period.

26	9	1993	
10	9	1	Sankata 8 x 8 x 10
6	7	1995	
20	2	0	Mangla 8 x 1 x 10
26	9	1995	
10	5	0	Pingla 8 x 2 x 10
6	3	1996	
0	8	0	Dhanya 8 x 3 x 10
6	11	1996	
20	10	0	Bhramari 8 x 4 x 10
26	9	1997	
10	1	1	Bhramari 8 x 5 x 10
6	11	1998	
0	4	1	Ulka 8 x 6 x 10
6	3	2000	
20	6	1	Siddha 8 x 7 x 10

The shortest sub period is of 10 days of Mangla / Mangla and the longest sub period is 1 year 9 months 10 days of Sankata / Sankata.

A ready table for sub period is given.

Table 4.1 – Sub Periods in Yogini Dasa - Mangla

Sub Periods	Sub Period Y M D	Total Period Y M D
Mangla	00 – 00 – 10	00 – 00 – 10
Pingla	00 – 00 – 20	00 – 01 – 00
Dhanya	00 – 01 – 00	00 – 02 – 00
Bhramari	00 – 01 – 10	00 – 03 – 10
Bhadrika	00 – 01 – 20	00 – 05 – 00
Ulka	00 – 02 – 00	00 – 07 – 00
Siddha	00 – 02 – 10	00 – 09 – 10
Sankata	00 – 02 – 20	01 – 00 – 00

Table 4.2 – Sub Periods in Yogini Dasa - Pingla

Sub Periods	Sub Period Y M D	Total Period Y M D
Pingla	00 – 01 – 10	00 – 01 – 10
Dhanya	00 – 02 – 00	00 – 03 – 10
Bhramari	00 – 02 – 20	00 – 06 – 00
Bhadrika	00 – 03 – 10	00 – 09 – 10
Ulka	00 – 04 – 00	01 – 01 – 10
Siddha	00 – 04 – 20	01 – 06 – 00
Sankata	00 – 05 – 10	01 – 11 – 10
Mangla	00 – 00 – 20	02 – 00 – 00

Table 4.3 – Sub Periods in Yogini Dasa - Dhanya

Sub Periods	Sub Period Y M D	Total Period Y M D
Dhanya	00 – 03 – 00	00 – 03 – 00
Bhramari	00 – 04 – 00	00 – 07 – 00
Bhadrika	00 – 05 – 00	01 – 00 – 00
Ulka	00 – 06 – 00	01 – 06 – 00
Siddha	00 – 07 – 00	02 – 01 – 00
Sankata	00 – 08 – 00	02 – 09 – 00
Mangla	00 – 01 – 00	02 – 10 – 00
Pingla	00 – 02 – 00	03 – 00 – 00

Table 4.4 – Sub Periods in Yogini Dasa - Bhramari

Sub Periods	Sub Period Y M D	Total Period Y M D
Bhramari	00 – 05 – 10	00 – 05 – 10
Bhadrika	00 – 06 – 20	01 – 00 – 00
Ulka	00 – 08 – 00	01 – 08 – 00
Siddha	00 – 09 – 10	02 – 05 – 10
Sankata	00 – 10 – 20	03 – 04 – 00
Mangla	00 – 01 – 10	03 – 05 – 10
Pingla	00 – 20 – 20	03 – 08 – 00
Dhanya	00 – 04 – 00	04 – 00 – 00

Table 4.5 – Sub Periods in Yogini Dasa - Bhadrika

Sub Periods	Sub Period Y M D	Total Period Y M D
Bhadrika	00 – 08 – 10	00 – 08 – 10
Ulka	00 – 10 – 00	01 – 06 – 10
Siddha	00 – 11 – 20	02 – 06 – 00
Sankata	01 – 01 – 10	03 – 07 – 10
Mangla	00 – 01 – 20	03 – 09 – 00
Pingla	00 – 03 – 10	04 – 00 – 10
Dhanya	00 – 05 – 00	04 – 05 – 10
Bhramari	00 – 06 – 20	05 – 00 – 00

Table 4.6 – Sub Periods in Yogini Dasa - Ulka

Sub Periods	Sub Period Y M D	Total Period Y M D
Ulka	01 – 00 – 00	01 – 00 – 00
Siddha	01 – 02 – 00	02 – 02 – 00
Sankata	01 – 04 – 00	03 – 06 – 00
Mangla	00 – 02 – 00	03 – 08 – 00
Pingla	00 – 04 – 00	04 – 00 – 00
Dhanya	00 – 06 – 00	04 – 06 – 00
Bhramari	00 – 08 – 00	05 – 02 – 00
Bhadrika	00 – 10 – 00	06 – 00 – 00

Table 4.7 – Sub Periods in Yogini Dasa - Siddha

Sub Periods	Sub Period Y M D	Total Period Y M D
Siddha	01 – 04 – 10	01 – 04 – 10
Sankata	01 – 06 – 20	02 – 11 – 00
Mangla	00 – 02 – 10	03 – 01 – 10
Pingla	00 – 04 – 20	03 – 06 – 00
Dhanya	00 – 07 – 00	04 – 01 – 00
Bhramari	00 – 09 – 10	04 – 10 – 10
Bhadrika	00 – 11 – 20	05 – 10 – 00
Ulka	01 – 02 – 00	07 – 00 – 00

Table 4.8 – Sub Periods in Yogini Dasa - Sankata

Sub Periods	Sub Period Y M D	Total Period Y M D
Sankata	01 – 09 – 10	01 – 09 – 10
Mangla	00 – 02 – 20	02 – 00 – 00
Pingla	00 – 05 – 10	02 – 05 – 10
Dhanya	00 – 08 – 00	03 – 01 – 10
Bhramari	00 – 10 – 20	04 – 00 - 00
Bhadrika	01 – 01 – 10	05 – 01 – 10
Ulka	01 – 04 – 00	06 – 05 – 10
Siddha	01 – 06 – 20	08 – 00 – 00

Yogini Dasha Results of Maha dasha

Mansagri have given the interpretation of Dasha Results of Yogini Maha dasha and antardasha (Sub periods). These are given here for the benefit of readers. The results given are in line with the names of the Yogini.

Four Yoginis are of benefic planets and four are of malefic planets. The results given in classic are auspicious or inauspicious according to the Yogini belonging to benefics or malefics.

These are not to be taken literally. We have demonstrated the correct method of analyzing the Yogini Dasha later in this book. It is the total horoscope that matters.

Mangla

During Mangla Dasha, the person will be religious. He will be devoted to gods, religious persons and his Guru. He will have gains of conveyance, riches, fame, and growth of family. Auspicious ceremonies at home, praise from ruler, gain of ornaments, comfort from wife and gain of knowledge.

Pingla

There will be physical and mental sufferings. Troubled by evil association. Suffer from blood disorder, bilious disease, heart problems, and immoral relation with a wicked woman. Suffering to children and servant. Loss of fame and reputation and have unfulfilled desires.

Dhanya

Gain of wealth and grains, business will increase. There will be all round happiness and good ceremonies in the family. The enemies will be destroyed; Gets honor from the king. Comfort from woman. Holy pilgrimages will be undertaken. The person is lucky to have this Dasha of Dhanya.

Bhramari

Aimless wondering in the places like mountains, and dense forests in scorching heat like a deer wanders in illusion. Even the king will sleep on the ground after loss of kingdom.

Bhadrika

There will be harmony in the family. The social status is elevated and the person mixes with eminent people thus improving his career. He develops business skills and benefits from the rulers. He will enjoy the company of beautiful woman.

Ulka

Ulka Dasha gives loss of fame, wealth, cattle's, conveyance, business and clothes. He will face punishment from ruler. He will be troubled by spouse, servants, children etc. He will develop disease of heart, ears, feet, teeth and eyes.

Siddha

All desires will be fulfilled. Gain of wealth, education, fame and prosperity. Authority granted by the ruler (status given by king). Expansion of business. Marriage of children. Gets company of friends and enjoys luxurious from king.

Sankata

The position or the kingdom is lost. Destruction due to fire in the house or village. Unworthy desires. Separation from the son and family. Loss of precious metals like gold. weakness of body and the fear of death.

Results of sub periods of Yoginis

Mangla Maha dasha

1. Mangla – This is giver of happiness from friends, sons, spouse and business. The sub period of Mangla in Mangla Maha dasha is giver of auspicious ceremonies.

2. Pingla – It is giver of enmity with friends and relatives. There is anxiety in mind. In this dasha all types of suffering will happen.

3. Dhanya – There will be gains of elephants, cows and wealth. Derives happiness from son, friends and relatives. There are all types of luxuries.

4.   Bhramari - There will be rift with wife and friends. Lives in other lands and there is loss of wealth. He will develop friendship with the rulers.

5.   Bhadrika – He will enjoy the wealth of all types with sons, wife, friends and relatives in a cordial way. He will have devotion to Gods. This will be a period of making merry.

6.   Ulka – Loss of wealth and fame. Children, wife, friends and animals will suffer. He will be in constant fear of punishment from the king.

7.   Siddha - He will have happiness from wife, children and wealth. All types of pleasure will be enjoyed. Friends and relatives will gather at his home.

8.   Sankata – There will be fear from water, fire, thieves and the king. He will suffer death like situation.

Pingla

1.   Pingla - He will develop addiction and will suffer from ailments, mental tension and have troublesome travelling.

2.   Dhanya – Will have wealth, plenty of food and gain of progeny. The sexual enjoyments will be there. He will acquire landed property and all desires will be fulfilled.

3.   Bhramari - He will live in foreign land and suffer loss due to house, village or city and from relatives. There will be discord in the family.

4.   Bhadrika – It will give all round prosperity. He will earn fame, profits from business and gain of son. The residence will be changed.

5.   Ulka – There is opposition from relatives and friends. Danger from king, thieves and trouble from society.

6.   Siddha – He will master the mantras. There will be gain of wealth and grains. He will suffer from respiratory problems and diabetes.

7. Sankata – Loss of wealth. Danger from king and enemies. He will have fear of some serious diseases.

8. Mangla – The person suffers from sorrows and unfounded fears. He gets various diseases and his longevity is affected.

Dhanya

1. Dhanya - The person gains property, lands, wealth and grains. There is earning from the king. Happiness from wife and children.

2. Bhramari - The travel will be troublesome. Loss of wealth. He gains by change of residence. He will oppose his friends and relatives.

3. Bhadrika – it is an auspicious time. He gets happiness from family and friends. He will gain conveyance and honor from the king. There will be acquisition of clothes.

4. Ulka – This is a troublesome period and suffers losses. He will experience pain in heart and waist.

5. Siddha – Will get great happiness from children. Many friends will visit his house and he gets many kinds of enjoyments and gets pleasure.

6. Sankata – This is a period of bondage. He will not be having interest in his work like business, policies and the works given by the king.

7. Mangla – All round happiness in the home. He will enjoy the comfort of food, wife, children and precious metals.

8. Pingla – There will be 'oss of property and wealth of many ways. There will be fear of king and he will have pains and ailments in his body. There is no enthusiasm in his work.

Bhramari

1. Bhramari - It will be a period of frightfulness. There will be trouble from poison. He will be shifted from his place. He will be away from friends, relatives and enemies.

2. Bhadrika – He will have association of friends and will travel abroad. Good education and gets honor from King.

3. Ulka - This dasha is giver of fever, pains and troubles from blood disorder. Sufferings to wife, children. There will be loss of wealth and other things.

4. Siddha – The desired things will be accomplished. This dasha will give the wealth of wisdom, education and relief from diseases and fears.

5. Sankata – Great death like sufferings and will have sorrow, sickness and attachments leading to disappointment. He faces theft charges in the court of king.

6. Mangla – Auspicious events will happen and there will be comfort and pleasure around. He will get prosperity and happiness by serving the king.

7. Pingla – The person will have disease of rectum, mouth, feet etc. There will be fear of injuries caused by animals like elephant, horses, buffaloes and tigers.

8. Dhanya – Accumulation of wealth, vehicles and pleasurable amenities. He will gain from the king. There will be losses on account of tribals.

Bhadrika

1. Bhadrika – He will receive honors and there will be gain of horses, cows etc. He will get freedom from wrong habits and sorrows and will get to know the correct path of life.

2. Ulka – In this dasha, there will be conflict with people, suffers ill wealth and loss of job or home. There will be loss of wealth and have great worries.

3. Siddha – Will have devotion to gods and Brahmins. There is happiness from wife, children and relatives. Well have comforts, enjoyments at home, village with celebration.

4. Sankata – Will face many troubles, sorrows, obstacles. There will be troubles in travelling abroad.

5.   Mangla – Will be honored and there is increase in land assets, business and the family will expand.

6.   Pingla – Have bilious disorders. He will get good advice from elders which will increase his agriculture, property and in many ways.

7.   Dhanya – Happiness from wife, children, friends and relatives. There will be auspicious celebrations at home. Have great gains of wealth and food.

8.   Bhramari – Diseases of blood, danger from fire. Death like fears. This dasha destroys a person who is the enemy in the village. He will have happiness from relatives.

Ulka

1.   Ulka – Sudden loss of wealth which is caused by enemy. Will have great fear of loss of kingdom.

2.   Siddha – This antardasha delivers unfavorable results and the auspiciousness of Venus is not felt. He will undertake journey to foreign countries.

3.   Sankata – Fear of death, children will suffer. There will be harm to wife, relatives and servants.

4.   Mangla – The person will have wrong notions. He gets happiness from wealth, friends, wife and wisdom. He will get rid of disease and wickedness.

5.   Pingla – Will be troubled by skin disease like leprosy and disease of head. He will be a wanderer or aimless traveler.

6.   Dhanya – No gains and no comforts. Diseases of wind and phlegm will trouble. There will be rift with wife, children and relatives.

7.   Bhramari - The mind will be agitated and there is fear or enemies. Many types of Sufferings are faced during this period.

8.   Bhadrika – There will be all round prosperity and gain of wealth. Will suffer loss of clothes and ornaments. He will have happiness from friends and relatives.

Siddha

1.   Siddha – Accomplishes all his undertakings. Gets happiness from relatives. There is increase in comforts of children and friends.

2.   Sankata – Faces confinement and loss of wealth through the king. It may be by way of penalty or by theft. He is under fear and made to leave the country.

3.   Mangla – Will enjoy sensual pleasures. His own people will give him happiness and will earn wealth through the king. There will be success all-round.

4.   Pingla – Will be given to anger and arrogance. He will have fear of fire and develop rift with his own people. He gets illegal income.

5.   Dhanya – The good results of good deeds done in past life will be bestowed. His all desires are fulfilled.

6.   Bhramari – Due to serious bad habits he has to desert his residence. He will face danger due to the anger from king's family.

7.   Bhadrika – Auspicious events at home. He indulges in sensual pleasures. There is increase of comfort, education and virtues. Success in all undertakings.

8.   Ulka – Destruction of wealth and grains. He faces troubles, sorrows and indulges in bad habits. Suffers from diseases of rectum.

Sankata

1.   Sankata – will have grave danger of death, losses due to the king. Have to leave the country and destruction of wealth.

2. Mangla – Suffering from many disease and ill health. Pains to wife. He will be addicted to many evil habits.

3. Pingla – There will be sudden financial loses. Grief from son. Danger from enemies and separation from near relatives.

4. Dhanya – Due to problems of spleen, he will suffer pain in stomach. Great happiness from son. Enjoys fame and popularity among the people of own country.

5. Bhramari - There will be travels in his own and foreign countries. Harm will be caused to his home, village or county. There is fear of loss of kingdom.

6. Bhadrika – The person will acquire knowledge and education. Increase in ornaments, fame and clothes. He will have quarrel with ordinary people.

7. Ulka – The accumulated wealth will be lost. The property will be lost and faces death like situations. The animals will suffer. There will be problems to maternal family.

8. Siddha - The person will be active. There will be birth of children and gets happiness from own progress. The person will be in elated state of mind.

Chapter 2

Research

The description given in chapter 1 is the classical method of computing Yogini Dasha. This method is also followed for our calculations also. We are following the classics but the interpretation of result is the tested research.

Yogini Dasha repeats every thirty six year. The events are not repeating every 36 years. Some people say that we should consider the age of the person. We agree but the nature of events should remain same. This is also not so. Suppose a person join service at the age of 24 years in a Yogini Dasha. The same Yogini will repeat at 60 years of age and the person retires from work. For example a person gets married at an age of 24 years. Will he marry again at 60?

The Yoginis are generated through the Nakshatra and this is the hidden secret of analyzing the Yogini. It is in the Nakshatra which generates the Yogini.

Thus we have to understand the Yogini Nakshatra.

The problem came while linking the Yoginis with Nakshatra sequence. There are twenty seven Nakshatra and twenty four yoginis in three cycles. Three Yogini dasha originate from four Nakshatra. Other five Yogini originate from three Nakshatra each.

The classics have laid down the sequence or Yogini dasha from Mangla to Sankata and cannot be altered. The solution came through the analysis of navamsha of Nakshatra. Thus three Nakshatra Ashwani, Bharani and Kritika were left before Rohini to maintain the sequence.

This is akin to the frog jumps of kalchakra dasha or mandook dasha.

We have taken Nakshatra lords as the Vimshottari lords. The Yogini dasha is microscopic view of Vimshottari. The unfolding of events is seen with a clear view since yogini dasha is of 36 years cycle and Vimshottari is 120 years. The dasha periods in Vimshottari are longer as compared to Yogini Dasha. To aid this further, we are having different progress lagna for each dasha according to the nakshatra generating the dasha. As the lagna changes, the role of the planets also changes.

A step by step method of working out the Yogini with Nakshatra is given.

1. Workout the Yogini dasha and the balance at birth.

2. Note down the Nakshatra and the Nakshatra lord of Moon at birth. (Vimshottari lord of Nakshatra).

3. Write the dasha at birth along with Nakshatra of Moon like Bhramari / Anuradha.

4. For next Yogini dasha write the next Nakshatra along with dasha. Continue writing dasha and Nakshatra for the subsequent dasha.

5. When you reach Revati, jump to Rohini for next dasha. The Yogini dasha for Revati is Ulka. So for next dasha of Siddha we jump to Rohini.

6. This way we have a Nakshatra for each Yogini dasha period. Each Yogini dasha will have its generating Nakshatra. For example we take Mangla dasha period. Mangla dasha repeats three times in 27 Nakshatra. Now each Mangla will have a different Nakshatra which is ruling a particular Mangla dasha.

7. For a Yogini dasha period, recast the birth chart keeping the sign of Nakshatra as Lagna / Ascendant. This recasted chart is called progress chart and the Lagna or Ascendant is called progress lagna (PL).

8.   Planets remain in the signs as occupied by them in birth chart.

9.   When a Nakshatra occupy two signs, the progress lagna will change to the next sign according to span of Nakshatra in each sign. The time of change will be in proportion to dasha period and span of Nakshatra in each sign.

     For example for Mrigshira Nakshatra, the dasha is of Sankata of eight years. Mrigshira falls in Taurus and Gemini. Two Padas are in Taurus and two Padas are in Gemini. So this Nakshatra is equally divided in these two signs. The Sankata dasha is of eight years. These eight years will be equally divided in Taurus and Gemini. Thus the progress lagna will change to Gemini after four years have passed in Sankata.

     This is applicable to Nakshatra of Sun and Jupiter. For dasha generated by a Nakshatra of Sun, we have one pada in one sign and three Padas in next sign. So the progress lagna will change after one – fourth dasha period of Yogini generated by the Nakshatra.

     Similarly for Nakshatra of Jupiter, there are three Padas in first sign and one pada in next sign. The progress lagna will change to next sign after three –fourth of the dasha period of the Yogini generated by the Yogini.

10. This way we have different lagans for each dasha. This progress chart now is interpreted for results and timing of events.

     We illustrate the method with an example:-

Example – Indira Gandhi 19th November, 1917, 23-11 Hrs. Allahabad

Left chart (Rasi – North Indian style):
- Ma, Ke at top
- 5, 6 on left; 3, 2 with Ju
- Sa in center upper
- 4
- 7, 1, 10
- Su Me, 8, 9, Ra Ve at bottom left
- Mo in center
- 12, 11 on right

Right chart (South Indian style):

		Ju	Ke
	Birth Chart		Sa
Mo	19 Nov. 1917 23-11-0 Allahabad		Ma
Ra Ve	Su Me		

Lag	**Sun**	**Mon**	**Mar**	**Mer**	**Jup**	**Ven**	**Sat**	**Rah**
27°22'	04°07'	05°35'	16°22'	13°13'	15°00'	21°00'	21°47'	09°12'

Longitude of Moon is 5° – 35' in Capricorn. The Nakshatra is Uttara Ashadha. The balance of Yogini Dasha at Birth is Sankata 2 years 7 months and 24 days. The dasha sequence will be –

D	M	Y	
19	11	1917	
24	07	2	Sankata / U.Ashadha
13	07	1920	
00	00	1	Mangla / Shravan
13	07	1921	
00	00	2	Pingla / Dhanishta
13	07	1923	
00	00	3	Dhanya / Shatbhisaj
13	07	1926	
00	00	4	Bhramari / P.Bhadrapad

13	07	1930	
00	00	5	Bhadrika/ U.Bhadrapad
13	07	1935	
00	00	6	Ulka / Revati
13	07	1941	
00	00	7	Siddha/ Rohini (note: The jump from Revati to Rohini)
13	07	1948	
00	00	8	Sankata / Mrigshira
13	07	1956	
00	00	1	Mangla / Ardra
13	07	1957	
00	00	2	Pingla / Punarvasu
13	07	1959	
00	00	3	Dhanya / Pushya
13	07	1962	
00	00	4	Bhramari / Ashlesha
13	07	1966	
00	00	5	Bhadrika / Magha
13	07	1971	
00	00	6	Ulka/ P.Phalguni
13	07	1977	
00	00	7	Siddha / U.Phalguni
13	07	1984	
00	00	8	Sankata / Hasta
13	07	1992	

A table for Nakshatra, Yogini and the sign of progress lagna is given.

Yogini Dasha	Years	Lord of Yogini	Nak--shatra	Nak--shatra Lord	Sign of PL	Change sign after
Bhramari	4	Mars	Ashwani	Ketu	Aries	X
Bhadrika	5	Mercury	Bharani	Venus	Aries	X
Ulka	6	Saturn	Kritika	Sun	Aries / Taurus	1 Y 6 M
Siddha	7	Venus	Rohini	Moon	Taurus	X
Sankata	8	Rahu	Mrigshira	Mars	Taurus/ Gemini	4 Y 0 M
Mangla	1	Moon	Ardra	Rahu	Gemini	X
Pingla	2	Sun	Punarvasu	Jupiter	Gemini/ Cancer	1Y 6 M
Dhanya	3	Jupiter	Pushya	Saturn	Cancer	X
Bhramari	4	Mars	Ashlesha	Mercury	Cancer	X
Bhadrika	5	Mercury	Magha	Ketu	Leo	X
Ulka	6	Saturn	P.Phalguni	Venus	Leo	X
Siddha	7	Venus	U.Phalguni	Sun	Leo / Virgo	1 Y 9 M
Sankata	8	Rahu	Hasta	Moon	Virgo	X
Mangla	1	Moon	Chitra	Mars	Virgo / Libra	0 Y 6 M
Pingla	2	Sun	Swati	Rahu	Libra	X
Dhanya	3	Jupiter	Vishakha	Jupiter	Libra / Scorpio	2 Y 3 M
Bhramari	4	Mars	Anuradha	Saturn	Scorpio	X
Bhadrika	5	Mercury	Jyeshtha	Mercury	Scorpio	X
Ulka	6	Saturn	Moola	Ketu	Sagittarius	X
Siddha	7	Venus	Poorva Ashadha	Venus	Sagittarius	X
Sankata	8	Rahu	Uttara Ashadha	Sun	Sagittarius/ Capricorn	2 Y 0 M
Mangla	1	Moon	Shravan	Moon	Capricorn	X
Pingla	2	Sun	Dhanishta	Mars	Capricorn/ Aquarius	1 Y 0 M
Dhanya	3	Jupiter	Shatbhisaj	Rahu	Aquarius	X
Bhramari	4	Mars	Poorva Bhadrapad	Jupiter	Aquarius/ Pisces	3 Y 0 M

Bhadrika	5	Mercury	Uttara Bhadrapad	Saturn	Pisces	X
Ulka	6	Saturn	Revati	Mercury	Pisces	X
Siddha	7	Venus	Rohini	Moon	Taurus	X

Note: Jump to Rohini after Revati (Ignore Ashwani, Bharani and Kritika)

If birth is in Ashwani or Bharani or Kritika then proceed in normal order.

Examination of Dasha Periods

1. The recasted chart for the running dasha is examined in totality.

2. The Nakshatra lord is important as well as the progress lagna.

3. We must identify the Nakshatra lord in the birth chart and the new role in the progress chart.

4. Any planet connected to a house in birth chart makes the connection with the house in progress chart assures the events of that house in the duration of dasha period of progress chart.

We illustrate this by an example.

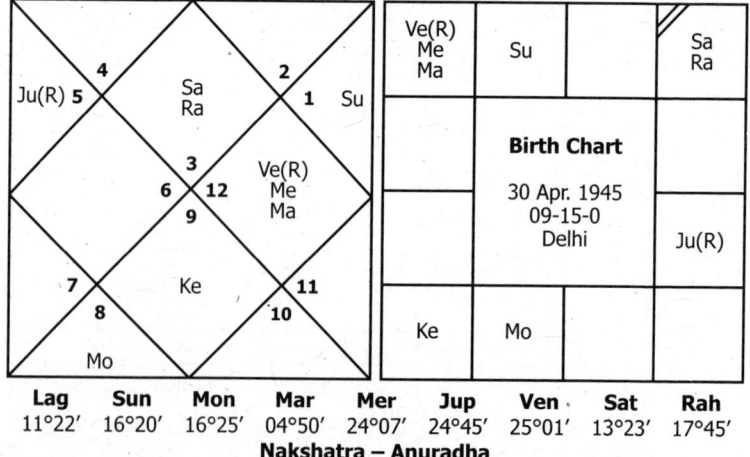

| Lag | Sun | Mon | Mar | Mer | Jup | Ven | Sat | Rah |
| 11°22′ | 16°20′ | 16°25′ | 04°50′ | 24°07′ | 24°45′ | 25°01′ | 13°23′ | 17°45′ |

Nakshatra – Anuradha

He was born in Bhramari / Anuradha. He was a class one
officer with ministry of Defence. The dasha sequence is

D	M	Y	
30	04	1945	
26	0	0	Bhramari / Anuradha
26	05	1945	
00	00	5	Bhadrika / Jyeshtha
26	05	1950	
00	00	6	Ulka / Moola
26	05	1956	
00	00	7	Siddha / P.Ashadha
26	05	1963	
00	00	8	Sankata / U.Ashadha
26	05	1971	

Here we illustrate selection in class I service in 1969. The
Nakshatra is U.Ashadha and its lord is Sun. The progress
lagna moves to Capricorn on 26.5.65 i.e. after two years
of Sankata. The progress chart is,

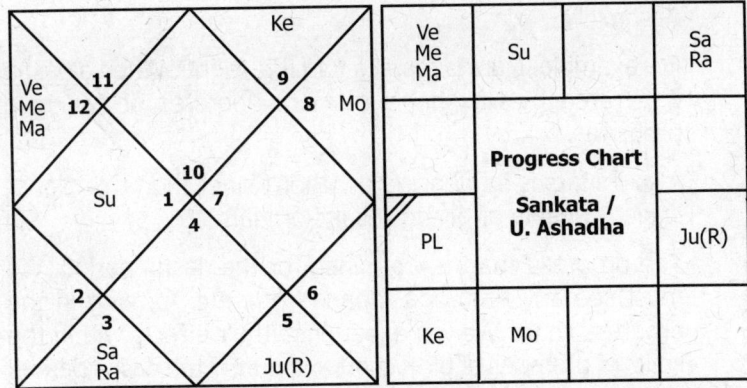

Sun is the Nakshatra Lord. It is influenced by Jupiter. Jupiter
is the tenth lord of birth chart. In the progress chart, Sun
is aspecting tenth house. The results of tenth are expected
thro' exalted Sun. The sub period was of Siddha. Venus is

in tenth house of birth Chart and is the tenth lord of progress chart.

If we move further and reach Bhramari of P.Bhadrapad from 26 May 1977 to 26 May 1981. The progress Lagna is Pisces from 26 May 1980. The star lord is Jupiter. Jupiter is birth tenth lord and also the progress tenth lord. Jupiter is in 6th from progress lagna. The tenth house is occupied by Ketu and aspected by Saturn. He resigned from class I job. The aspect of Jupiter on Sagittarius gave another job.

5. A planet is related to a house in birth chart. Now in progress chart, another planet is related to the same house in progress chart. If these two planets are related then event signified by the house materializes. Suppose Mars is seventh lord of birth chart. In progress chart Jupiter is the seventh lord. Mars is aspecting Jupiter; the marriage will take place during the currency of progress chart.

6. Work out the significators of an event and note these planets. During a dasha period if the same planets become the significator of the event in progress chart, it will take place. The significator can be the Nakshatra lord of the dasha.

    For example, Mars is maraca for Libra lagna. When a dasha generated by Nakshatra of Mars operates, it can give problems.

    Also if Mars is influencing another planet then this planet is also capable of giving results of Mars.

7. The progress chart is examined for the dasha period. We must see any Raj Yoga, dhana Yoga etc. forming in the progress chart. We will experience their effects within the limits of promises of birth chart and during the dasha period.

8. In the progress chart, if we see any serious affection to any house, it is a danger signal for the significations of that house. In the example given in point 4 of this chapter,

the progress Lagna is Pisces. The fourth house has Saturn and Rahu. It indicates change of house and it happened. The problems were faced in the new rented house.

9.   The sub period of events will be of the planets related to the house. They may be lord of the house; the planets placed in the house or aspecting it and associated with lord.

10. The sub period of Nakshatra Lord and the planets related to it is also important.

11. Any planet who is related to Nakshatra lord and the lord of the house gives the events of that house.

12. Rahu and Ketu acts as their dispositor and the planet associated with them.

13. The events promised by Ketu are given in sub period of Sankata.

Chapter - 3

Mangla

Mangla Yogini dasha is of one year duration. As the name implies, this is considered auspicious. It is not always so.

Mangla dasha belongs to three Nakshatra. These are Ardra, Chitra, and Shravan. The table below gives the Nakshatra lord etc. for each of Mangla Yogini period.

Nakshatra	Nakshatra Lord	Sign of Nakshatra	Remarks
Ardra	Rahu	Gemini	For entire period Progress Lagna is Gemini
Chitra	Mars	Virgo / Libra	First six months PL is Virgo and for last six months PL is Libra.
Shravan	Moon	Capricorn	PL is Capricorn. The Nakshatra and dasha lord are same.

We will examine some charts for each of Mangla period.

Mangla / Ardra

Rahu is the Nakshatra lord. Rahu do not have lordship of any sign. It gives results of the sign lord occupied by it and of the planet conjunct with it. Gemini is the progress lagna. Placement of Rahu in Kendra /Trikona from Gemini as well as

from birth lagna makes it give good results. Association of Rahu
with lords of trine is also auspicious.

Example 1: S.L.Shakdhar

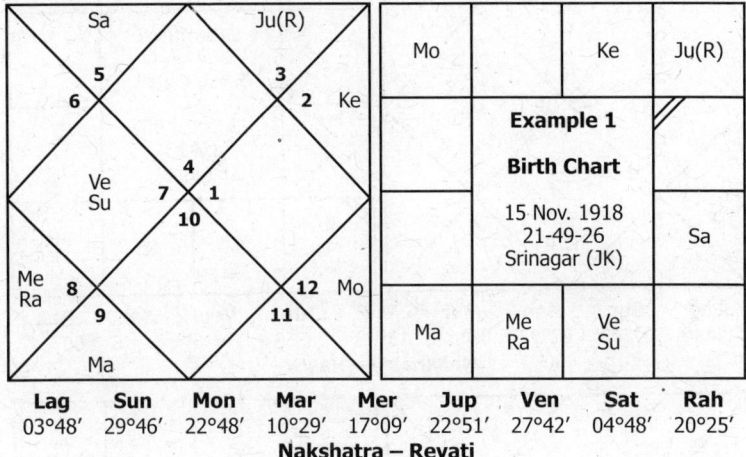

Lag	Sun	Mon	Mar	Mer	Jup	Ven	Sat	Rah
03°48'	29°46'	22°48'	10°29'	17°09'	22°51'	27°42'	04°48'	20°25'

Nakshatra – Revati

He got married on 7 May 1937 in the Yogini Dasha period
of Mangla / Ardra. The progress chart is casted. (Note - In
progress Yogini we go to Rohini after Revati).

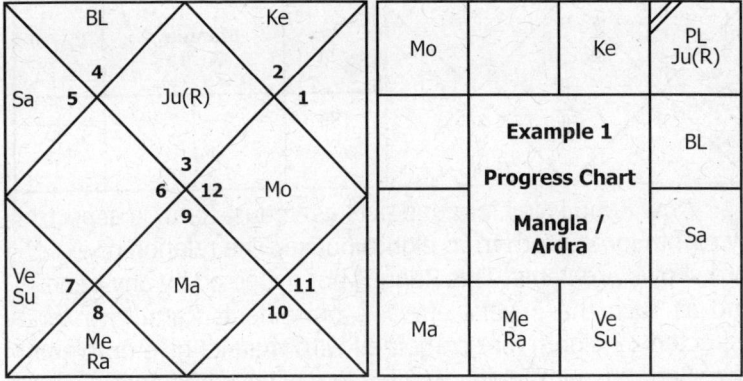

Rahu is in Scorpio and with Mercury. It acts as Mars. From
progress Lagna, Mars is placed in seventh house and aspected
by seventh lord Jupiter. Marriage took placed in Mangla /
Bhramari or Moon / Mars.

Example 2: Charan Singh

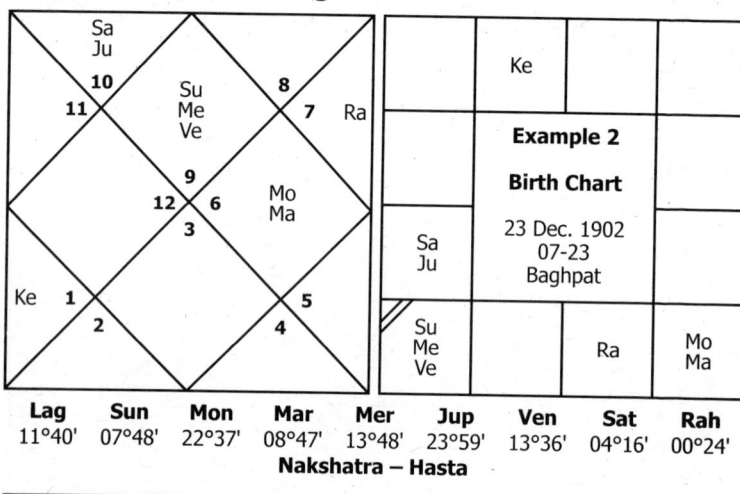

Lag	Sun	Mon	Mar	Mer	Jup	Ven	Sat	Rah
11°40'	07°48'	22°37'	08°47'	13°48'	23°59'	13°36'	04°16'	00°24'

Nakshatra − Hasta

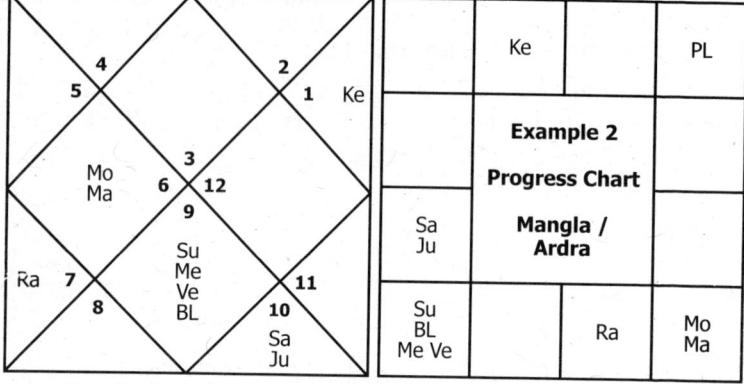

Now Rahu is in Libra and acts as Venus. Rahu is aspected by eighth lord Saturn from eighth house. The relation of eighth lord shows problems. This Rahu is not aspected by any benefic and as such the malefic effect is prominent. Rahu in a trine aspected by eighth lord conjoined with maraca give problems. Here Saturn is with Jupiter which is lord of seventh house. Saturn is in Pasha / Nigada Dreshkana. Saturn is maraca of birth chart. The star lord is now afflicted. Birth lagna lord is in eighth house. Progress lagna lord is with twelfth lord and aspected by Mars. He remained in jail during emergency of 1975.

Example: 3

This chart belongs to Sri Sri Ravi Shankarji. He got Mangla / Ardra at a very early age of four years.

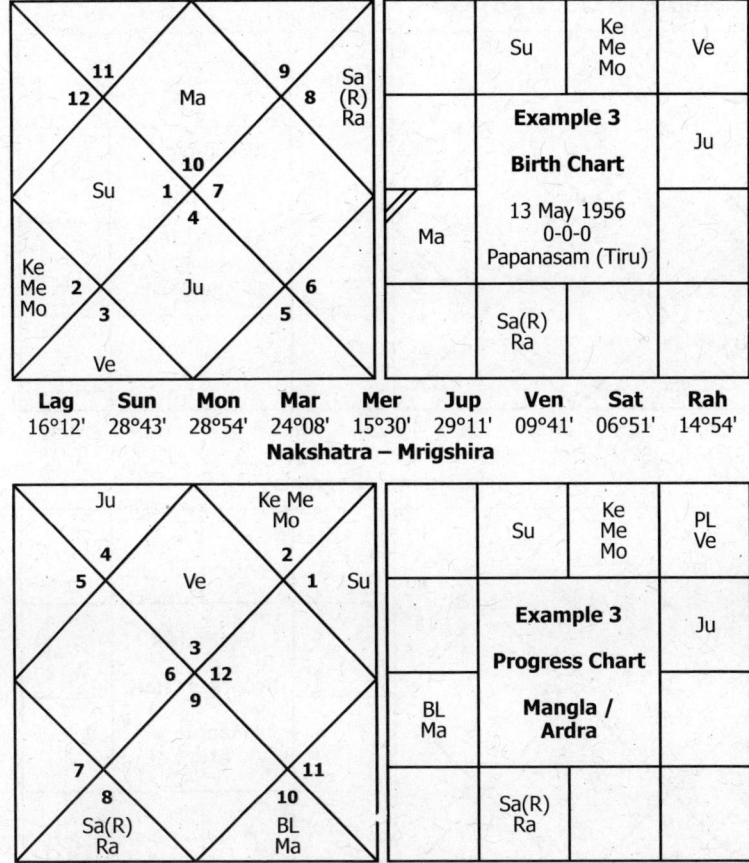

	Su	Ke Me Mo	Ve
	Example 3 **Birth Chart**		Ju
Ma	13 May 1956 0-0-0 Papanasam (Tiru)		
	Sa(R) Ra		

	Lag	Sun	Mon	Mar	Mer	Jup	Ven	Sat	Rah
	16°12'	28°43'	28°54'	24°08'	15°30'	29°11'	09°41'	06°51'	14°54'

Nakshatra – Mrigshira

	Su	Ke Me Mo	PL Ve
	Example 3 **Progress Chart**		Ju
BL Ma	**Mangla /** **Ardra**		
	Sa(R) Ra		

Basic chart is very strong with three exalted planets in Kendra. Mercury and Venus exchange sign. Moon is exalted. Ketu is with ninth lord and aspected by lagna lord. There is an exchange of lagna lord and eleventh lord.

Mangla / Ardra operated in 1961 when Sri Sri Ji was four years. In the progress chart Rahu is in sixth house and is placed with ninth lord Saturn. Sixth house shows efforts and is the house of Sadhna. Rahu is aspected by lagna lord Mercury and exalted Moon and Jupiter. He could recite the entire Bhagwat Gita during this Mangla Period.

Example 4: Govt. Officer

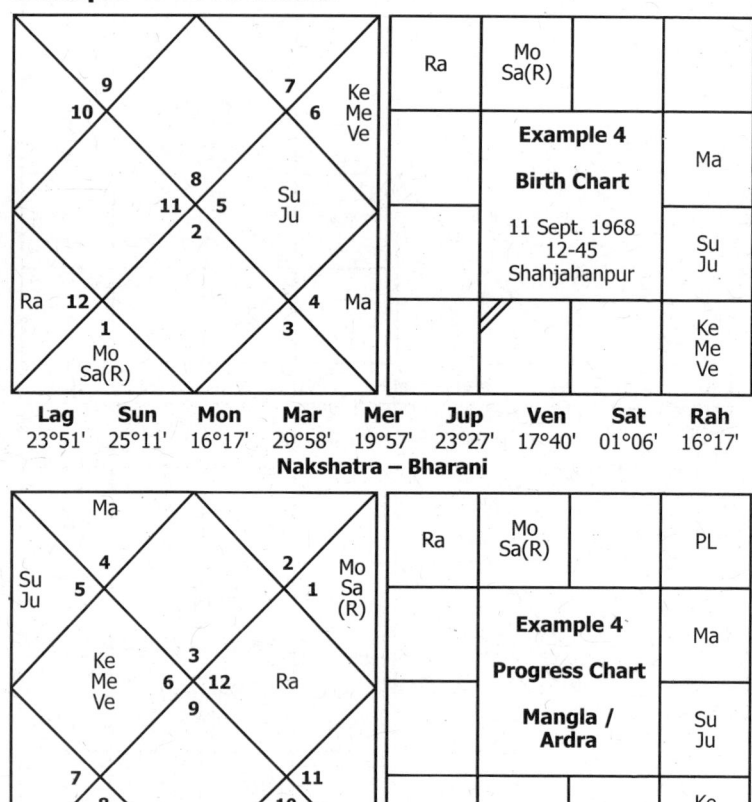

Lag	Sun	Mon	Mar	Mer	Jup	Ven	Sat	Rah
23°51'	25°11'	16°17'	29°58'	19°57'	23°27'	17°40'	01°06'	16°17'

Nakshatra – Bharani

He started his service on 1 September, 1993 in the Yogini Dasha of Moon/ Jupiter. Jupiter sub period started on 1st September, 1993.

The Nakshatra lord Rahu is placed in tenth house from progress Lagna. Rahu acts as Jupiter. In the birth chart Jupiter is placed in tenth house with tenth lord. The job was started in Moon / Jupiter.

Example 5: Child Birth

This horoscope is of a lady who is a school teacher. Her husband is an executive working in Dubai. She got a baby girl on 22.5.2004 in Mangla / Pingla.

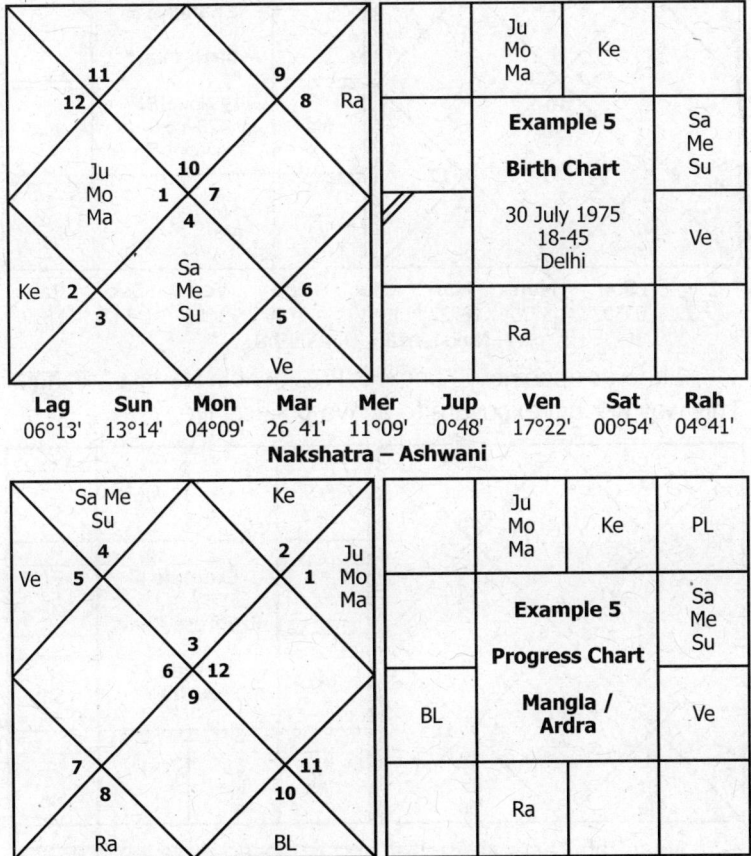

Lag	Sun	Mon	Mar	Mer	Jup	Ven	Sat	Rah
06°13'	13°14'	04°09'	26 41'	11°09'	0°48'	17°22'	00°54'	04°41'

Nakshatra – Ashwani

Rahu acts as Mars. Mars is in eleventh house and aspects fifth house and Rahu. The ninth lord Saturn is aspecting Mars and Moon.

Example 6: Indira Gandhi

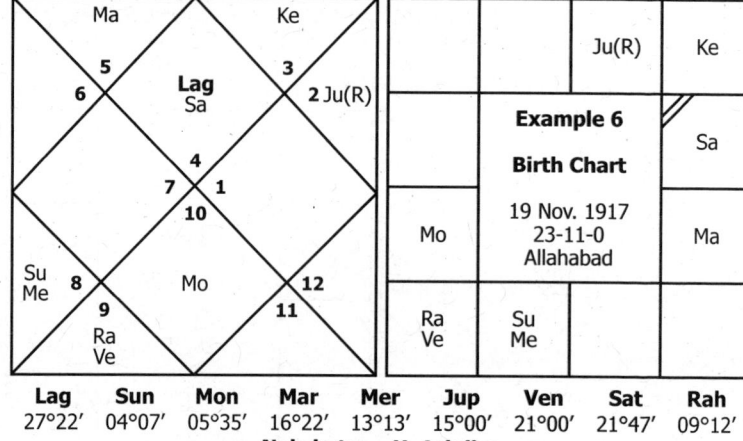

Lag	Sun	Mon	Mar	Mer	Jup	Ven	Sat	Rah
27°22'	04°07'	05°35'	16°22'	13°13'	15°00'	21°00'	21°47'	09°12'

Nakshatra – U. Ashdha

She was appointed Congress President in Mangla / Mangla. This was her big exposure to active political life.

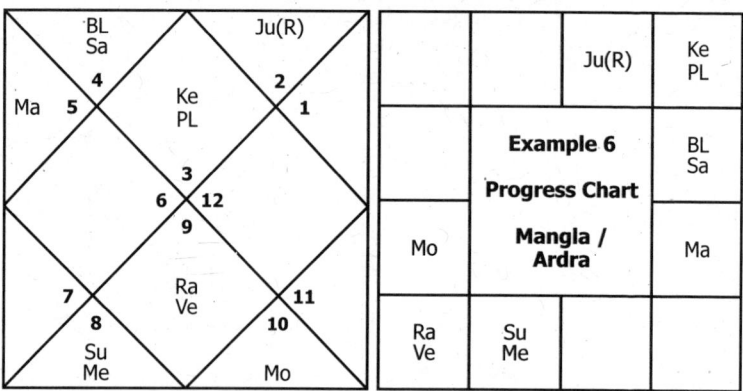

Now Rahu acts as Jupiter and is placed in seventh house. Conjunction of Venus with Rahu is like raj yoga of Kendra and Trikona. Moon is aspected by ninth and tenth lord of progress lagna.

Mangla / Chitra

Mars is the lord of the progress Nakshatra. Chitra Nakshatra falls in Virgo and Libra. Two pada are in Virgo and two Padas are in Libra. Thus the dasha period covers two signs. The first six months of Mangla (Chitra) will have Virgo as progress lagna and for last six months the progress lagna is Libra.

When Virgo is the progress lagna, Mars is the lord of third and eighth house indicating suddenness and efforts. Mercury is the lord of tenth and lagna.

With Libra is the progress lagna, Mars is the seventh and second lord. Badly placed Mars can give ill health even death. As Kendra lord when with good association can give position and wealth.

Example 7: Hillary Clinton

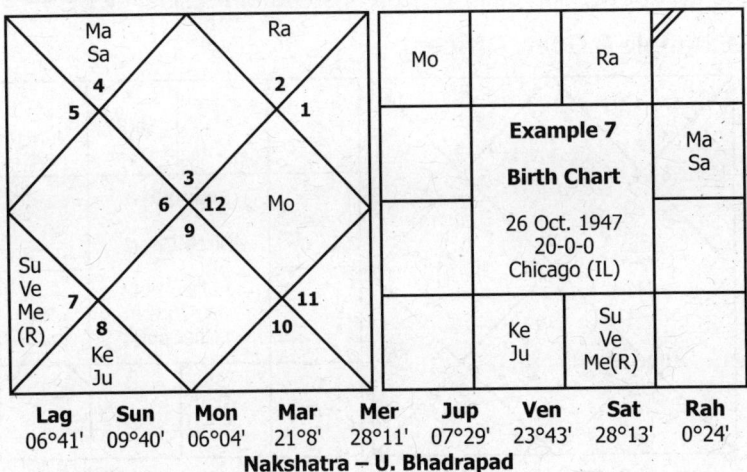

Lag	Sun	Mon	Mar	Mer	Jup	Ven	Sat	Rah
06°41'	09°40'	06°04'	21°8'	28°11'	07°29'	23°43'	28°13'	0°24'

Nakshatra – U. Bhadrapad

She was appointed secretary of state on 20th Jan. 2009. The Yogini dasha was Mangla / Bhramari. The progress chart for Mangla / Chitra is given. The Mangla dasha started on 16 Oct 2008 and the progress lagna will be Virgo up 16 April 2009.

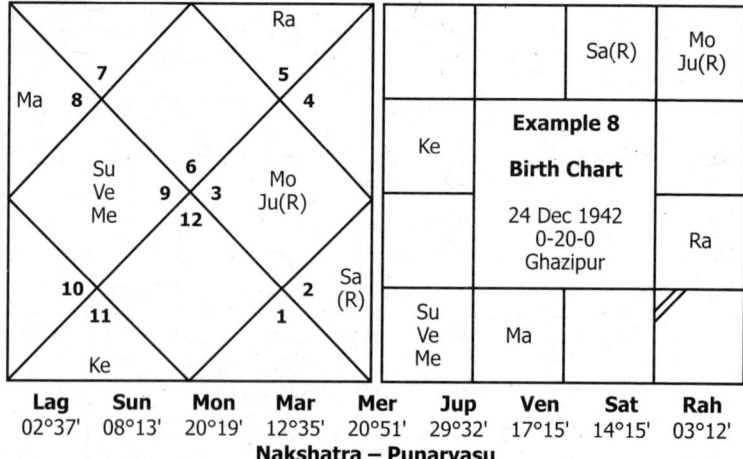

Mars is the lord of eighth and third house and is debilitated. The lords of third and eighth give yogkarak results when they are debilitated. From Virgo the ninth and tenth lord is making excellent Raj Yoga but with Sun. Sun is twelfth lord and she had to accept the secretary of state instead of Presidency.

Example 8 Govt. Officer

Lag	Sun	Mon	Mar	Mer	Jup	Ven	Sat	Rah
02°37'	08°13'	20°19'	12°35'	20°51'	29°32'	17°15'	14°15'	03°12'

Nakshatra – Punarvasu

He got promotion in Mangla / Bhadrika. The Mangla / Chitra started on 5 Dec. 1977 and Virgo will be the progress lagna till 5 June 1978.

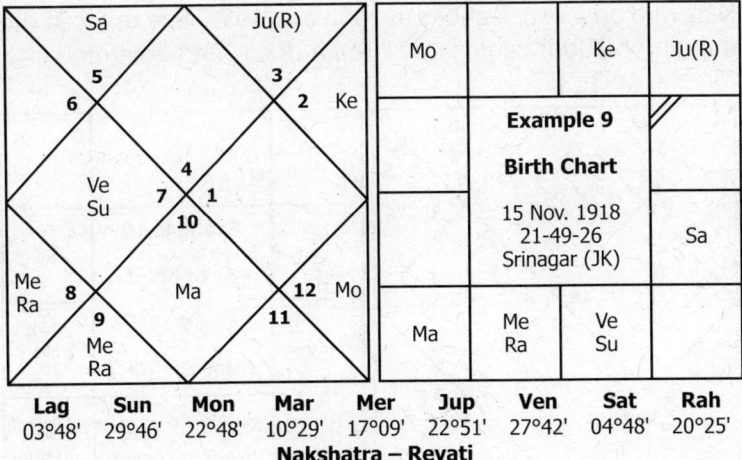

From progress lagna, the lord of tenth Mercury is aspecting tenth house. Venus and Mercury are forming Raj yoga. Mars is in third house in its own sign and aspects tenth house. The promotion came with transfer.

Example 9 S.L.Shakdhar

He was appointed as General Secretary of Lok Sabha in Mangla / Siddha. Please note that in Mangla / Ardra he got married.

Lag	Sun	Mon	Mar	Mer	Jup	Ven	Sat	Rah
03°48'	29°46'	22°48'	10°29'	17°09'	22°51'	27°42'	04°48'	20°25'

Nakshatra – Revati

The Progress lagna is Libra.

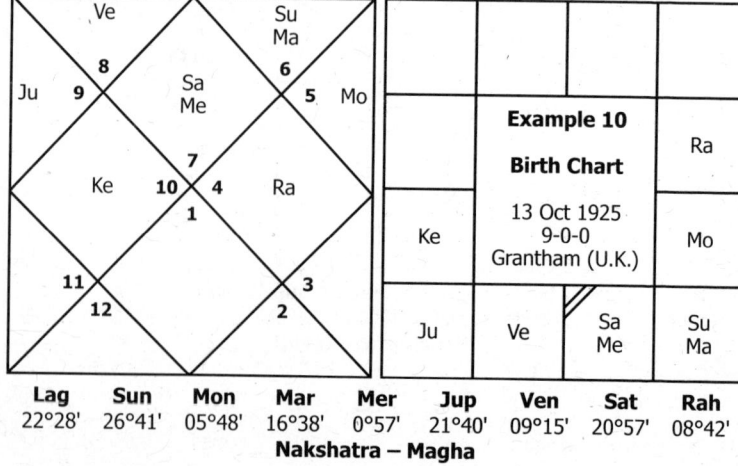

With Virgo progress lagna, the lord of tenth house, Mercury is afflicted by Rahu. With Libra as progress lagna, the tenth house is aspected by Nakshatra lord Mars. (With Virgo also the tenth house is aspected by Mars) Now the lord of tenth house Moon is also aspected by Mars. The lagna is occupied by its lord Venus. The sub period was Siddha.

Example 10 Margret Thatcher

She was conservative candidate for the safe labour seat Dart ford and lost elections in 1950 and 1951. She reduced the margin of labour candidate Norman dodds and emerging as a force in politics.

Lag	Sun	Mon	Mar	Mer	Jup	Ven	Sat	Rah
22°28'	26°41'	05°48'	16°38'	0°57'	21°40'	09°15'	20°57'	08°42'

Nakshatra – Magha

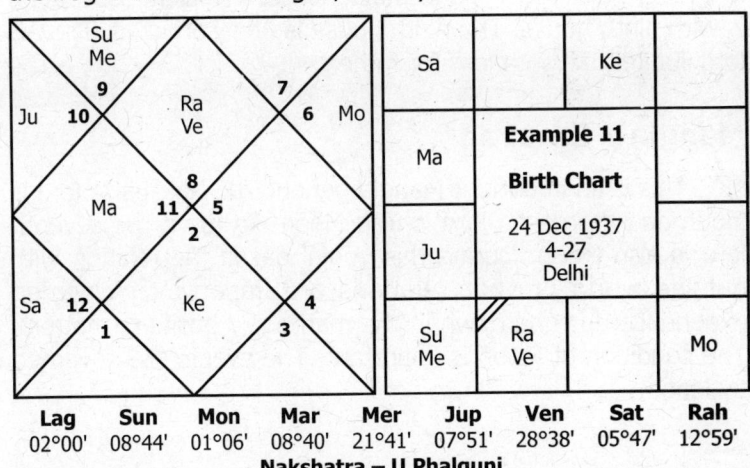

	BL Sa Me		Mo				
Ve 8	7	PL Su Ma	5	4 Ra		Example 10	Ra
	Ju 9	6 3				Progress Chart	
		12			Ke	Mangla / Chitra	Mo
Ke 10	11		2	1	Ju	Ve	BL Sa Me	PL Su Ma

The star lord Mars is not connected with tenth house or tenth lord Mercury. Mars is with twelfth lord Sun. The dasha lord is in twelfth. Next progress lagna is Libra and again Mars is in twelfth. The gain of position is not seen.

Example 11 Death of father

He is an advocate and his father died on 15 Oct 1950 in the Yogini dasha of Mangla / Dhanya.

	Su Me				Sa		Ke	
Ju 10	9	Ra Ve	7	6 Mo		Example 11	
	Ma 11	8	5		Ma	Birth Chart	
			2		Ju	24 Dec 1937 4-27 Delhi	
Sa 12	1	Ke		4 3	Su Me	Ra Ve		Mo

Lag	Sun	Mon	Mar	Mer	Jup	Ven	Sat	Rah
02°00'	08°44'	01°06'	08°40'	21°41'	07°51'	28°38'	05°47'	12°59'

Nakshatra — U Phalguni

Mangla / Chitra started on 25 Aug 1950. The progress lagna will be Virgo for first six months i.e. up to 25 April 1951.

BL Ra Ve 7 8	Mo PL	5 4	
	Su Me 9 6 3 12		
Ju 10 11	Sa	2 1	Ke
	Ma		

Sa		Ke	
Ma	**Example 11**		
	Progress Chart		
Ju	**Mangla / Chitra**		
Su Me	BL Ra Ve		Mo PL

Ninth house from progress lagna is afflicted by Ketu and is aspected by Saturn and Mars. Eighth lord from Taurus is Jupiter and is aspecting it. The karaka of father is in fourth house which is eighth from ninth. Sun is with Mercury that is maraca of father i.e. Second lord from ninth house. The dasha Nakshatra lord Mars is also aspecting the ninth house. All malefic association is with ninth house. The ninth house is badly afflicted. The AD lord Jupiter is eighth lord for father.

Mangla / Shravan

This is an important Mangla period. The Nakshatra lord is Moon and the dasha lord is also Moon. To top it the seventh lord is also Moon. During this Yogini dasha the relation with outside world or your relations are important. A person experience ups and down in the marriage / business matters. The condition of Moon is important. The events are governed by Moon.

Example 12 Affair

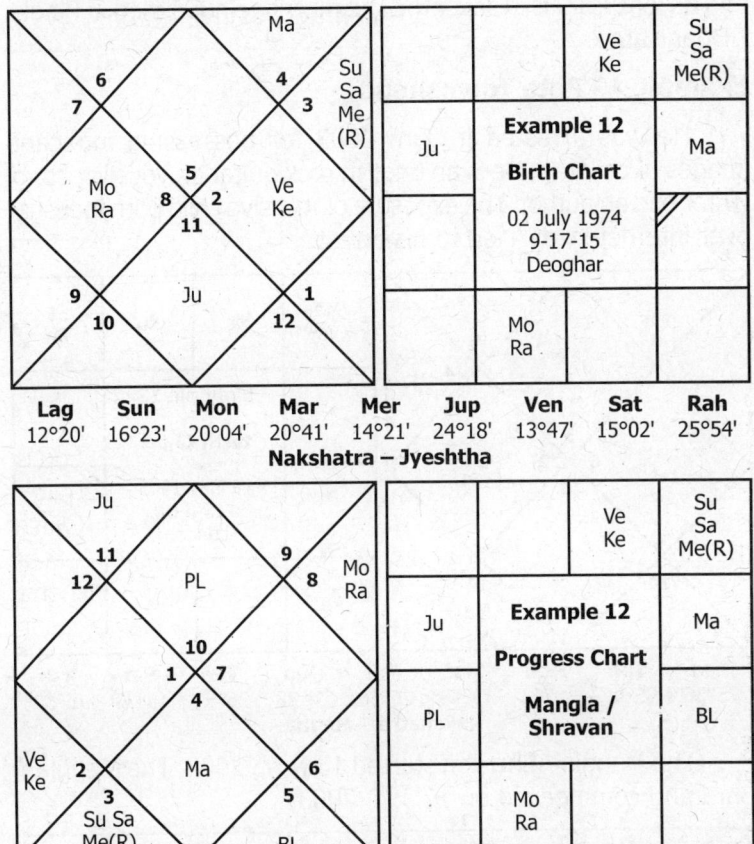

Lag	Sun	Mon	Mar	Mer	Jup	Ven	Sat	Rah
12°20'	16°23'	20°04'	20°41'	14°21'	24°18'	13°47'	15°02'	25°54'

Nakshatra – Jyeshtha

The Mangla / Shravan operated from 24 March 1999 to 24 Mar 2000. The person was running his twenty fifth year of age. This age is the right age for marriage and affairs. The birth Moon will be in Jyeshtha / Moola for this dasha to operate at marriageable age.

Here Moon is debilitated and afflicted by Rahu / Ketu axis. The fifth and seventh lords are in mutual aspect and both are in Rahu / Ketu axis. No benefic is aspecting this combination and as such possibility of marriage is not present. This person had an intense affair throughout Mangla period which ended with this period. For next period of Pingla, the Nakshatra is Dhanishta and its lord Mars is in seventh. The marriage happened in Pingla / Dhanishta.

Example 13 Pete Townshend

He was arrested in Jan. 2003 for possessing indecent images of children. He is an English rock guitarist, vocalist, song writer and an author. The exposure of massive child porn industry over internet in USA led to his arrest.

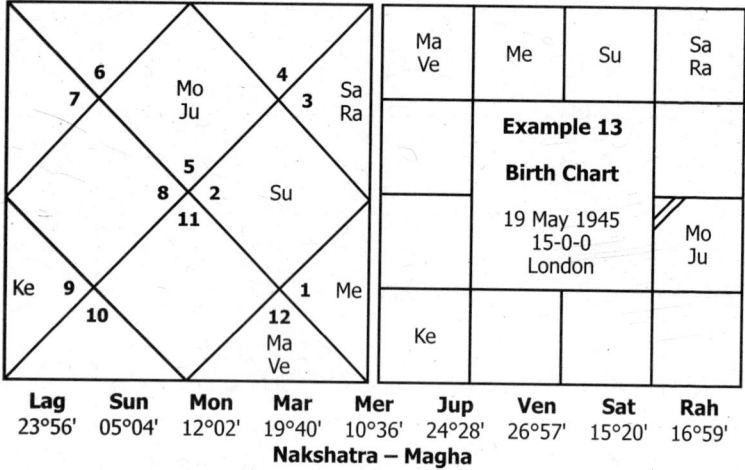

Ma Ve	Me	Su	Sa Ra
	Example 13		
	Birth Chart		Mo Ju
	19 May 1945 15-0-0 London		
Ke			

Lag	Sun	Mon	Mar	Mer	Jup	Ven	Sat	Rah
23°56'	05°04'	12°02'	19°40'	10°36'	24°28'	26°57'	15°20'	16°59'

Nakshatra – Magha

The Mangla / Shravan started 13 Nov., 2002. The Mangla / Bhramari commenced on 12 Jan, 2003.

Ma Ve	Me	Su	Sa Ra
	Example 13		
	Progress Chart		Mo Ju BL
PL	**Mangla / Shravan**		
Ke			

The age of the person is now 57 years. The Moon is in eighth house of the progress chart. It is with Jupiter and aspected by Saturn. Since Saturn is the progress Lagna lord not much damage was caused. He was jailed on 13 Jan, 2003, a day after Bhramari sub-period started. Mars is in eighth from Moon.

Example 14 Job started

He started his career in Moon / Bhramari. In the above example 13, the person was arrested in the same period. The placement of Mars / and Moon made the difference. In example 13 Moons is in eighth house from PL. The birth lagna is also in eighth.

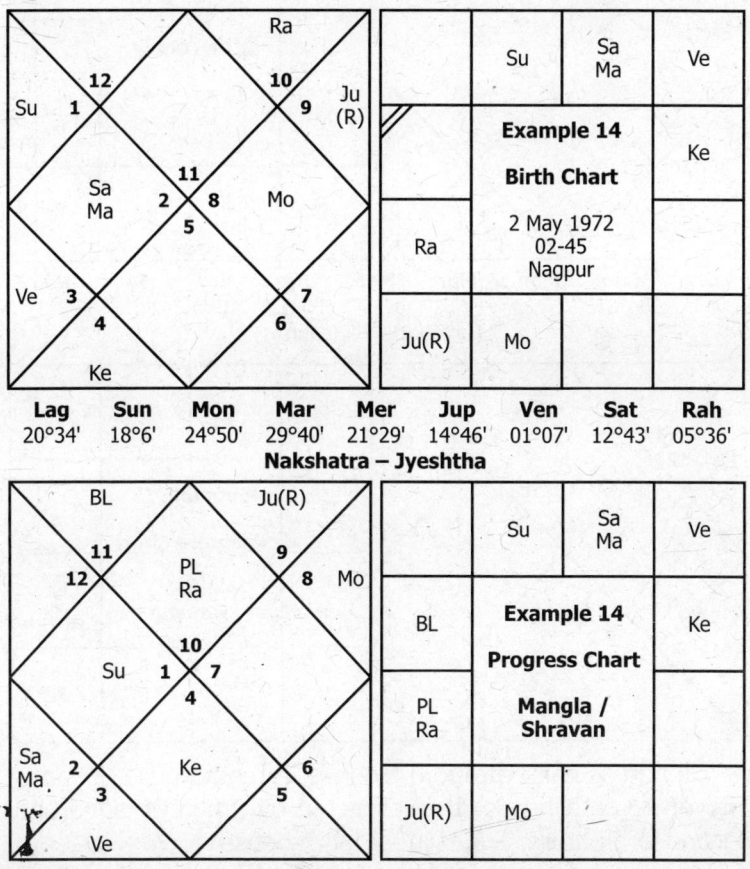

Lag	Sun	Mon	Mar	Mer	Jup	Ven	Sat	Rah
20°34'	18°6'	24°50'	29°40'	21°29'	14°46'	01°07'	12°43'	05°36'

Nakshatra – Jyeshtha

Moon is in eleventh house of progress chart. Moon is aspected by Mars and Saturn. Saturn is lagna lord of birth and progress chart. He started his job in July 1995 in the Bhramari sub period. Mars is the tenth lord of birth chart and aspect its own sign Scorpio which is now eleventh house.

Example 15 Promotion

He got a jump in March 1981. The sub period was of Pingla.

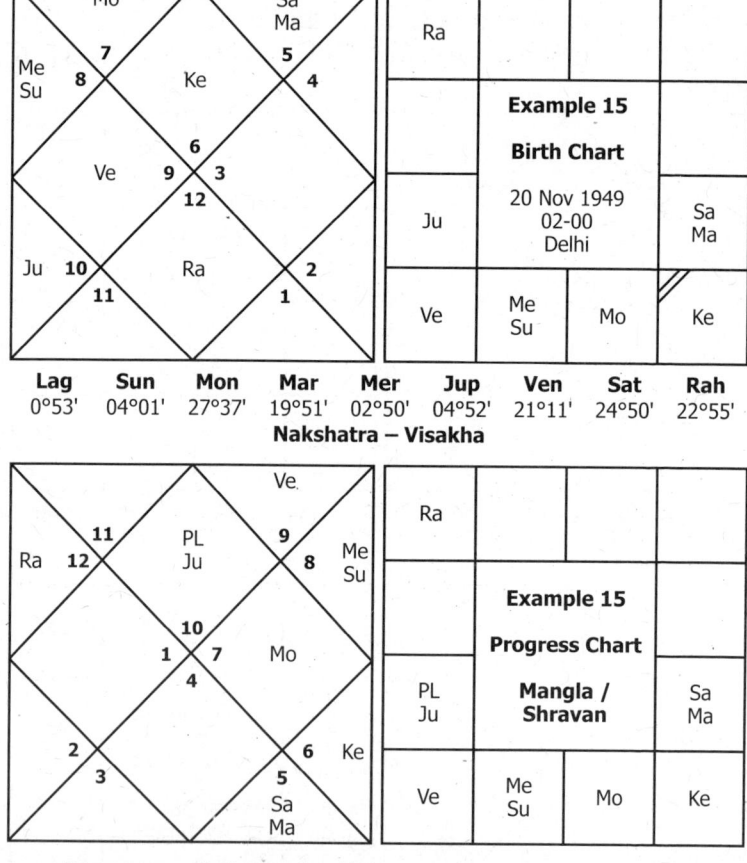

Lag	Sun	Mon	Mar	Mer	Jup	Ven	Sat	Rah
0°53'	04°01'	27°37'	19°51'	02°50'	04°52'	21°11'	24°50'	22°55'

Nakshatra – Visakha

Progress nakshatra lord Moon is in tenth house. Moon is lord of seventh house. It is aspected by progress lagna and second lord Saturn. Sun is in eleventh house.

Example 16 Profession

This chart belongs to a highly placed executive. The Mangla Shravan period started on 9th Aug. 2007.

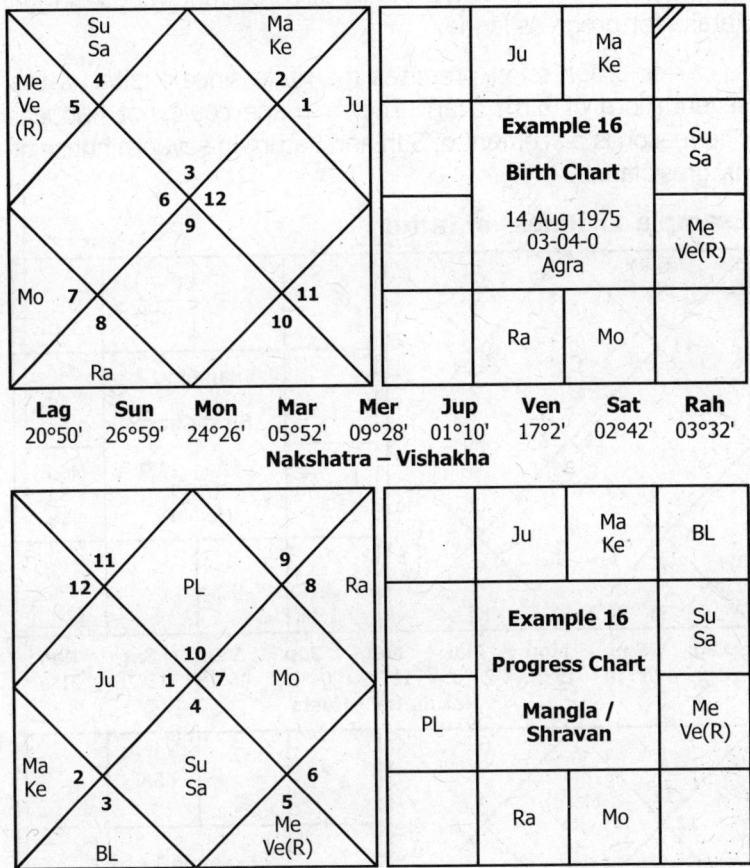

Lag	Sun	Mon	Mar	Mer	Jup	Ven	Sat	Rah
20°50'	26°59'	24°26'	05°52'	09°28'	01°10'	17°2'	02°42'	03°32'

Nakshatra – Vishakha

Now Moon is placed in tenth house. It is aspected by Jupiter who is tenth lord of birth chart.

She was working with an MNC and was posted abroad. In Mangla / Mangla, she resigned from that job and returned to

India to take up job with another American MNC at a much higher salary. In progress chart Jupiter is third and twelfth lord from progress lagna. Also the progress tenth lord is retrograde and is in eighth house. We should also see that Venus is Yoga karaka for progress lagna.

This progression promises marriage since Jupiter is the seventh lord of birth chart. The marriage could not happen. The reason is placement of Sun and Saturn in seventh house of progress lagna.

Example 17 illness of father

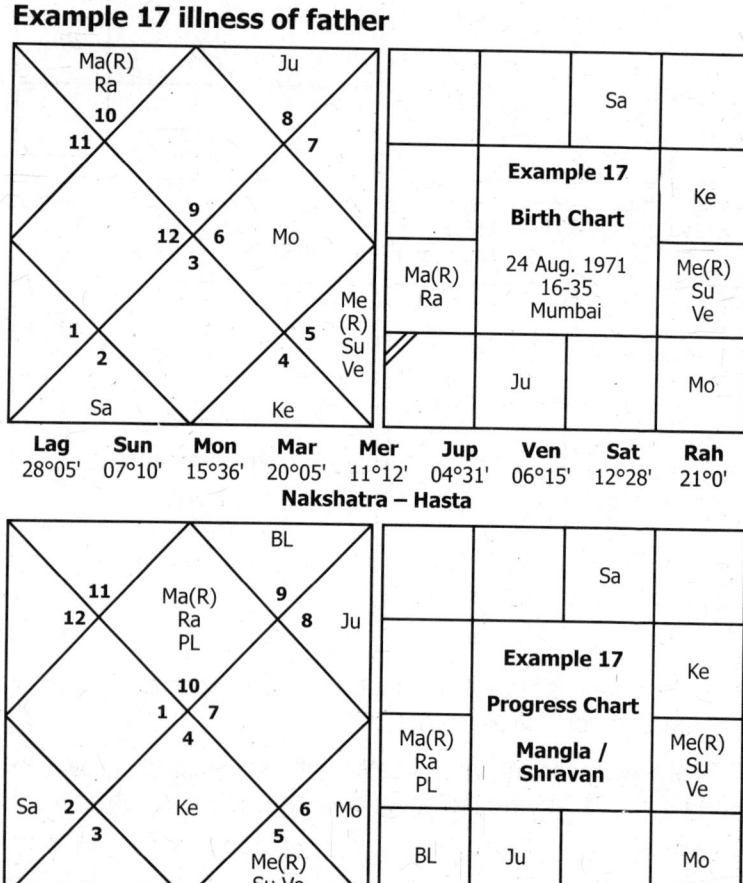

Lag	Sun	Mon	Mar	Mer	Jup	Ven	Sat	Rah
28°05'	07°10'	15°36'	20°05'	11°12'	04°31'	06°15'	12°28'	21°0'

Nakshatra – Hasta

Moon is now in ninth house. The attention is on ninth house. The ninth lord Mercury is in eighth house from PL. It is with Sun who is the significator of father. It is aspected by afflicted Mars. The sixth lord of birth chart also joins Sun and Mercury in eighth house. Father got seriously ill in Mangla / Pingla.

Chapter 4

Pingla

Pingla dasha is of two years. This can operate in three Nakshatra. This dasha is not considered a benefic in classics. However the results depend upon the Nakshatra lord.

Punarvasu, Swati and Dhanishta generate this dasha. Table below gives the Nakshatra and lords etc. for Pingla Yogini dasha.

Nakshatra	Nakshatra Lord	Sign of Nakshatra	Remarks
Punarvasu	Jupiter	Gemini / Cancer	For first one year six months, The progress lagna is Gemini and last six months it is cancer.
Swati	Rahu	Libra	Libra is the progress Lagna.
Dhanishta	Mars	Capricorn / Aquarius	For first one year progress lagna is Capricorn and for last one year it is Aquarius.

Pingla / Punarvasu

Punarvasu Nakshatra has three Padas in Gemini and one pada in cancer. In Gemini it is from 20° to 30°. In cancer it is from 0 to 3° – 20'. The navamsha signs are Aries, Taurus, Gemini and cancer.

Progress lagna is Gemini for first eighteen months of Pingla / Punarvasu. Jupiter is the lord of seventh and tenth house. The area of focus will be related to partner and profession. The position of Jupiter in the birth chart is also important.

For Cancer progress lagna, Jupiter is sixth and ninth lord. The focus now is on these houses.

Jupiter should normally make relation to the house and house lord for any event related to a house.

Example: Hillary Clinton

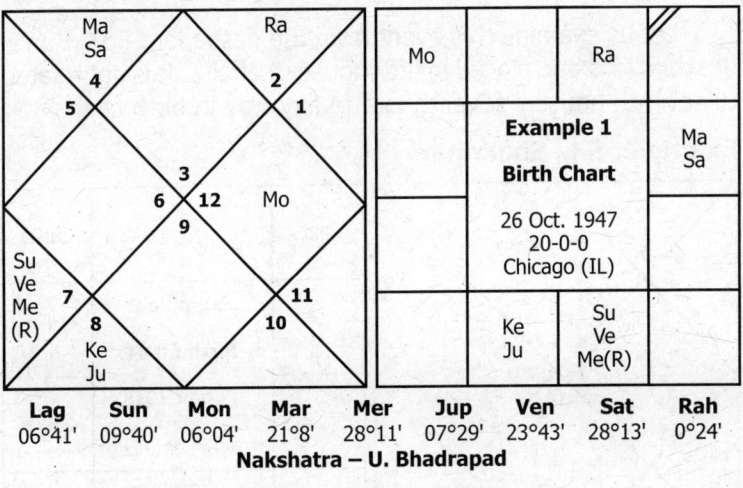

Lag	Sun	Mon	Mar	Mer	Jup	Ven	Sat	Rah
06°41'	09°40'	06°04'	21°8'	28°11'	07°29'	23°43'	28°13'	0°24'

Nakshatra – U. Bhadrapad

She got married on 11 Oct 1975 in the dasha of Pingla / Mangla. The progress lagna is cancer.

We first examine it from Gemini progress lagna. Jupiter is seventh lord but placed in sixth house. It is not making any relation with seventh house or the lagna. Since Jupiter is seventh lord and is afflicted, it gave relationship but could not convert it in marriage.

With cancer progress lagna, the stage is now set. Jupiter is the seventh lord of birth chart and now aspects lagna lord, lagna and seventh lord of progress chart.

Let us examine this event from the dasha lord Sun. Sun is the third lord and placed in fifth house of affairs. It is not related to seventh house / seventh lord in any way in birth chart.

Example: S.L. Shakdhar

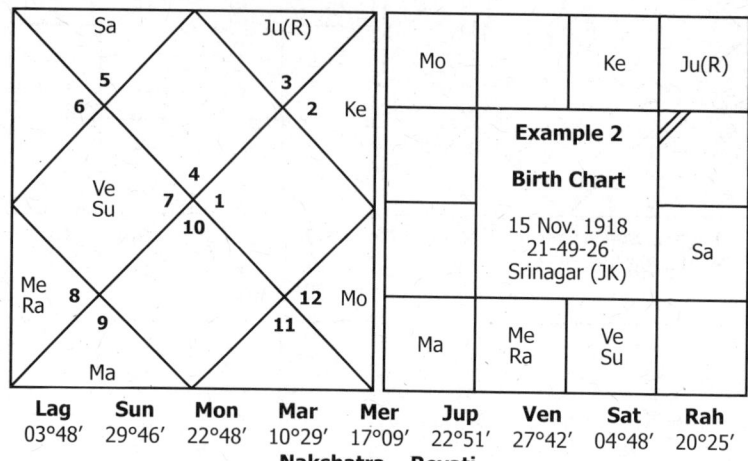

Lag	Sun	Mon	Mar	Mer	Jup	Ven	Sat	Rah
03°48′	29°46′	22°48′	10°29′	17°09′	22°51′	27°42′	04°48′	20°25′

Nakshatra – Revati

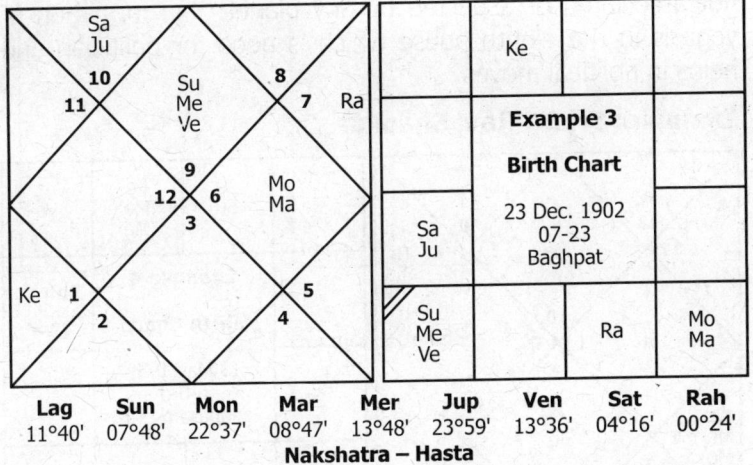

Jupiter is now tenth lord and placed in Lagna. Jupiter is aspected by Mars who is now eleventh lord. Mars is the tenth lord of birth chart. Mars is also aspecting the progress tenth house. Mars is the lord of sixth house indicating service. He started his career as an LDC in Pingla/ Pingla. Sun is aspected by Jupiter.

Example: Charan Singh

Lag	Sun	Mon	Mar	Mer	Jup	Ven	Sat	Rah
11°40'	07°48'	22°37'	08°47'	13°48'	23°59'	13°36'	04°16'	00°24'

Nakshatra – Hasta

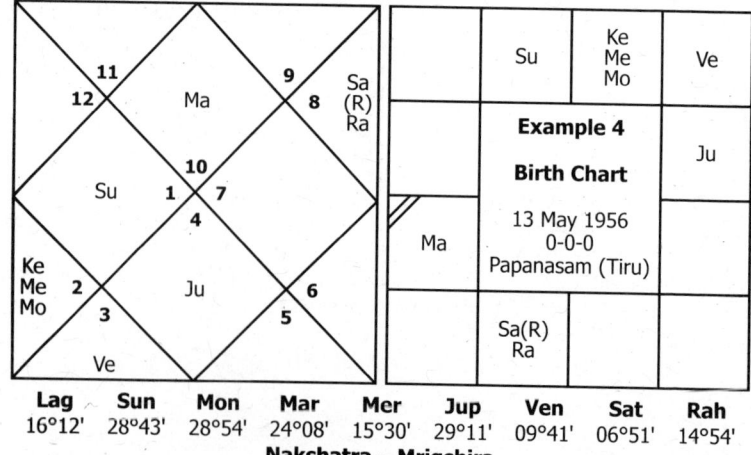

He became Deputy Prime Minister of India on 24th March 1977 and remained DPM till 28.7.79. After that he was Prime Minister till 14th Jan. 1980.

The Pingla dasha started on 25 May, 1976. For first one year six months i.e. till 25 November, 1978 the progress lagna is Gemini. The Nakshatra lord Jupiter is the lord of tenth house and forms a powerful Raj Yoga with ninth Lord Saturn. This is not associated or aspected by any planet. The formation of yoga is in the eighth house which is good for politician and helps in political moves.

Example: Sri Sri Ravi Shankar

Lag	Sun	Mon	Mar	Mer	Jup	Ven	Sat	Rah
16°12'	28°43'	28°54'	24°08'	15°30'	29°11'	09°41'	06°51'	14°54'

Nakshatra – Mrigshira

<table>
<tr><td></td><td></td><td></td></tr>
</table>

	Su	Ke Me Mo	Ve
		Example 4 **Progress Chart**	PL Ju
Ma BL		**Pingla /** **Punarvasu**	
		Sa(R) Ra	

(North Indian chart at left contains: Ve at top; 5, 6 at upper left; Ju; 3, 2 Ke Me Mo at upper right; 4; 7, 1 Su; 10; Sa(R) Ra 8, 9 at lower left; 12, 11 Ma BL at lower right)

The Nakshatra lord is ninth lord and is exalted in lagna. The ninth and tenth lords are in mutual aspect. The fifth and lagna lords are exalted. A wonderful placement of lords of dharma trikona. He mastered the Rig Veda at the young age starting with this dasha at an age of six years.

Example: Marriage

She was married on 18th Nov. 1995 in the progress lagna of Gemini

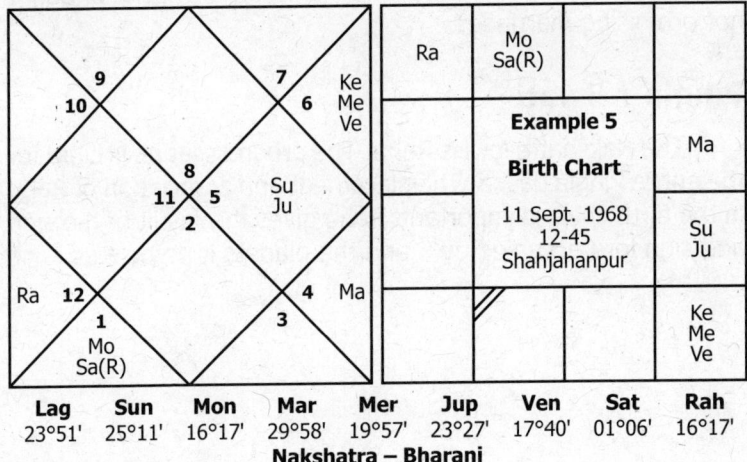

	Lag	Sun	Mon	Mar	Mer	Jup	Ven	Sat	Rah
	23°51'	25°11'	16°17'	29°58'	19°57'	23°27'	17°40'	01°06'	16°17'

Nakshatra – Bharani

Ra	Mo Sa(R)		PL
	Example 5 **Progress Chart** **Pingla / Punarvasu**		Ma
			Su Ju
	BL		Ke Me Ve

(Left chart — North Indian diamond style)

```
        Ma
     4        2      Mo
Su  5        1       Sa
Ju                   (R)
     Ke    3
     Me  6  12  Ra
     Ve    9
    7           11
       8      10
         BL
```

Pingla / Punarvasu started on 1st Aug 1994. In the progress Yogini Dasha we go to Rohini after Revati.

The Nakshatra lord Jupiter is seventh lord and aspects seventh house. The sub period was of Siddha. It will be interesting to examine Sun for its promise to give marriage during Pingla dasha. Sun is the tenth lord placed in tenth house in the birth chart. It is associated with Jupiter. Jupiter is not the lord of seventh house but fifth and second lord of birth chart. Sun is not related to seventh house or lord. The dasha of Sun is not promising marriage.

Pingla / Swati

The Nakshatra lord is Rahu. The progress lagna is Libra for the entire Pingla dasha. The placement and association of Rahu in the birth chart is important. Rahu gives the result of the sign and sign lord occupied by it and the planets it associates.

Example: Harivanash Rai Bachchan

First wife died on 17.11.1936 in the dasha of Pingla / Siddha.

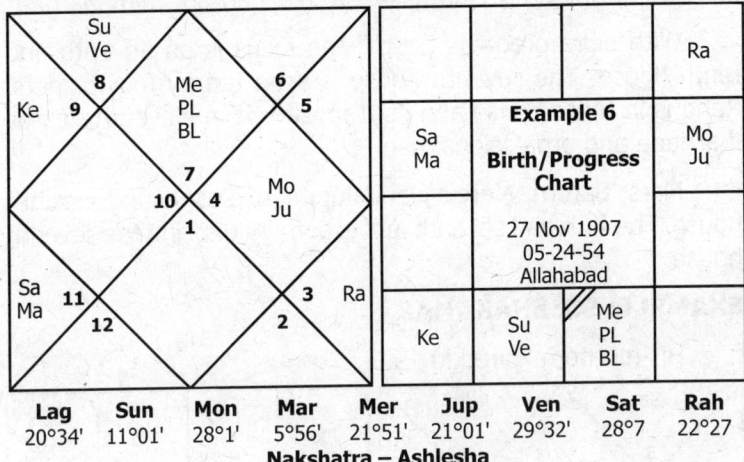

Lag	Sun	Mon	Mar	Mer	Jup	Ven	Sat	Rah
20°34'	11°01'	28°1'	5°56'	21°51'	21°01'	29°32'	28°7	22°27

Nakshatra – Ashlesha

The progress and birth lagna is same as Libra. The seventh house and seventh lord are afflicted. From seventh house, Venus is the lord of second and seventh and is placed in second house.

Example : - Margret Thatcher

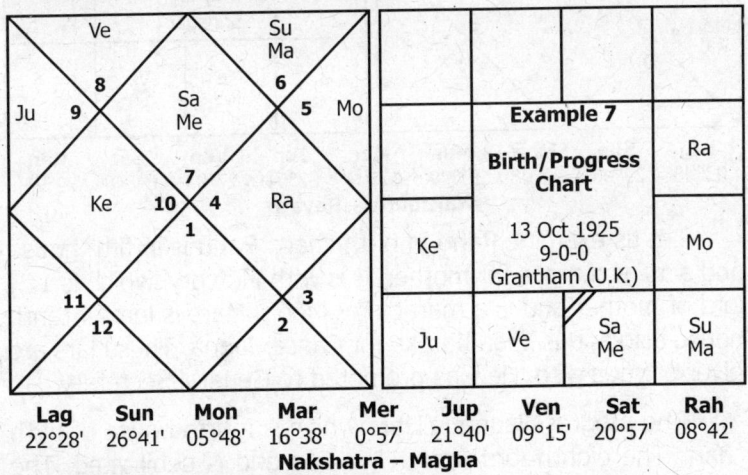

Lag	Sun	Mon	Mar	Mer	Jup	Ven	Sat	Rah
22°28'	26°41'	05°48'	16°38'	0°57'	21°40'	09°15'	20°57'	08°42'

Nakshatra – Magha

She married Sir Denis Thatcher on 13 Dec. 1951. They had met in Feb 1949. Sir Thatcher was ten years senior to her and had married three times before his marriage with Margret.

With Libra progress Lagna, the focus is on Seventh and tenth house. The seventh house is aspected by four planets. Rahu is in tenth house and its dispositor is in eleventh. It was marriage and professional rise.

Mars, Saturn, Mercury and Jupiter are aspecting seventh house. The fifth and seventh lord is both influencing the seventh house.

EXAMPLE: S.L.SHAKDHAR

His mother expired in 1974.

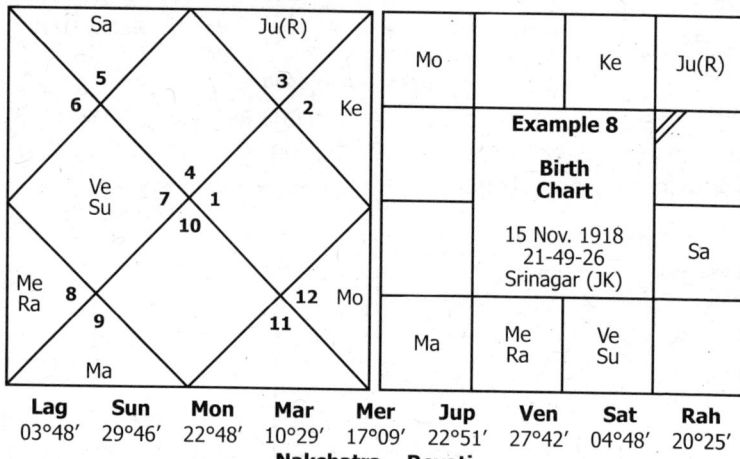

Lag	Sun	Mon	Mar	Mer	Jup	Ven	Sat	Rah
03°48′	29°46′	22°48′	10°29′	17°09′	22°51′	27°42′	04°48′	20°25′

Nakshatra – Revati

Let us examine Rahu in birth chart. Rahu is in fifth house and acts as maraca for mother. It is with Mercury, which is 12th lord of mother and is a maraca for Moon. Mars is lord of tenth house also and is Yoga Karaka for Cancer lagna. Thus Mars are giver of yoga also. He was promoted to General Secretary.

The progress lagna is Libra which is fourth house of birth chart. The eighth lord from 4th is Sun and is debilitated. The eighth house from 4th house is occupied by Saturn. The fourth

lord of progress chart is in eighth from fourth. Mother died in
Pingla / Pingla.

Mo		Ke	Ju(R)
	Example 8 **Progress Chart** **Pingla /** **Swati**		BL
			Sa
Ma	Me Ra	Ve Su PL	

Let us see why mother did not expire in Mangla of Ardra
Nakshatra. The progress lagna was Gemini. The fourth lord is in
sixth house of PL and can give illness only.

Pingla / Dhanishta

Dhanishta Nakshatra occupies Capricorn and Aquarius. First
two pada of Dhanishta falls in Capricorn and last two in Aquarius.
Therefore, for first half dasha period i.e. one year the progress
lagna will be Capricorn and for last one year the progress lagna
will be Aquarius. This change happens in Ulka Sub period.

For both progress lagna, Saturn is the lord of lagna and
Venus is the yogkarak. Therefore, attention should be given to
these planets also.

For Capricorn, Mars is the lord of fourth and eleventh house
and activates these houses. The lordship and placement of Mars
in natal chart is important.

For Aquarius, Mars is the lord of third and tenth house.
The matters regarding profession, father, travels etc. come into
play.

Example Serious Accident

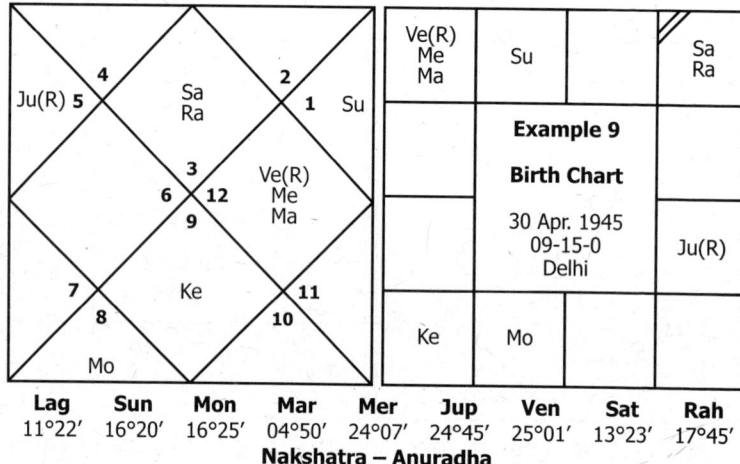

Lag	Sun	Mon	Mar	Mer	Jup	Ven	Sat	Rah
11°22′	16°20′	16°25′	04°50′	24°07′	24°45′	25°01′	13°23′	17°45′

Nakshatra – Anuradha

A near fatal accident happened in Sept., 1972 when he was driving a Jeep. Four other co passengers were hurt. The dasha was Pingla / Bhramari

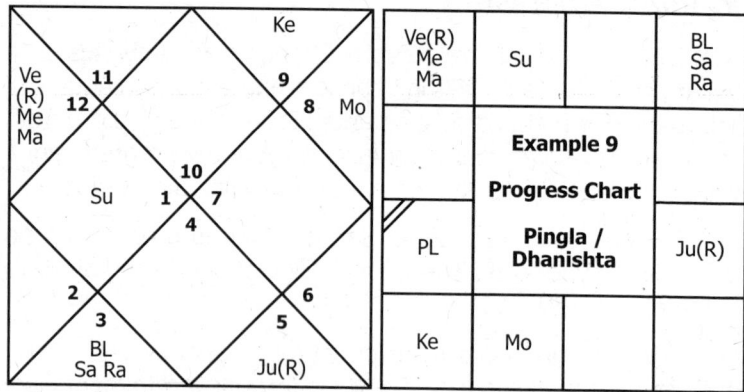

Eighth house is the progress lagna. Mars is the sixth lord of the birth chart.

In the progress chart Mars is fourth lord and is placed with sixth lord of Progress chart. A very serious accident involving sixth and fourth Lords of Birth and progress chart happened in Sept. 1972.

The saving grace came from the conjunction of Mars with fifth and ninth lord and aspect of lagna lord.

He remained hospitalized for six months and recovered when the progress lagna moved to Aquarius.

It will be of interest to see the changes which happened after the progress lagna moved to Aquarius. Daughter was born on 22 Dec. 1973 in the sub period of Sankata.

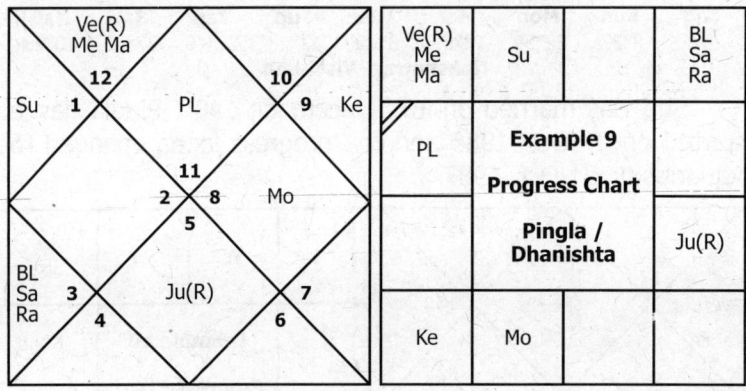

Now also Mars is with fifth, ninth and aspected by Lagna Lord. The relation with sixth lord of progress is not there.

Saturn and Rahu are in fifth house. The effect of trine lords is still present. After the birth of daughter he was transferred. Mars is third and tenth lord now.

Example Benazir Bhutto

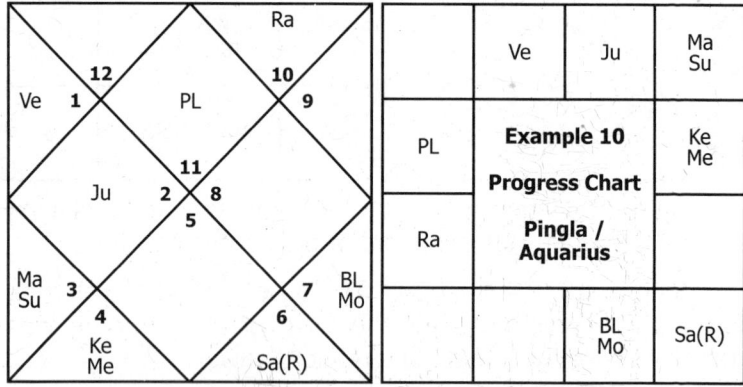

	Lag Sun Mon Mar Mer Jup Ven Sat Rah							

Lag	Sun	Mon	Mar	Mer	Jup	Ven	Sat	Rah
25°4'	8°27'	22°59'	12°59'	3°29'	17°12'	22°46	27°20	10°28

Nakshatra – Vishakha

She was married on 18th December, 1987. Pingla dasha started on 21 Oct. 1986 and the progress lagna changed to Aquarius on 21 Oct. 1987.

Mars is the seventh lord of birth chart. In the progress chart it is with seventh lord of the progress chart. It is aspected by lord of lagna Saturn. The marriage was in Pingla / Siddha. Venus is the birth lagna lord placed in seventh house in birth chart.

Example: Chief Minister

He became chief Minister of Orissa in Pingla / Bhadrika in the progress lagna of Aquarius.

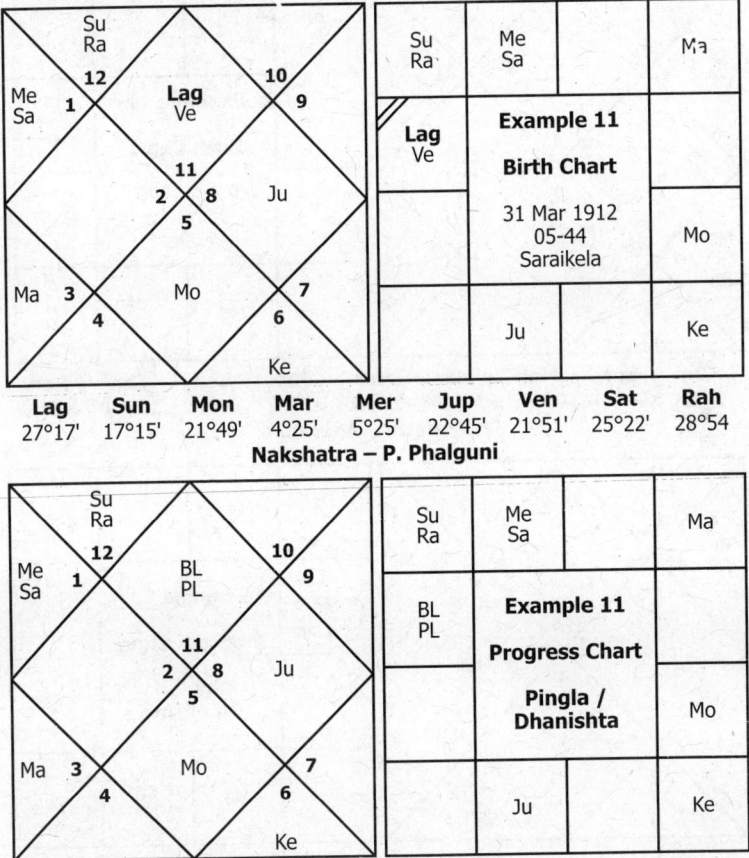

Lag	Sun	Mon	Mar	Mer	Jup	Ven	Sat	Rah
27°17'	17°15'	21°49'	4°25'	5°25'	22°45'	21°51'	25°22'	28°54

Nakshatra – P. Phalguni

Mars is the tenth lord. Mars is aspected by lagna lord Saturn. There is exchange of fifth and third lord. Mercury is the fifth lord and this is raj yoga of fifth and tenth lord.

Example: Pt. Ravi Shankar

This Period of Pingla/Dhanishta brought him into lime light.

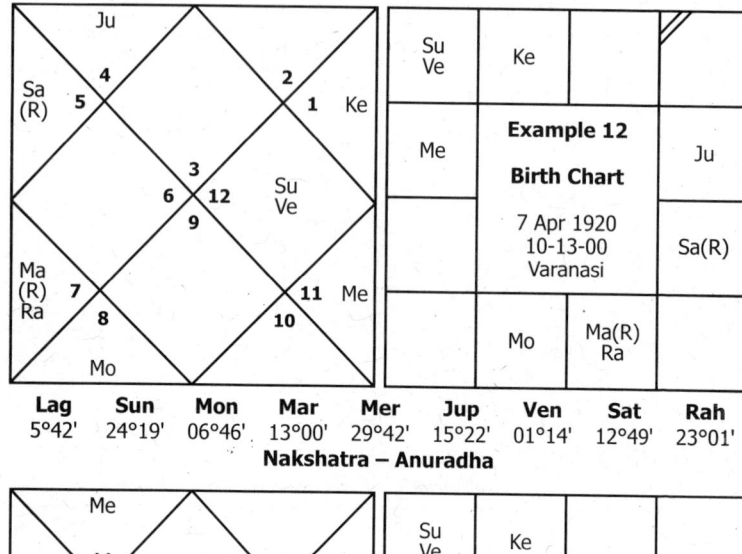

Lag	Sun	Mon	Mar	Mer	Jup	Ven	Sat	Rah
5°42'	24°19'	06°46'	13°00'	29°42'	15°22'	01°14'	12°49'	23°01'

Nakshatra – Anuradha

He was Music Director with All India Radio. He composed music for Aputrilogy of Satyajit Ray and got international acclaim.

Nakshatra lord Mars is in tenth house with Rahu. It isaspected by lagna lord Saturn.

Example: Marriage

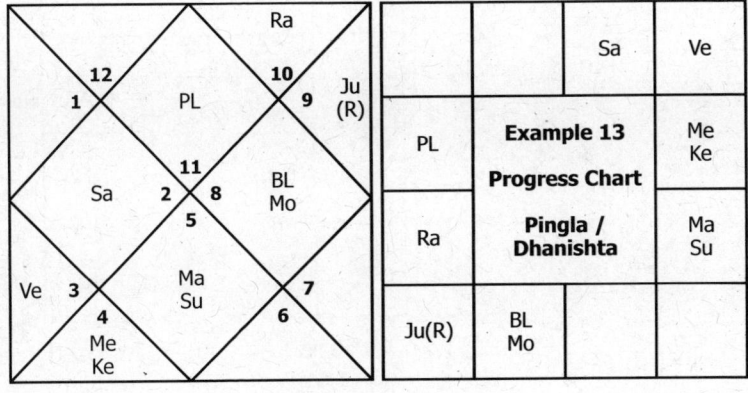

Lag	Sun	Mon	Mar	Mer	Jup	Ven	Sat	Rah
5°59'	1°56'	15°24'	8°34'	16°59'	5°5'	16°28'	25°18'	2°11'

Nakshatra – Anuradha

Marriage took place in Jan 2001. The Pingla dasha started on 3rd Jan, 2000 and the progress Lagna moved to Aquarius in Jan. 2001.

A clear picture emerges. Mars is the birth lagna lord. In the progress chart, it is in seventh house with seventh lord and aspected by Jupiter. Saturn is the lagna lord and aspects lagna. Saturn is in seventh house of birth chart.

With the traditional approach in the birth chart Sun is in tenth house making no relation with seventh house or seventh lord. Only when we progress Yogini with the Nakshatra, the promise comes out clear and loud.

Chapter 5

Dhanya

Dhanya Maha dasha is generated by three Nakshatra. The lord of Dhanya Yogini is Jupiter and classics have rated Jupiter as the most benefic planets and give mostly auspicious results during this period.

The Nakshatra of Dhanya Dasha are given:

Nakshatra	Lord	Sign of Nakshatra	Remarks
Pushya	Saturn	Cancer	Cancer in progress lagna
Vishakha	Jupiter	Libra / Scorpio	First two years 3 months progress lagna in Libra. Last 9 months progress lagna is Scorpio.
Shatbhisaj	Rahu	Aquarius	Aquarius is the progress Lagna.

Dhanya / Pushya

Pushya Nakshatra is considered auspicious. Both heavy weights and the ninth and tenth lord of Kaalpurush are controlling this period.

It is our experience that this Yogini period **brings major changes which have lifelong effects.**

Example: Queen Victoria

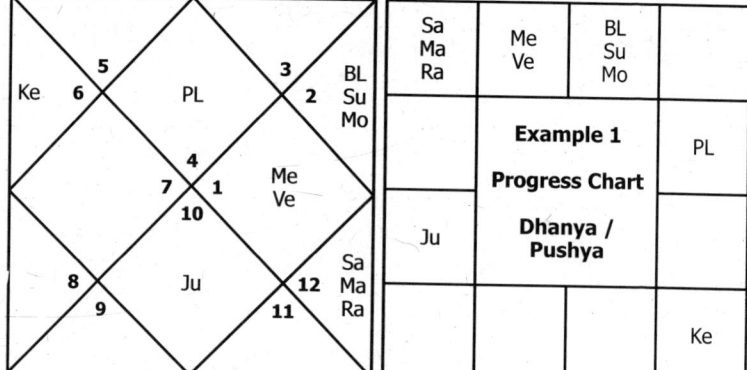

	North Indian chart		
Sa Ma Ra	Me Ve	Lag Su Mo	
	Example 1		
	Birth Chart		
Ju	24 May 1819 02-26-54 London		
			Ke

Lag	Sun	Mon	Mar	Mer	Jup	Ven	Sat	Rah
13°17'	10°47'	12°20'	26°19'	17°36'	25°35'	5°14'	7°24'	28°24'

Nakshatra – Rohini

	North Indian chart		
Sa Ma Ra	Me Ve	BL Su Mo	
	Example 1		PL
	Progress Chart		
Ju	**Dhanya / Pushya**		
			Ke

She was coroneted on 20 June 1836 at age of 18 years. She remained queen till her death on 22 Jan 1901.

She was fifth in the line of succession to the throne but the turn of events made her the queen. Dhanya/ Pushya changed the life.

Saturn is the yoga Karaka ninth lord of birth chart and has become the dasha Nakshatra. Examine the progress chart. The lagna lord Moon is exalted in eleventh house. Both Lagna and lagna lord are aspected by Jupiter. Jupiter is debilitated ninth lord and shows death of father.Saturn and Jupiter have exchanged seventh and ninth houses.

The coronation came in Dhanya/ Ulka.

Example: - Permanent Shift

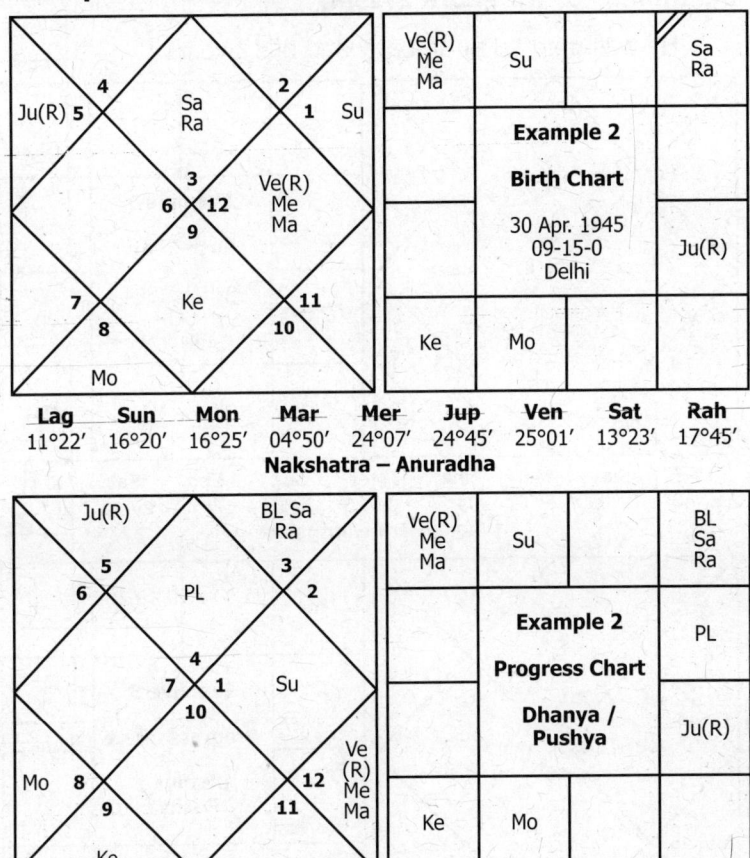

Lag	Sun	Mon	Mar	Mer	Jup	Ven	Sat	Rah
11°22′	16°20′	16°25′	04°50′	24°07′	24°45′	25°01′	13°23′	17°45′

Nakshatra – Anuradha

Dhanya/Pushya commenced on 26 May2010. In May 2012 he shifted out of Delhi to settle in Gurgaon at the age of 67 years and it should be the home for rest of life. This is a major change for the person born in Delhi and lived in Delhi throughout.

Saturn and the birth lagna are in 12th house. Saturn is with Rahu and aspected by Mars. It is a big disturbance and affliction to Nakshatra lord. Venus is the fourth lord of progress lagna. Both fourth lords of birth chart and progress chart are afflicted. The change came in Dhanya/Siddha. Jupiter and Venus are retrograde but Saturn in not.

Example: - Dr Rajendra Prasad

He was married at an early age of 12 years

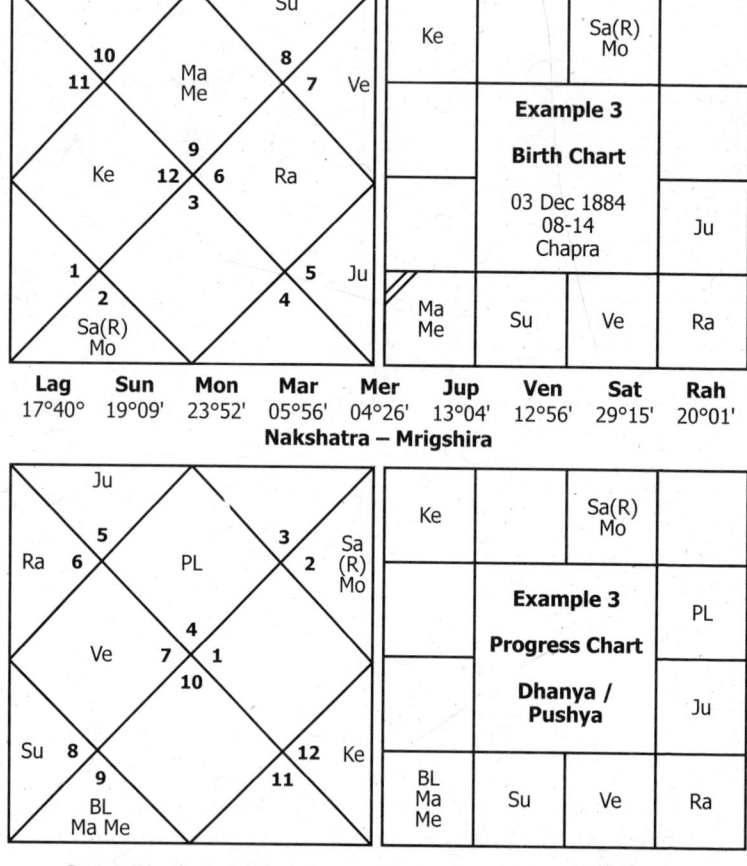

Lag	Sun	Mon	Mar	Mer	Jup	Ven	Sat	Rah
17°40°	19°09'	23°52'	05°56'	04°26'	13°04'	12°56'	29°15'	20°01'

Nakshatra – Mrigshira

Saturn is the seventh lord of progress chart. It is with Lagna lord of progress chart. Both are placed in eleventh house.

Example: Indira Gandhi

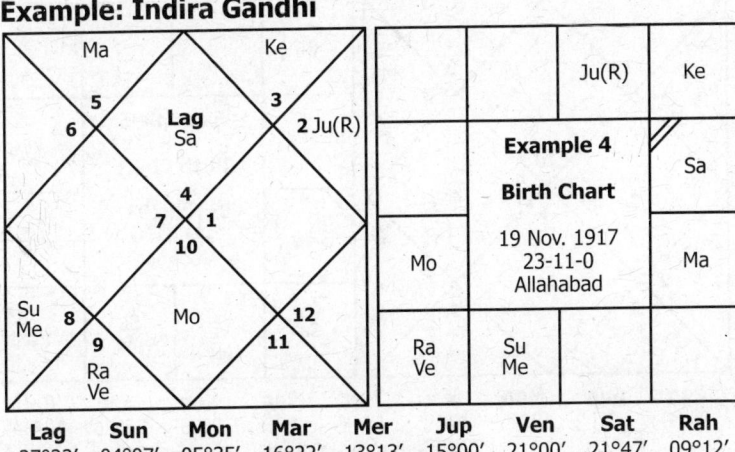

Lag	Sun	Mon	Mar	Mer	Jup	Ven	Sat	Rah
27°22'	04°07'	05°35'	16°22'	13°13'	15°00'	21°00'	21°47'	09°12'

Nakshatra – U. Ashdha

The progress chart for Dhanya / Pushya is same as birth chart.

The Nakshatra Lord Saturn is the seventh and the eighth lord of Birth Chart. In progress chart, we take seventh house as the house of spouse. The maraca for husband is Saturn and Moon. Both are in natural aspect in one/seven axis.

Firoz Gandhi died on 8th September 1960 in the sub period of Ulka i.e. Saturn.

Example: L. M. Singhvi

Laxmi Mal Singhvi was the longest serving high Commissioner to U.K. He expired on 13 Oct 2007 in Dhanya / Pingla.

Saturn is the second lord of Birth Chart. In the progress chart Saturn is again the seventh and eighth lord. The maraca status of Saturn is confirmed. For earlier dasha generated by Saturn Nakshatra did not reconfirm the maraca status of Saturn.

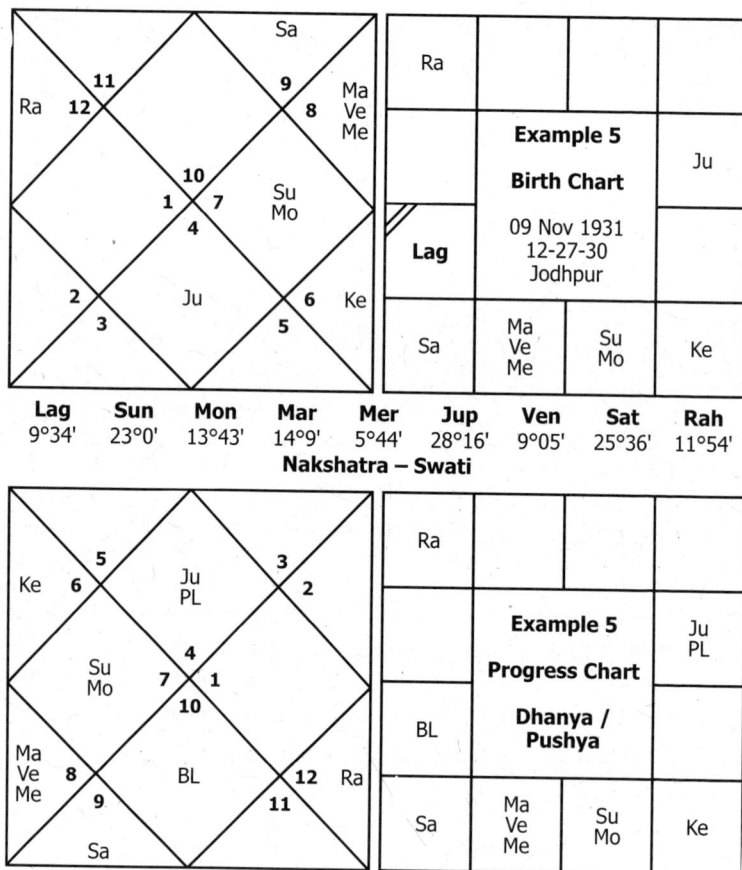

Lag	Sun	Mon	Mar	Mer	Jup	Ven	Sat	Rah
9°34'	23°0'	13°43'	14°9'	5°44'	28°16'	9°05'	25°36'	11°54'

Nakshatra – Swati

Sun is the eighth lord of birth chart and the second lord of progress chart. The end came in Dhanya / Pingla.

Example: Promotion

He got an excellent promotion on 23 Jan. 1992 in the dasha of Dhanya/ Dhanya. Dhanya started on 21 Jan. 1992.

Saturn is aspecting tenth house in the birth chart. It is aspected by lord of fifth house Mars.

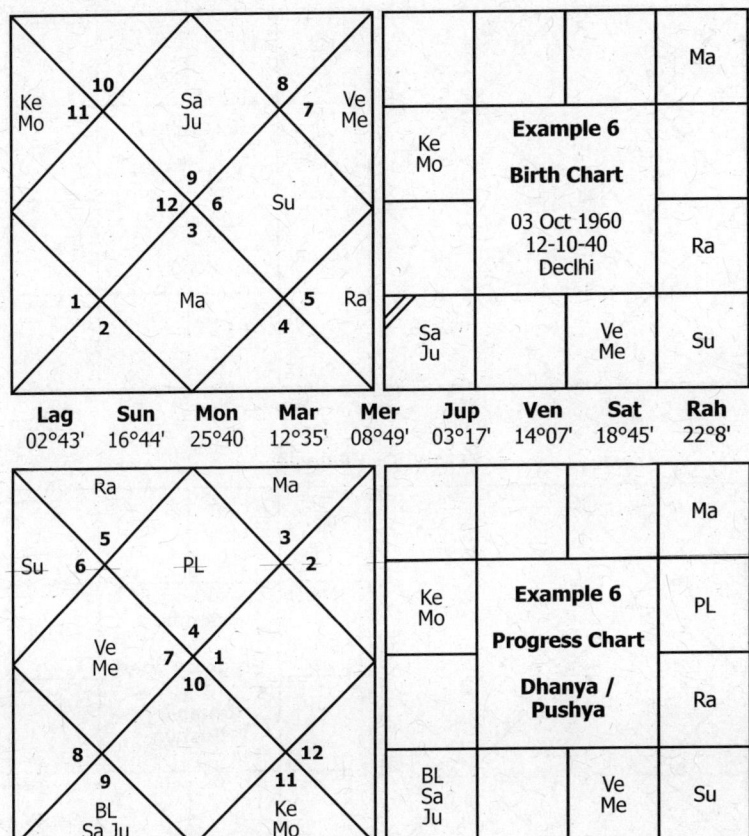

Lag	Sun	Mon	Mar	Mer	Jup	Ven	Sat	Rah
02°43'	16°44'	25°40	12°35'	08°49'	03°17'	14°07'	18°45'	22°8'

In the progress chart it again is making relation with progress tenth lord Mars. Jupiter is aspecting the progress tenth lord and tenth house. Jupiter is the dasha lord and is with Nakshatra Lord.

Example: Promotion

We take another case of a government officer who got promoted on 13 Aug. 1986.

Saturn is aspected by Mars in the birth chart. Mars is the tenth lord in the progress chart.

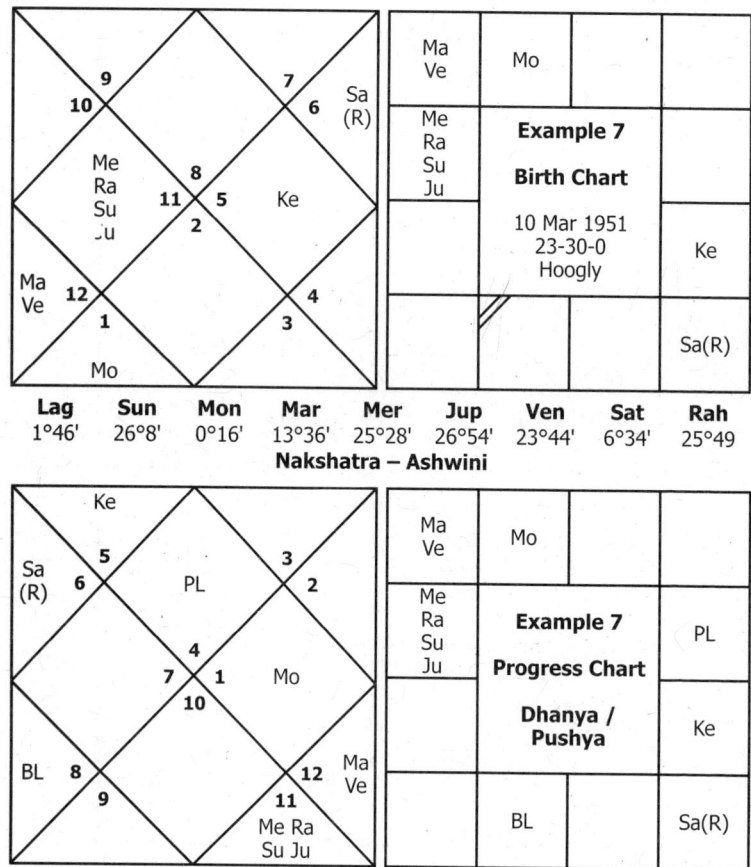

Lag	Sun	Mon	Mar	Mer	Jup	Ven	Sat	Rah
1°46'	26°8'	0°16'	13°36'	25°28'	26°54'	23°44'	6°34'	25°49

Nakshatra – Ashwini

Rahu act as Saturn and give result of Saturn also. It is conjoined with tenth lord of birth chart.

The promotion came in Sankata sub period.

Example: Jailed

He was with Merchant Navy. In Jan 2006 he was arrested in a foreign country on the charge of murder and was jailed.

Saturn is fifth and sixth lord of birth chart and is placed in tenth home. It is with Ketu.

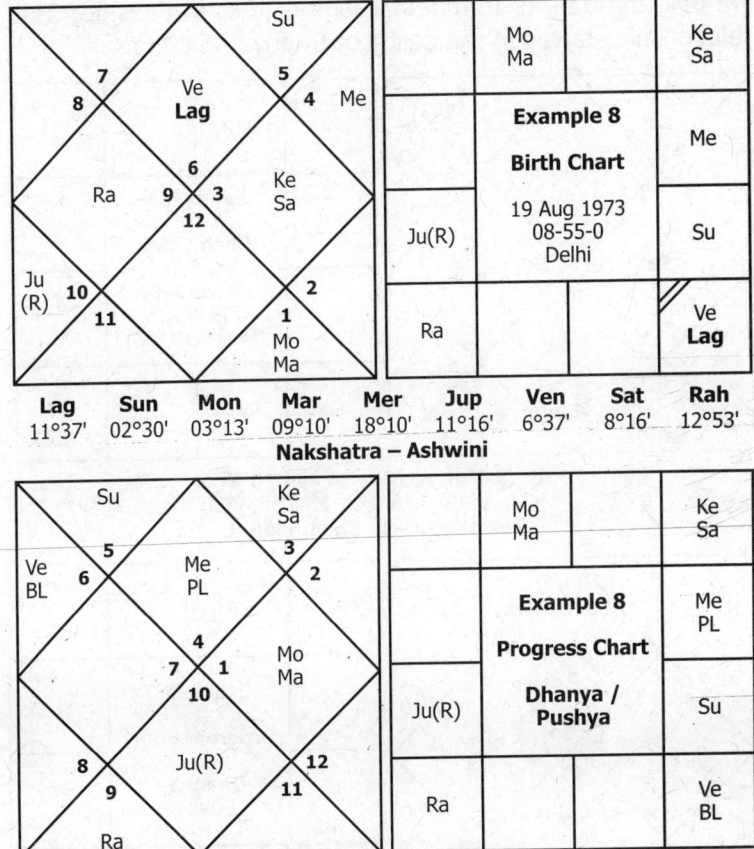

	Mo Ma		Ke Sa
		Example 8	Me
		Birth Chart	
Ju(R)		19 Aug 1973 08-55-0 Delhi	Su
Ra			Ve Lag

Lag	Sun	Mon	Mar	Mer	Jup	Ven	Sat	Rah
11°37'	02°30'	03°13'	09°10'	18°10'	11°16'	6°37'	8°16'	12°53'

Nakshatra – Ashwini

	Mo Ma		Ke Sa
		Example 8	Me PL
		Progress Chart	
Ju(R)		Dhanya / Pushya	Su
Ra			Ve BL

In the progress chart, Saturn is in twelfth house in Rahu / Ketu axis. Lagna is in Papa Kartari and is a typical bandana yoga. Saturn is not having any benefic relation. Twelfth house is also the house of confinement. Mars is eighth lord of birth chart and is in tenth house of progress chart.

Example: Catherine Zeta Jones

She is the British Film actor. She married Michael Douglas in 2000. The formal marriage was performed on 18 November 2000. Her first child was born on 8 Aug 2000 much before her formal marriage. What should now be the date of marriage. Do we take the date of formal marriage or the relationship? The relationship started in the dasha of Dhanya / Siddha.

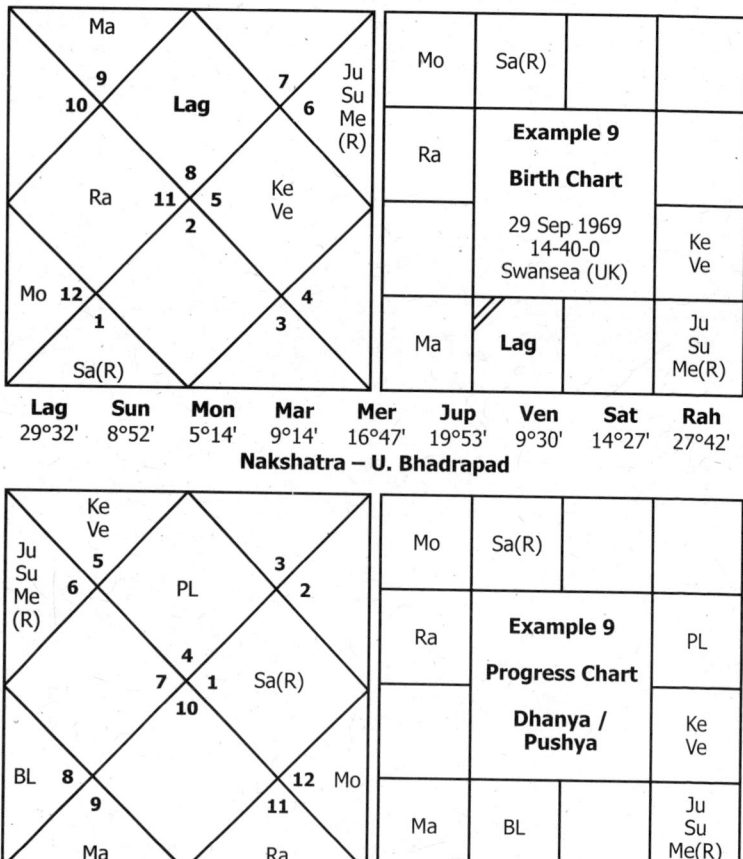

Lag	Sun	Mon	Mar	Mer	Jup	Ven	Sat	Rah
29°32'	8°52'	5°14'	9°14'	16°47'	19°53'	9°30'	14°27'	27°42'

Nakshatra – U. Bhadrapad

The nakshatra lord Saturn is in tenth house and aspects progress seventh house. It is also the seventh lord. The sub period of Venus gave the actual marriage since it is birth seventh lord.

Dhanya Vishakha

Jupiter is the dasha as well as the Nakshatra Lord. The results given by Jupiter are prominent. Vishakha Nakshatra is in Libra and Scorpio sign. First three Padas are in Libra and the last pada is in Scorpio. Dhanya Dasha is of three years and as such for first two years and three months the progress lagna will be Libra and for last nine months, the progress lagna is Scorpio. The progress Lagna changes to Scorpio in Sankata sub period.

With Libra progress lagna, Jupiter is lord of third and sixth house and is a malefic. It high lights the effect of these houses and is good for competition, service etc.

With Scorpio progress lagna, Jupiter is lord of second and fifth house and the results of Jupiter improve.

Jupiter is the planet for spirituality. In Dhanya / Vishakha, it should turn the person towards spirituality.

Example: Margret Thatcher

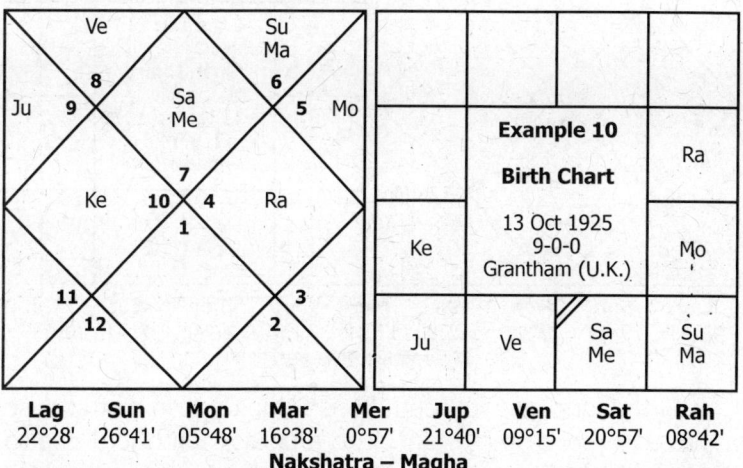

Lag	Sun	Mon	Mar	Mer	Jup	Ven	Sat	Rah
22°28'	26°41'	05°48'	16°38'	0°57'	21°40'	09°15'	20°57'	08°42'

Nakshatra – Magha

Twins were born on 15 Aug. 1953. The dasha was Dhanya / Ulka.

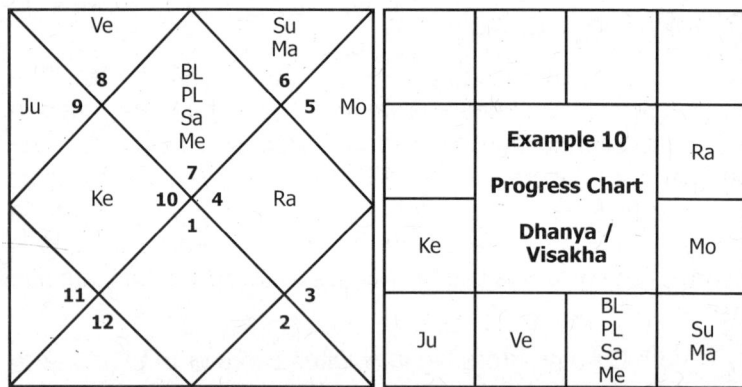

Jupiter is placed in third house and aspects ninth house. It is under the aspect of Saturn. Saturn is the fifth lord of birth and progress chart. Twins were born in the sub period of Saturn.

Example: S.L. Shakdhar

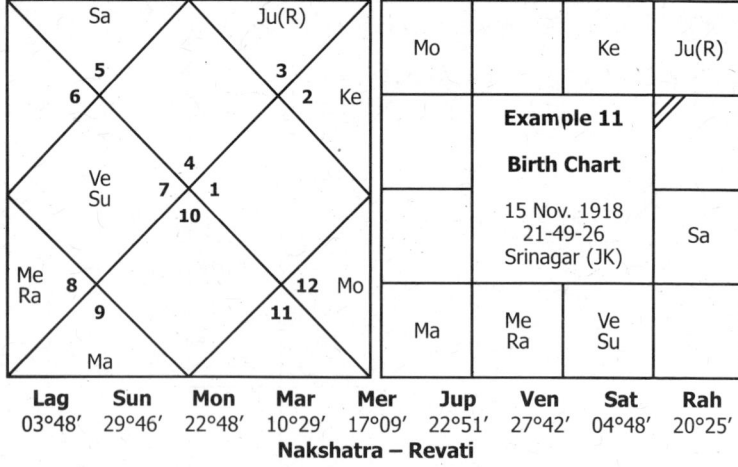

Lag	Sun	Mon	Mar	Mer	Jup	Ven	Sat	Rah
03°48'	29°46'	22°48'	10°29'	17°09'	22°51'	27°42'	04°48'	20°25'

Nakshatra – Revati

Birth lagna goes to tenth house. Jupiter is in ninth house aspected by birth tenth lord. The progress tenth lord is also aspected by birth tenth lord. Mars aspected tenth house also.

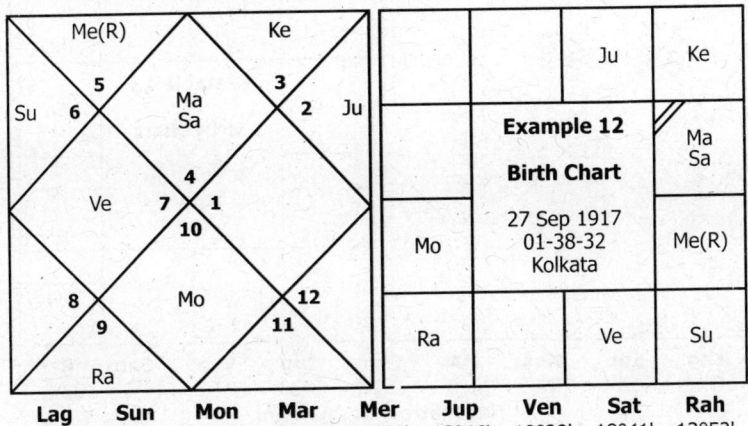

He was appointed Chief Election Commissioner in Dhanya/ Ulka on 17 June, 1977. The approval came in Dhanya / Bhramari.

Example: Naina Devi

A great singer died in Oct. 1993.

Lag	Sun	Mon	Mar	Mer	Jup	Ven	Sat	Rah
12°47'	10°25'	13°59'	16°7'	26°59'	18°46'	19°29'	18°41'	13°52'

Jupiter is in eighth house of progress lagna. Saturn is the maraca of birth chart and Mars is the maraca of progress chart. Both are placed in tenth house. The end came in Dhanya / Ulka.

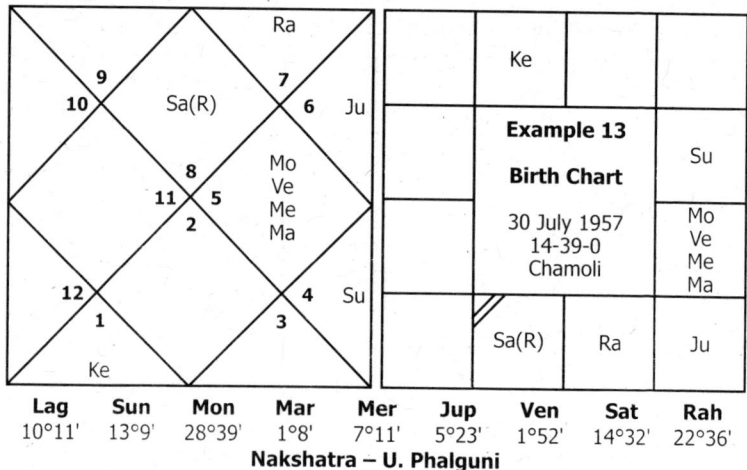

Example: Started Job

He started his career on 28 Aug. 1976 in the sub period of Sankata.

Lag	Sun	Mon	Mar	Mer	Jup	Ven	Sat	Rah
10°11'	13°9'	28°39'	1°8'	7°11'	5°23'	1°52'	14°32'	22°36'

Nakshatra – U. Phalguni

Dhanya started on 13 July 1974. For first two years and three month the progress lagna is Libra. It will change to Scorpio on 13 Oct., 1976.

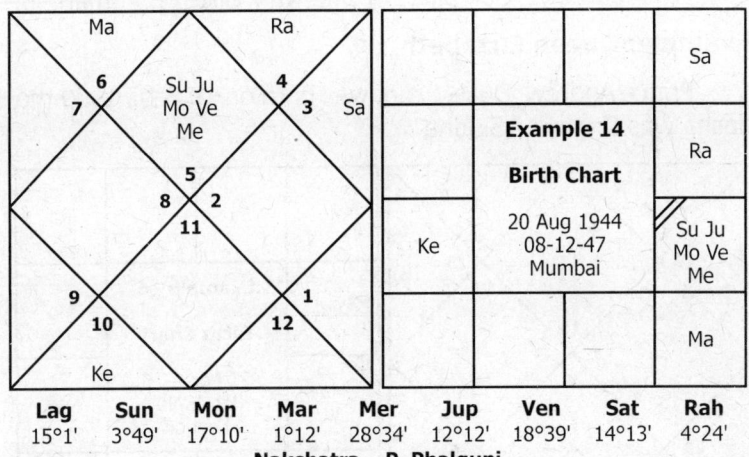

Jupiter is in twelfth house and aspecting its own sign in sixth house. Birth tenth lord is in progress tenth house. Tenth and eleventh lords of progress chart have exchanged places. Start of professional career is seen. Placement of Jupiter indicates movement out of birth place.

Example: Rajiv Gandhi

Lag	Sun	Mon	Mar	Mer	Jup	Ven	Sat	Rah
15°1'	3°49'	17°10'	1°12'	28°34'	12°12'	18°39'	14°13'	4°24'

Nakshatra – P. Phalguni

He married Edvige Antonia Albina Mario in 1968. The progress lagna was Libra.

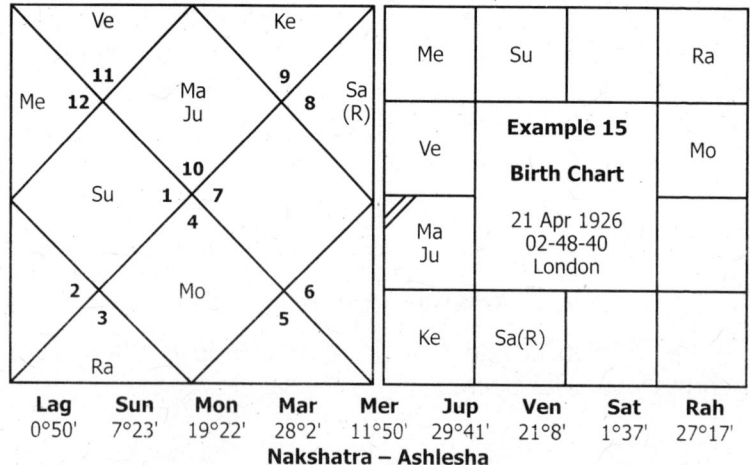

Jupiter is the birth fifth and eighth lord. It is aspected by the birth seventh lord Saturn. The conjunction of three benefics with this Jupiter promised love marriage.

Seventh house of progress chart is aspected by progress seventh Lord. In April, 1968 the Sub was of Mars.

The marriage took place in Dhanya / Ulka / Bhramari.

Example: Queen Elizabeth

Prince Andrew, Duke / York was born on 19 Feb., 1960 the dasha was Dhanya / Siddha

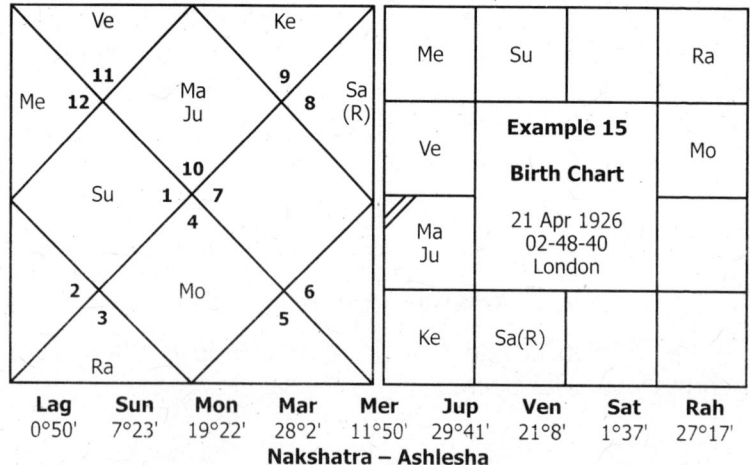

Lag	Sun	Mon	Mar	Mer	Jup	Ven	Sat	Rah
0°50'	7°23'	19°22'	28°2'	11°50'	29°41'	21°8'	1°37'	27°17'

Nakshatra – Ashlesha

Birth Chart (North Indian diamond):

```
        Sa(R)
      8        6
 Ke 9    PL     5
    BL    7
    Ma  10  4  Mo
    Ju   1
 Ve 11   Su    3  Ra
     12      2
        Me
```

Progress Chart (South Indian square):

Me	Su		Ra
Ve	**Example 15**		Mo
BL Ma Ju	**Progress Chart** **Dhanya / Visakha**		
Ke	Sa(R)	PL	

In birth chart Jupiter is in Lagna with exalted Mars and aspected by Moon.

In the progress chart the lord of fifth house of birth chart is in fifth house of progress chart. Jupiter is Karaka of children. The sub period is of Venus.

Dhanya / Shatbhisaj

The progress Lagna is Aquarius. Rahu is the Progress nakshatra. Placement of Rahu is important and also the progress chart with Aquarius lagna.

For Aquarius lagna Venus is Yoga karaka. Jupiter is the lord of second and eleventh house. Its relation with Venus, Saturn or Mercury gives dhana and Raj yoga in their periods.

Mercury is eighth lord of progress chart also. Its relation with lords of trik house lords of birth chart can give problems like accidents etc.

Example: Benazir Bhutto

She became Prime Minister of Pakistan on 4 December 1988 in Dhanya / Dhanya.

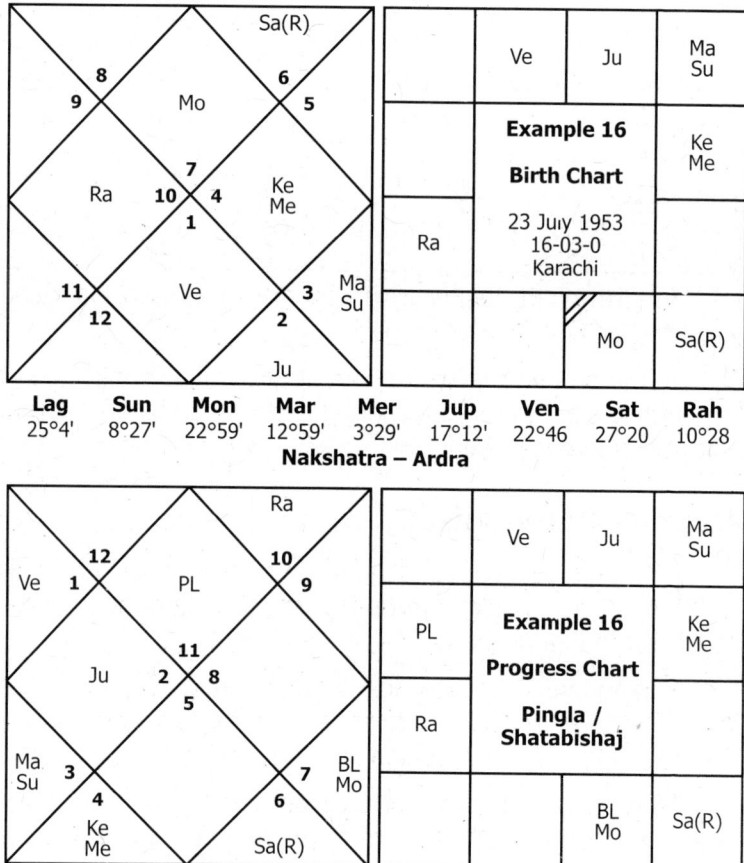

Lag	Sun	Mon	Mar	Mer	Jup	Ven	Sat	Rah
25°4'	8°27'	22°59'	12°59'	3°29'	17°12'	22°46	27°20	10°28

Nakshatra – Ardra

Rahu acts as Saturn and is placed in fourth house in birth chart.

In the progress chart , the tenth lord of progress chart is aspecting Rahu and thus Rahu is again connected with tenth house. Eleventh lord Jupiter aspects tenth house. The tenth lord Mars is aspected by Saturn, which is the lagna lord of progress lagna and Yoga Karaka of birth chart.

Example: Lata Mangeshkar

She was conferred the honor of Bharat Ratna in Jan. 2001. The dasha was Dhanya / Sankata. Sankata is the Nakshatra Lord.

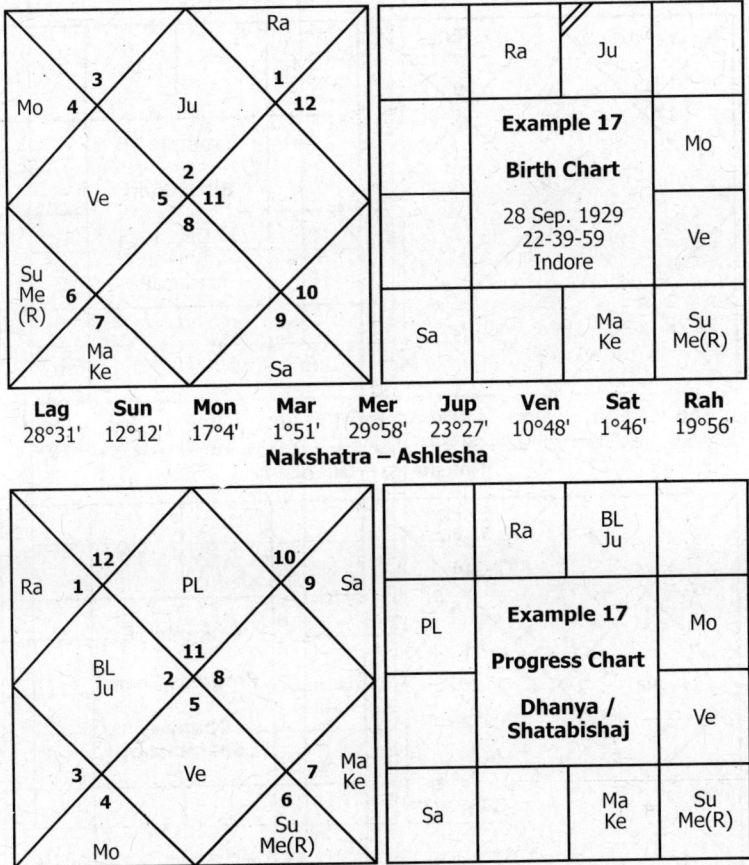

Lag	Sun	Mon	Mar	Mer	Jup	Ven	Sat	Rah
28°31'	12°12'	17°4'	1°51'	29°58'	23°27'	10°48'	1°46'	19°56'

Nakshatra – Ashlesha

Tenth house of birth chart rises as Progress lagna. Lagna lord Saturn is aspecting lagna. Saturn is the birth tenth lord.

Mars is tenth lord of progress chart and aspects the nakshatra lord. Progress lagna is aspected by yoga karaka Venus.

Can we see this event from regular Yogini Dasha? Jupiter is the dasha lord and is the eighth lord of chart. It is aspected by afflicted Mars from sixth house. Jupiter is not connected to tenth house.

Example: Narrow Escape

This young toddler drowned but was saved.

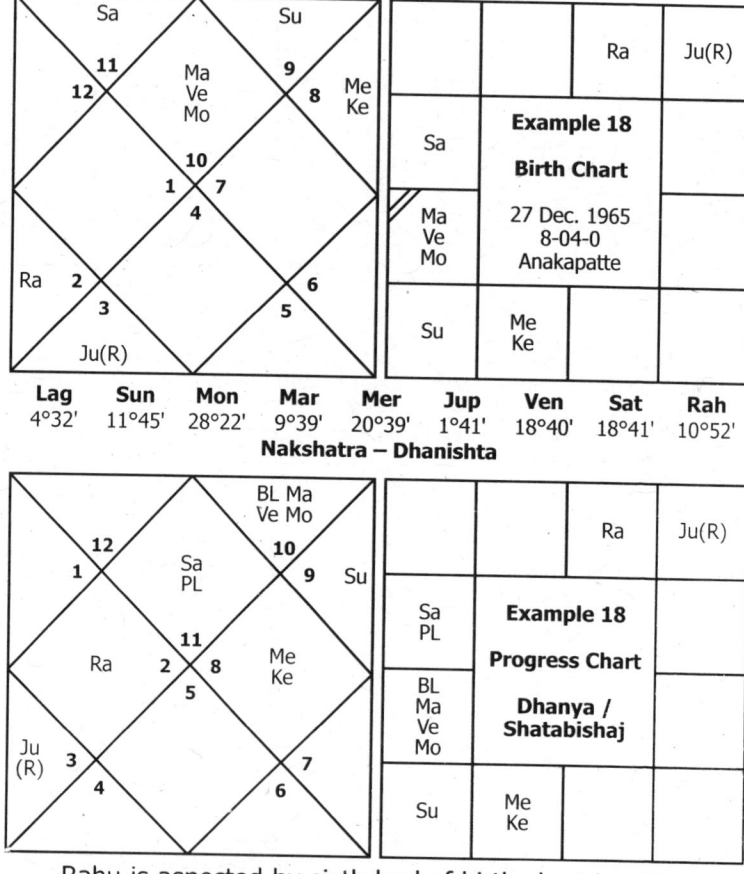

Lag	Sun	Mon	Mar	Mer	Jup	Ven	Sat	Rah
4°32'	11°45'	28°22'	9°39'	20°39'	1°41'	18°40'	18°41'	10°52'

Nakshatra – Dhanishta

Rahu is aspected by sixth lord of birth chart i.e. Mercury. Mercury is the eighth lord of progress chart.

Thus the Nakshatra Lord Rahu is connected with sixth lord of Birth Chart and eighth lord of progress chart.

The accident happens in Dhanya / Bhadrika in November 1967.

Example: Posting Abroad

He was transferred to Hongkong immediately after start of Dhanya on 9th April 1998. He joined in May 1998.

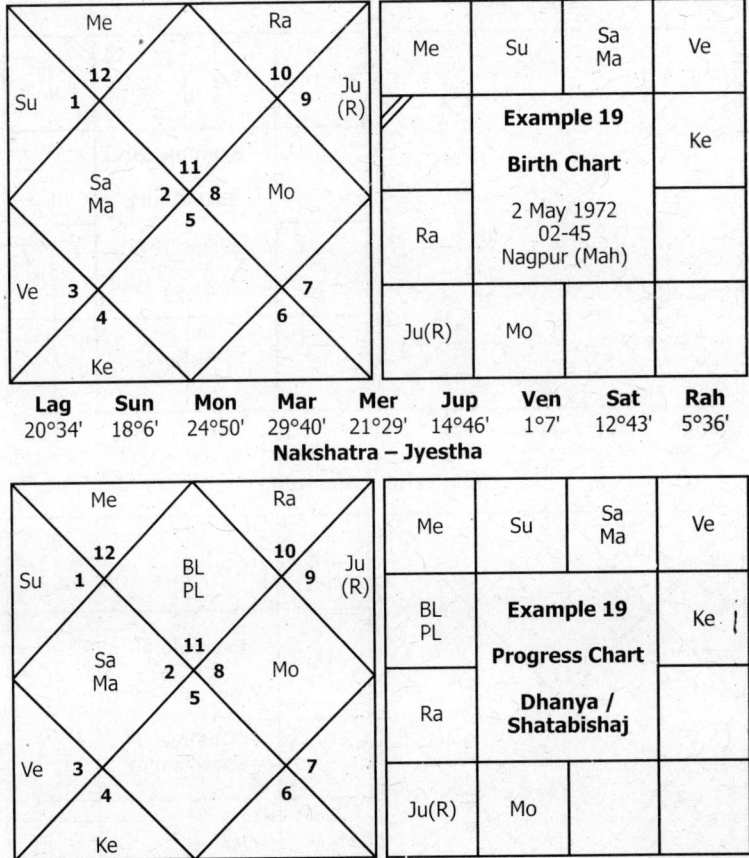

Lag	Sun	Mon	Mar	Mer	Jup	Ven	Sat	Rah
20°34'	18°6'	24°50'	29°40'	21°29'	14°46'	1°7'	12°43'	5°36'

Nakshatra – Jyestha

A clear indication of transfer and change of residence. The nakshatra lord Rahu is in twelfth house of both birth and progress chart. It is in the sign of Saturn who is in fourth house and with tenth lord and aspected by sixth lord. The shift to a foreign land is seen.

Example : Higher Education

He was a central government officer with Ministry of Defence. In 1975 July, he was nominated to pursue post graduate study in a prestigious IIT.

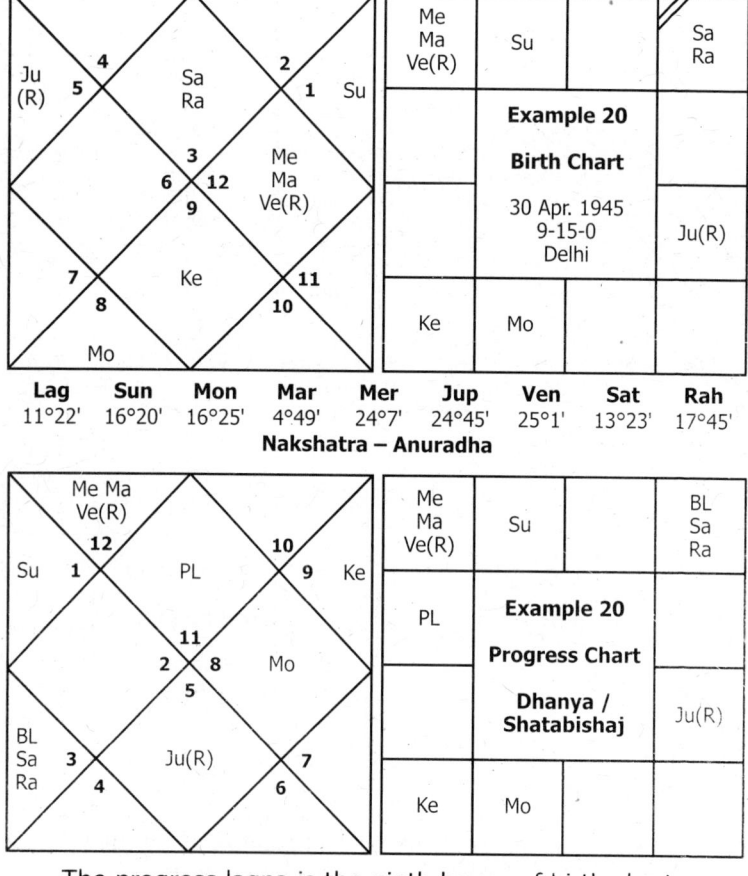

Lag	Sun	Mon	Mar	Mer	Jup	Ven	Sat	Rah
11°22'	16°20'	16°25'	4°49'	24°7'	24°45'	25°1'	13°23'	17°45'

Nakshatra – Anuradha

The progress lagna is the ninth house of birth chart.

Rahu is now in fifth house with lagna lord and aspected by 10th lord Mars. The dasha period was Dhanya/Ulka. Saturn is in fifth house.

As the fifth house is prominent during this dasha, daughter was born in the same period on 14 Aug1975.

Can the normal interpretation of yogini lead us to this conclusion?

Chapter 6

Bhramari

Bhramari dasha is generated by four nakshatras i.e. Ashwini Ashlesha, Anuradha and P.Bhadrapad.

Nakshatra	Nakshatra Lord	Sign	Remarks
Ashwini	Ketu	Aries	Progress Lagna is Aries
Ashlesha	Mercury	Cancer	Progress lagna is Cancer
Anuradha	Saturn	Scorpio	Progress Lagna is Scorpio
P.Bhadrapad	Jupiter	Aquarius / Pisces	For first three years progress Lagna is Aquarius. For last one year progress lagna is Pisces.

Bhramari / Ashwini

The dasha can only be operative in the four years period at the birth. In this system of progress yogini, we jump to Rohini after Revati nakshatra.

During infancy we can only see the health, death or the problems to parents and shift of residence. This is a period generally said to be related to the past karma of mother.

We cannot find many examples for this dasha. Two examples are taken from Astro data Bank.

Example: Adoption

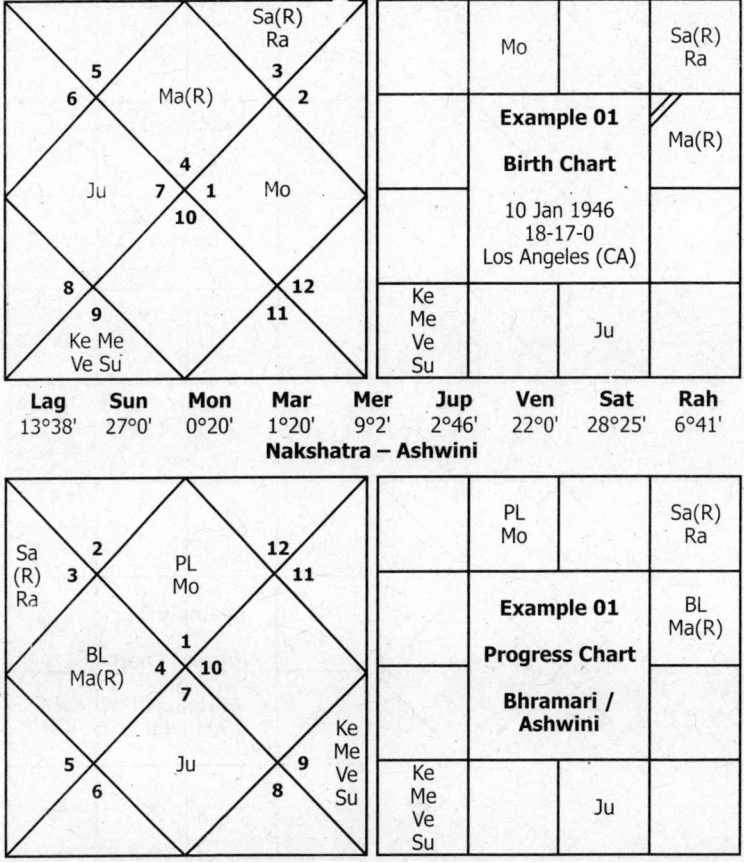

Lag	Sun	Mon	Mar	Mer	Jup	Ven	Sat	Rah
13°38'	27°0'	0°20'	1°20'	9°2'	2°46'	22°0'	28°25'	6°41'

Nakshatra – Ashwini

In the birth chart, the ninth house is aspected by retrograde eighth lord Saturn. The ninth lord is in eighth from ninth and aspected by retrograde debilitated Mars.

The progress chart gives confirmation to this effect. Ninth house is again afflicted in Rahu / Ketu axis and aspected by Saturn. The Jupiter is aspected by Mars who is again eighth lord. Mars is now lagna lord also and ensure life to father. He was adopted and moved out of home.

Example: Infant Mortality

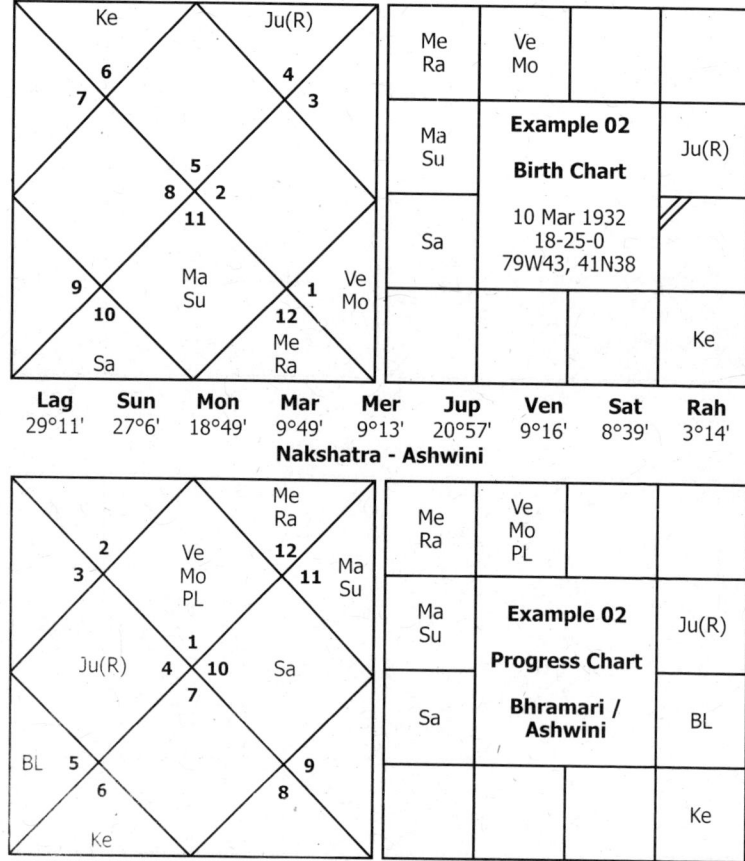

Lag	Sun	Mon	Mar	Mer	Jup	Ven	Sat	Rah
29°11'	27°6'	18°49'	9°49'	9°13'	20°57'	9°16'	8°39'	3°14'

Nakshatra - Ashwini

Let us first examine birth chart for longevity. The eight house is with Rahu and aspected by Saturn. The aspect of Jupiter to its own sign should be the saving factor. The dasha at birth was Ketu. Both maracas are connected with eighth house. Lagna is aspected by its lord and yoga karaka Mars. The lagna is strong.

In the progress chart, the eighth house is vacant. Now we see lagna. Venus is the maraca now and is placed in lagna. The nakshatra lord Ketu is in sixth house of illness. He developed Pneumonia and died on 17 Jan 1933. The sub period was Rahu.

Since Ketu do not have any dasha period in Yogini, we can take Rahu in its place.

Bhramari / Ashlesha

Mercury is the nakshatra lord and cancer is the progress lagna. Mars is the yoga karaka for progress chart. Saturn is lord of seventh and eighth house. Generally good results will be experienced during this dasha period.

Example. Indira Gandhi

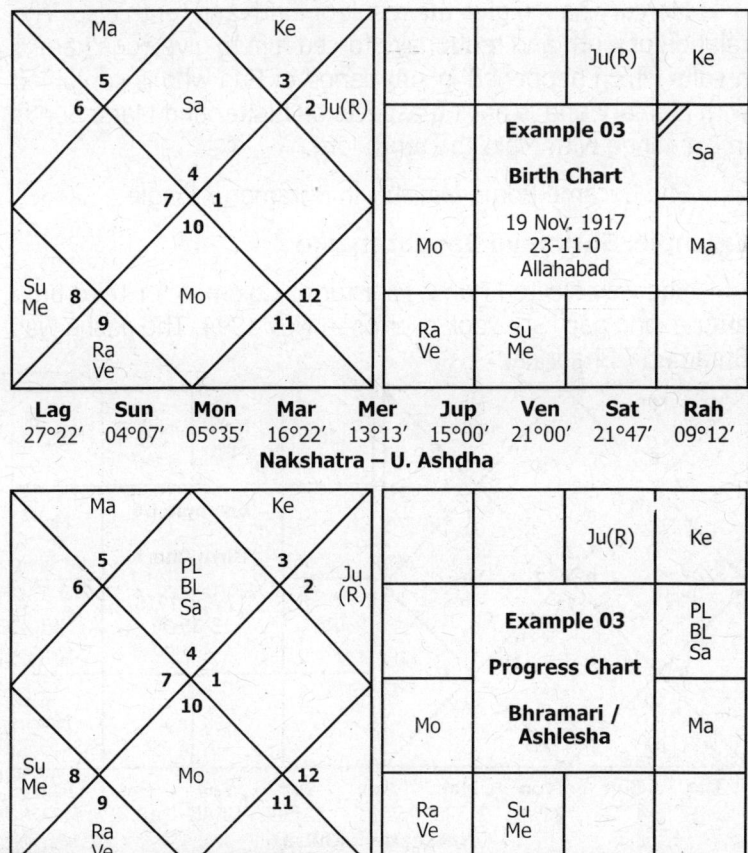

Lag	Sun	Mon	Mar	Mer	Jup	Ven	Sat	Rah
27°22'	04°07'	05°35'	16°22'	13°13'	15°00'	21°00'	21°47'	09°12'

Nakshatra – U. Ashdha

Her father expires on 27th May 1964 and she became prime Minister of India on 24 Jan. 1966. All happened in Bhramari / Ashlesha.

Mercury is nakshatra lord and is aspected by ninth and tenth lord. Ninth lord is retrograde.

For father Mars and Mercury are maracas. Venus is the third and eighth lord. Both dasha and nakshatra are maracas for father. Venus is afflicted in 6th house. Father died in the sub period of Venus after illness.

Mercury has to give the result of ninth and tenth also. The relation of ninth and tenth have forced him to give Yoga karaka results which happened in sub period of Sun who is conjoined with Mercury and is having aspects of Jupiter and Mars. Sun is in exchange with Mars the tenth lord.

She became Prime Minister in Bhramari / Pingla

Example. Shrimavo Bandaranaike

She was elected Prime Minister of Colombo for third time after a long gap. She took over on14 Nov 1994. The dasha was Bhramari / Bhadrika.

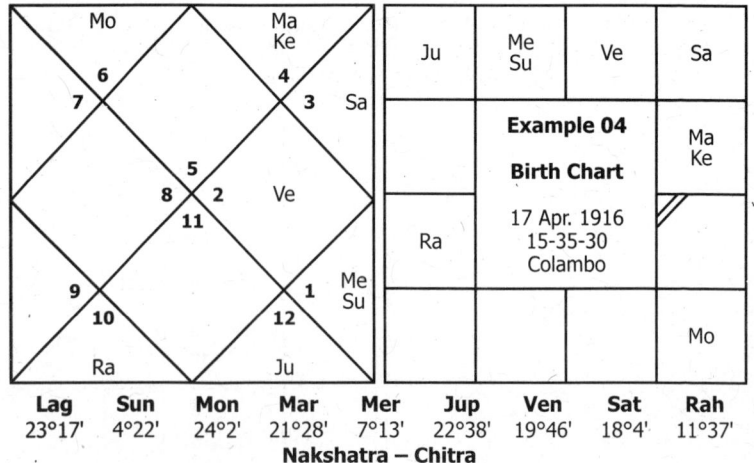

Lag	Sun	Mon	Mar	Mer	Jup	Ven	Sat	Rah
23°17'	4°22'	24°2'	21°28'	7°13'	22°38'	19°46'	18°4'	11°37'

Nakshatra – Chitra

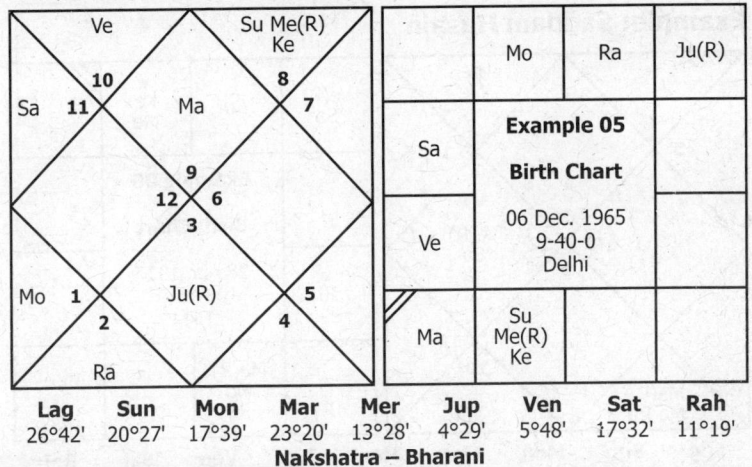

Mercury is in tenth house with exalted Sun. Sun is the lagna lord of birth chart. The tenth lord is in lagna and aspected by ninth lord Jupiter.

Regular analysis of Bhramari dasha gives no idea of this elevation. Mars is in twelfth house and afflicted by Ketu. The eighth lord Jupiter aspects Mars which is good for politicians.

Example: Brain Cancer

He died on the operation table during the brain surgery. Dasha was Bhramari / Bhadrika.

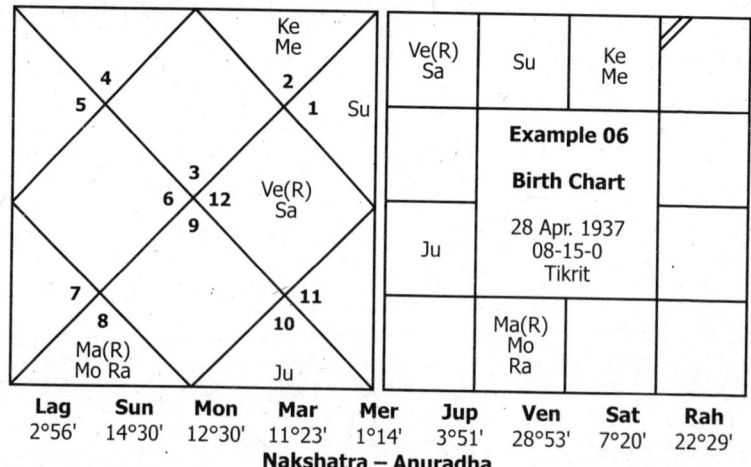

	Mo	Ra	Ju(R)
Sa	**Example 05** **Progress Chart**		PL
Ve	**Bhramari / Ashlesha**		
Ma	Su Me(R) Ke		

A very clear picture of this unfortunate event is seen in progress chart.

Mercury and Saturn are maracas of birth chart. This dasha belongs to Mercury.

In the progress chart Saturn and Sun are the maracas. Mercury is with Ketu. Sun joins it and Saturn aspects it from eighth house. All the maracas are influencing Mercury who is the nakshatra lord.

The end came in Mercury sub period.

Example: Saddam Husain

Ve(R) Sa	Su	Ke Me	
Ju	**Example 06** **Birth Chart**		
	28 Apr. 1937 08-15-0 Tikrit		
	Ma(R) Mo Ra		

Lag	Sun	Mon	Mar	Mer	Jup	Ven	Sat	Rah
2°56'	14°30'	12°30'	11°23'	1°14'	3°51'	28°53'	7°20'	22°29'

Nakshatra – Anuradha

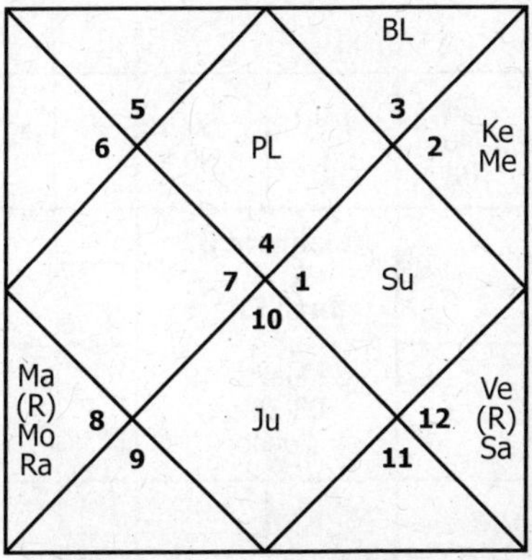
BL
5
6
PL
3
2
Ke
Me
4
7
1
Su
10
Ma
(R)
Mo
Ra
8
Ju
9
12
11
Ve
(R)
Sa

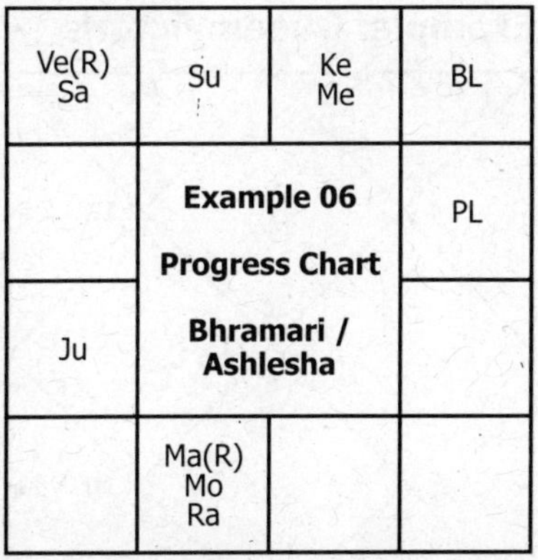
Ve(R)
Sa
Su
Ke
Me
BL
Example 06
Progress Chart
Bhramari /
Ashlesha
PL
Ju
Ma(R)
Mo
Ra

He was hanged to death on 30 December, 2006 in the dasha of Bhramari / Bhramari.

A freighting situation emerges. Moon and Jupiter are maraca in the birth chart. In the progress chart Sun and Saturn are maraca. Saturn is more serious planet.

Mercury is the progress nakshatra. It is with Ketu and aspected by Mars and Saturn. Jupiter is aspecting lagna. The nakshatra lord is badly afflicted by the maracas.

Mars is the participating planet with nakshatra lord. The end came in Mars period.

Bhramari / Anuradha

The progress lagna is Scorpio and the Nakshatra lord is Saturn.

Sun and Moon are the lords of tenth and ninth house of progress chart. Their relation gives good yoga. Also Saturn and Jupiter are fourth and fifth lord.

Mercury is the malefic planet and its relation with a planet can be harmful to the effects of the planet and more so if Saturn is also related.

Example: Queen Victoria

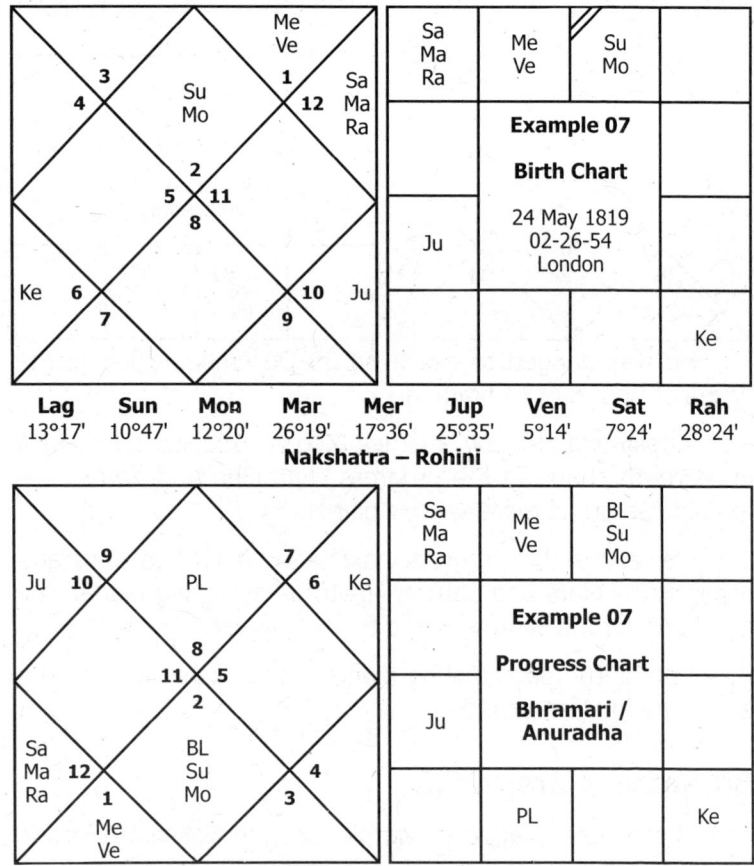

Lag	Sun	Mon	Mar	Mer	Jup	Ven	Sat	Rah
13°17'	10°47'	12°20'	26°19'	17°36'	25°35'	5°14'	7°24'	28°24'

Nakshatra – Rohini

She started using the title of Empress of India from 1st May 1876. It was a feather in her crown.

Sun and Moon are in seventh house. The lords of ninth and tenth house are conjoined.

Nakshatra lord Saturn is the ninth and tenth lord of birth chart. Saturn aspects Sun and Moon. It is with Mars.

The antardasha was of nakshatra lord Saturn. Third and fifth lords are in exchange of sign. It was a calculative move.

Example: K.R.Bhatnagar

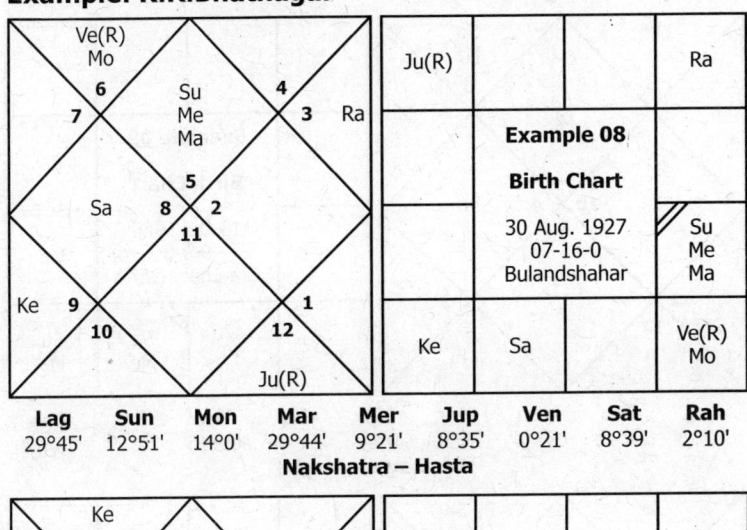

Lag	Sun	Mon	Mar	Mer	Jup	Ven	Sat	Rah
29°45'	12°51'	14°0'	29°44'	9°21'	8°35'	0°21'	8°39'	2°10'

Nakshatra – Hasta

His father expired in Bhramari / Bhramari.

Saturn is in the eighth house from ninth house in the birth chart. Venus is the maraca of father in birth chart.

In the progress chart, Saturn, the nakshatra lord is lord of seventh and eighth house from ninth house. The birth maraca is with progress ninth lord. Saturn is aspecting Sun, Mars and Mercury which are placed in tenth house i.e. maraca house for father.

Thus the maracas are influenced by Saturn.

Example: Margret Thatcher

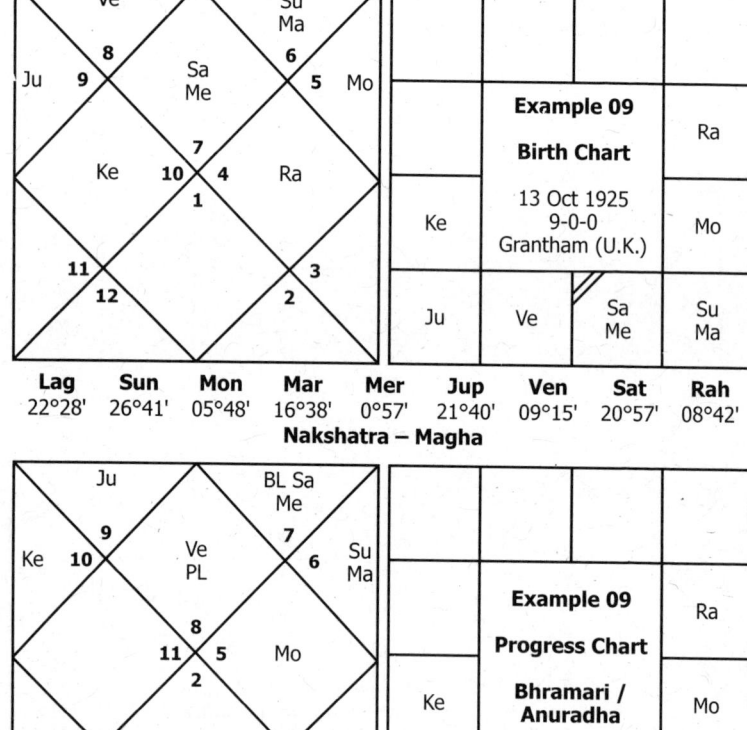

	Lag	Sun	Mon	Mar	Mer	Jup	Ven	Sat	Rah
	22°28'	26°41'	05°48'	16°38'	0°57'	21°40'	09°15'	20°57'	08°42'

Nakshatra – Magha

She was elected MP for the first time in the general elections held on 8 Oct. 1959 after a big struggle.

Saturn is the yoga karaka of birth chart. It aspects the tenth house and is with ninth lord Mercury. Thus Saturn is involved in Raj Yoga in birth chart.

In progress chart, ninth lord is in tenth an aspected by Jupiter. Seventh house is aspected by Venus.

She was elected in Bhadrika Sub. Mercury is involved in Yoga in birth chart.

Example H.R. Bachchan

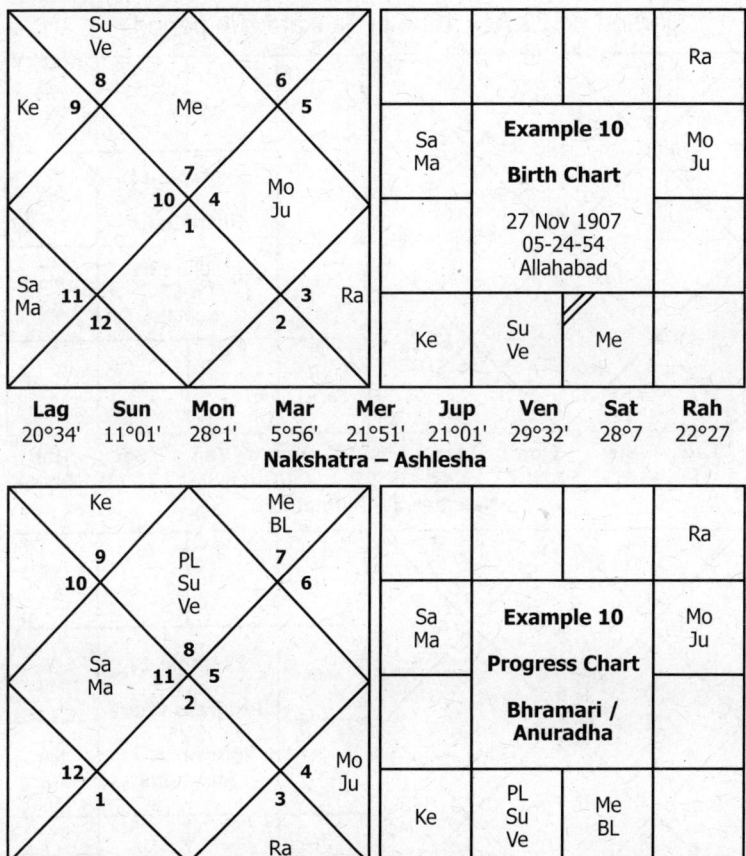

Lag	Sun	Mon	Mar	Mer	Jup	Ven	Sat	Rah
20°34'	11°01'	28°1'	5°56'	21°51'	21°01'	29°32'	28°7	22°27

Nakshatra – Ashlesha

Saturn is the Yogkarak of birth Chart and is placed in fifth house.

The star lord is Saturn in the progress chart. It is aspecting Venus and Sun. Fifth Lord Jupiter is in Ninth house with ninth lord. The promise of fifth and fourth house are highlighted.

Amitabh was born in Bhramari / Siddha. Venus is aspected by Saturn.

Example : Marriage

Married on 22 Nov 1986 in Sankata sub period.

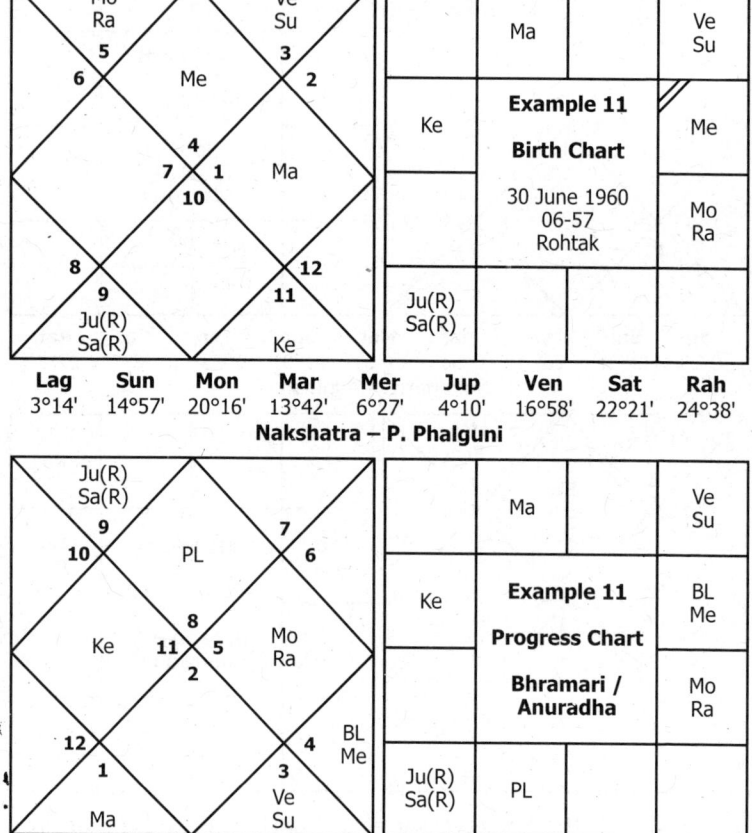

Lag	Sun	Mon	Mar	Mer	Jup	Ven	Sat	Rah
3°14'	14°57'	20°16'	13°42'	6°27'	4°10'	16°58'	22°21'	24°38'

Nakshatra – P. Phalguni

In the birth chart, Saturn is seventh lord and eighth lord. It is influencing Venus, Sun, Ketu and Mars. For Ketu we take Rahu or Sankata.

In the progress chart, seventh lord is Venus and is under the influence of Saturn. Now Saturn is placed in second house which is the secondary house for marriage.

The placement of Venus in eighth house is not good but it is with Sun. Rahu acts as Sun also. It was an intercaste marriage.

Example: Business Expansion

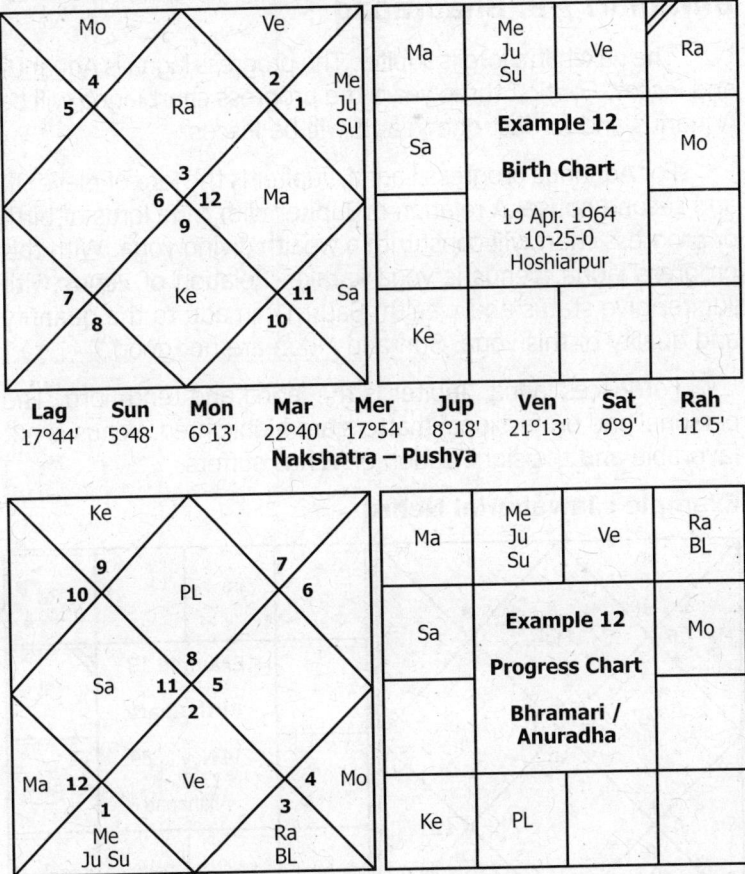

Lag	Sun	Mon	Mar	Mer	Jup	Ven	Sat	Rah
17°44'	5°48'	6°13'	22°40'	17°54'	8°18'	21°13'	9°9'	11°5'

Nakshatra – Pushya

In birth chart Saturn is lord of eighth and ninth and placed in ninth house of Bhagya. It influences Mercury, Jupiter and Sun. Mars is in tenth house.

In the progress chart, Saturn is in fourth house and activate tenth house. Sun is the tenth lord and is under influence of Saturn.

He expanded his business in Jan. 2003 and started another factory. Dasha was Bhramari / Bhramari.

Bhramari / P. Bhadrapad

The nakshatra lord is Jupiter. The progress lagna is Aquarius and Pisces. For first three years the progress chart lagna will be Aquarius and for last one year it will be Pisces.

For Aquarius progress Lagna, Jupiter is the lord of eleventh and second house. A relation of Jupiter with trine lords of birth or progress chart will constitute a wealth giving yoga. With this progress lagna, Venus is yoga karaka. Relation of Venus with Jupiter give status and wealth. Saturn can add to the quantity and quality of this yoga. Sun and Moon are not good.

For Pisces lagna, Jupiter is the lagna and tenth lord. The personal and professional matters are highlighted. Venus is not favorable and the signification of Venus suffers.

Example : Jawaharlal Nehru

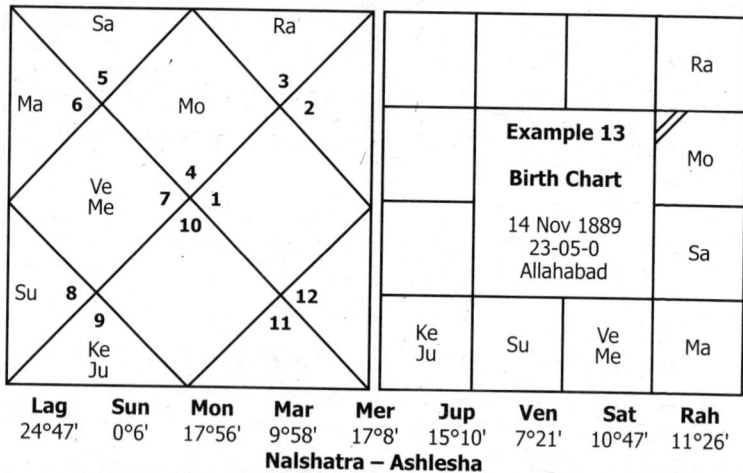

Lag	Sun	Mon	Mar	Mer	Jup	Ven	Sat	Rah
24°47'	0°6'	17°56'	9°58'	17°8'	15°10'	7°21'	10°47'	11°26'

Nalshatra – Ashlesha

Jupiter is sixth lord in the birth chart and is placed in sixth house with Ketu.

North Indian chart (houses 1–12):
- PL (top), Ke Ju (house 9/10 area), Su, Ve Me, Ra (house 3), Sa (center), Ma, Mo BL (house 4)

South Indian – Example 13:

			Ra
PL	Example 13		Mo BL
	Progress Chart		Sa
	Bhramari / P. Bhadrapad		
Ke Ju	Su	Ve Me	Ma

This Jupiter in the progress chart is the second lord and is a maraca. Mars is aspecting Jupiter from eighth house.

Jupiter influences Rahu / Ketu and Saturn. The end came in sub period of Sankata.

Example: Benazir Bhutto

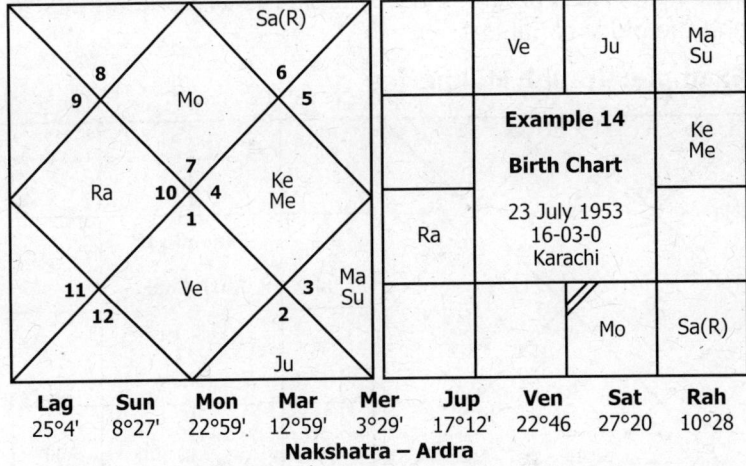

South Indian – Example 14:

	Ve	Ju	Ma Su
	Example 14		Ke Me
	Birth Chart		
Ra	23 July 1953 16-03-0 Karachi		
		Mo	Sa(R)

Lag	Sun	Mon	Mar	Mer	Jup	Ven	Sat	Rah
25°4'	8°27'	22°59'	12°59'	3°29'	17°12'	22°46	27°20	10°28

Nakshatra – Ardra

Jupiter is not related to tenth house or tenth lord in birth chart. It is sixth lord placed in eighth causing Vipreet Raj Yoga. There is no aspect or conjunction with this Jupiter. This gives Yoga during its dasha. The rise and fall are sudden.

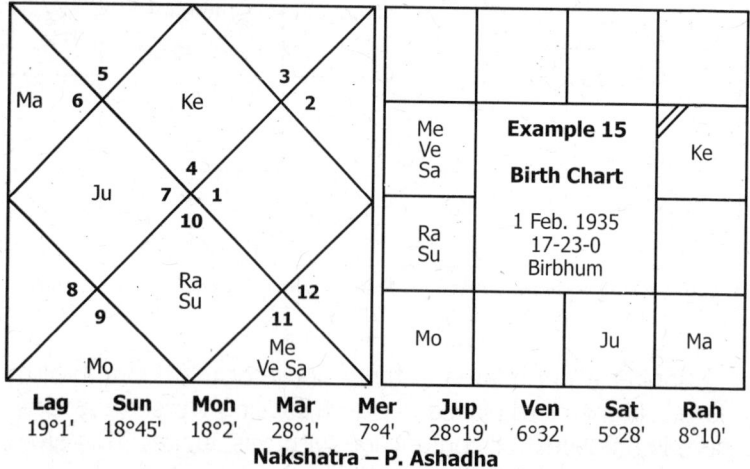

	Ve	Ju	Ma Su
PL	**Example 14** **Progress Chart**		Ke Me
Ra	**Bhramari /** **P. Bhadrapad**		
		BL Mo	Sa(R)

In the progress chart Jupiter is in fourth house and aspects tenth house. Jupiter is aspecting Saturn and Rahu. Both of these can give results of Jupiter.

She was elected Prime Minister for the second term and assumed office on 19 Oct. 1993.

With Pisces progress lagna, Jupiter is lord of tenth house and the office continues.

Example: Pranab Mukherjee

	Me Ve Sa	**Example 15** **Birth Chart**	Ke
	Ra Su	1 Feb. 1935 17-23-0 Birbhum	
	Mo	Ju	Ma

Lag	Sun	Mon	Mar	Mer	Jup	Ven	Sat	Rah
19°1'	18°45'	18°2'	28°1'	7°4'	28°19'	6°32'	5°28'	8°10'

Nakshatra – P. Ashadha

PL			
Me Ve Sa	**Example 15** **Progress Chart** **Bhramari /** **P. Bhadrapad**		BL Ke
Ra Su			
Mo		Ju	Ma

In the birth chart Jupiter is lord of ninth and sixth house and is placed in Kendra causing Yoga.

In the progress chart, Jupiter is in eighth house. It is influencing Mercury and Saturn. Mercury is the seventh lord of progress chart and Saturn is the seventh lord of birth chart.

He was married on 13 July, 1957 in the sub Period of Sankata. Rahu is in seventh house of birth chart.

Example: Srimavo Bandaranaike

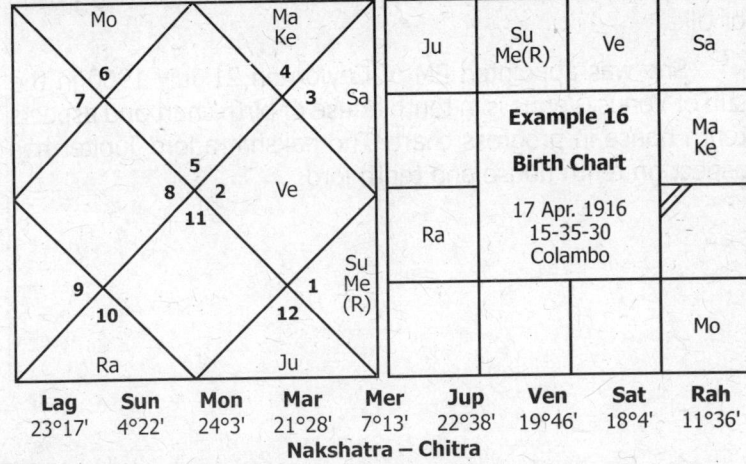

Ju	Su Me(R)	Ve	Sa
	Example 16 **Birth Chart** 17 Apr. 1916 15-35-30 Colambo		Ma Ke
Ra			
			Mo

Lag	Sun	Mon	Mar	Mer	Jup	Ven	Sat	Rah
23°17'	4°22'	24°3'	21°28'	7°13'	22°38'	19°46'	18°4'	11°36'

Nakshatra – Chitra

Ju	Me Su	Ve	Sa
PL	**Example 16** **Progress Chart**		Ma Ke
Ra	**Bhramari /** **P. Bhadrapad**		BL
			Mo

Her husband Solomon was assassinated by a Buddhist monk on 26 Sept. 1959.

For husband we take seventh house as lagna. Jupiter and Sun are maracas. Jupiter is a strong maraca as it is in eighth house in own sign.

The progress nakshatra lord is Jupiter. In the progress chart, it is in second house. The maracas of husband are Mercury and Saturn in the progress chart.

Saturn is aspecting Jupiter. The assassination was in sub of Ulka.

She was appointed PM of Ceylon on 21 July 1960 in the sub of Venus. Venus is in tenth house of birth chart and aspects tenth house in progress chart. The nakshatra lord Jupiter has aspect on tenth house and tenth lord.

Example : Loss of Govt. Job

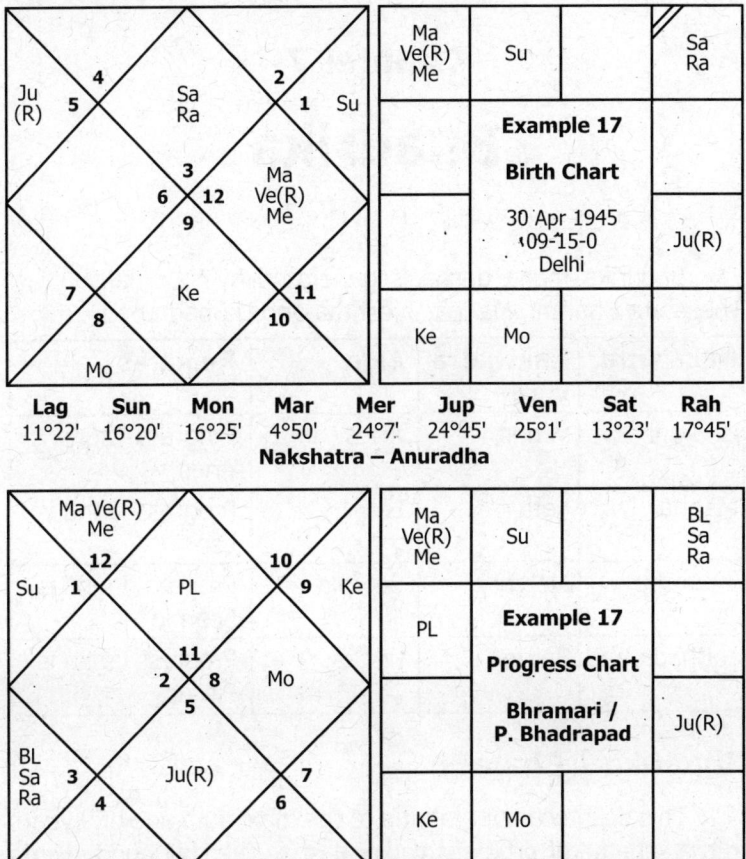

Lag	Sun	Mon	Mar	Mer	Jup	Ven	Sat	Rah
11°22'	16°20'	16°25'	4°50'	24°7'	24°45'	25°1'	13°23'	17°45'

Nakshatra – Anuradha

He was a Class I gazetted officer with Government of India. He resigned from Job on 19th Nov. 1979 to work with a private company.

The Nakshatra lord Jupiter is tenth lord of birth chart. It is retrograde and is a fallen planet. During this Jupiter the reversal of job is expected. In progress chart Jupiter is eleventh and second lord.

Planets in fifth house can cause loss of job being eighth from tenth. He resigned in Bhramari / Sankata.

Chapter 7

Bhadrika

Bhadrika maha dasha is generated by four nakshatras. These are Bharani, Magha, Jyeshtha and U.Bhadrapad.

Nakshatra	Nakshatra Lord	Sign	Remarks
Bharani	Venus	Aries	Progress Lagna is Aries
Magha	Ketu	Leo	Progress lagna is Leo
Jyeshtha	Mercury	Scorpio	Progress lagna is Scorpio
U.Bhadrapad	Saturn	Pisces	Progress lagna is Pisces.

Bhadrika / Bharani

This dasha can operate up to the maximum age of 9 years in the scheme of progress yogini dasha. The childhood events relating to family, parents, home etc. are seen in this dasha.

The progress lagna is Aries and the nakshatra lord Venus is the second and seventh lord of progress chart. The placement of Venus in a house highlights the events of the house. Malefic relation with Venus does not go well.

Example: Birth of younger brother

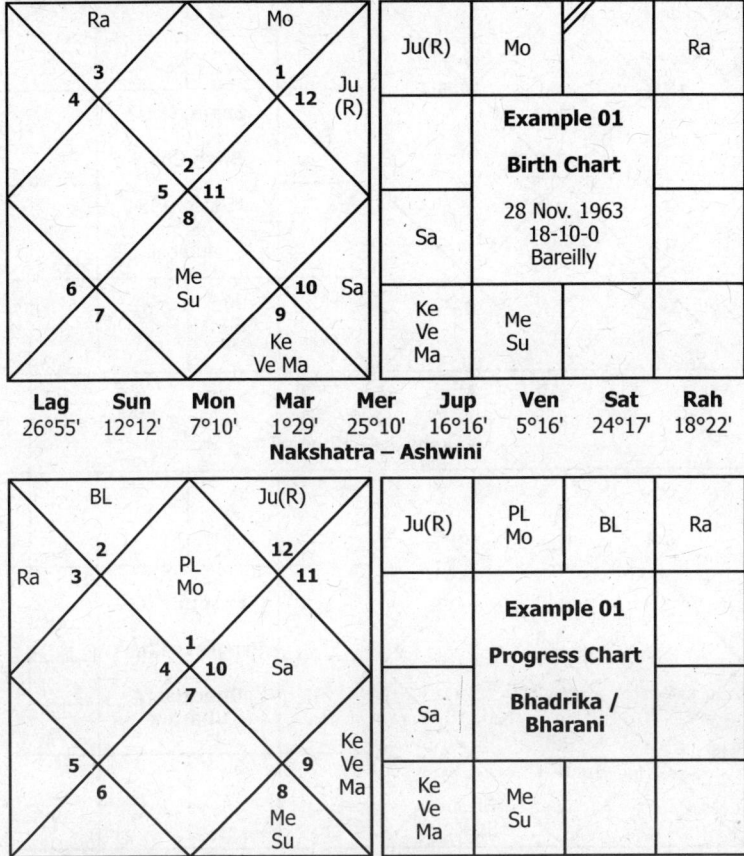

	Lag	Sun	Mon	Mar	Mer	Jup	Ven	Sat	Rah
	26°55'	12°12'	7°10'	1°29'	25°10'	16°16'	5°16'	24°17'	18°22'

Nakshatra – Ashwini

Younger brother was born on 20 Sept. 1969 in the dasha of Bhadrika / Pingla.

Venus is the nakshatra Lord and is placed in ninth house. It is influencing the third house and can give results of third house. It is conjoined with Mars and Ketu and indicates problems to co born also. In Bhadrika / Sankata there should be loss of co born.

The sub period was Pingla when younger brother was born. Sun is with the progress third lord.

Example: Death of Father

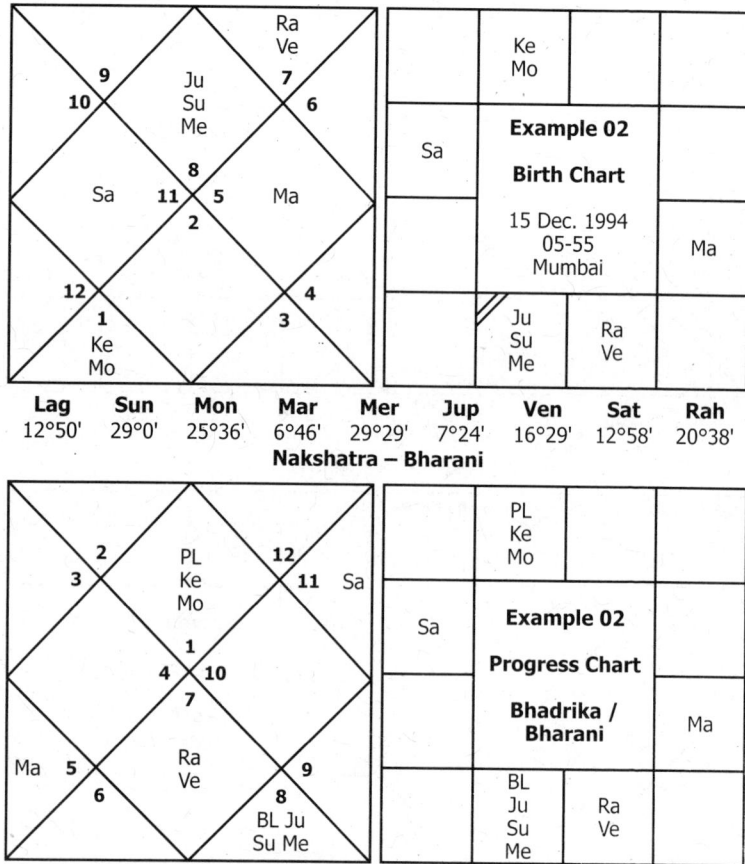

Lag	Sun	Mon	Mar	Mer	Jup	Ven	Sat	Rah
12°50'	29°0'	25°36'	6°46'	29°29'	7°24'	16°29'	12°58'	20°38'

Nakshatra – Bharani

This boy was adopted soon after his birth. His father was not known and was feared dead. He was adopted by an Indian doctor based in Dubai. The doctor was issueless.

In the birth chart, the ninth lord is in sixth house. It is with Ketu and aspected by Saturn. The ninth house is also aspected by Jupiter.

This is confirmed in the progress chart. The nakshatra lord Venus is with Rahu. The ninth lord Jupiter is in eighth and aspected by Saturn and Mars. The ninth lord is seriously related to eighth house and lords.

The progress chart with nakshatra lord gives a clearer picture.

Example: Bill Clinton

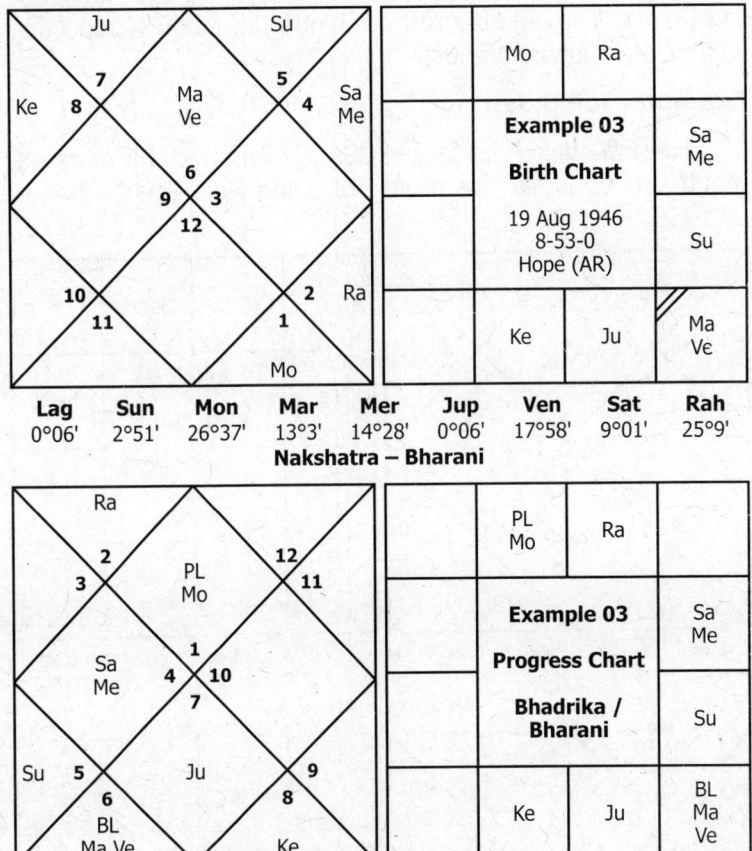

Lag	Sun	Mon	Mar	Mer	Jup	Ven	Sat	Rah
0°06'	2°51'	26°37'	13°3'	14°28'	0°06'	17°58'	9°01'	25°9'

Nakshatra – Bharani

His father expired three months before his birth. The dasha was Bhadrika / Bhramari.

In the birth chart Rahu is placed in ninth house. The ninth lord is Venus and is with eighth lord Mars and aspected by Saturn.

Venus is the lord of ninth house of birth chart and is afflicted.

In the progress chart, this afflicted Venus is now in sixth house. It is again with the eighth lord of progress chart. For father we take the ninth house as lagna. Saturn and Mercury are maracas for father and both are together in the eighth house from ninth. The eighth lord from ninth, i.e. Moon is aspecting Jupiter. Mars is with Venus.

Example: Joe Biden

He is the Vice President of USA. He lived with his maternal grandparents as his father was not doing well. This continued till 1956.

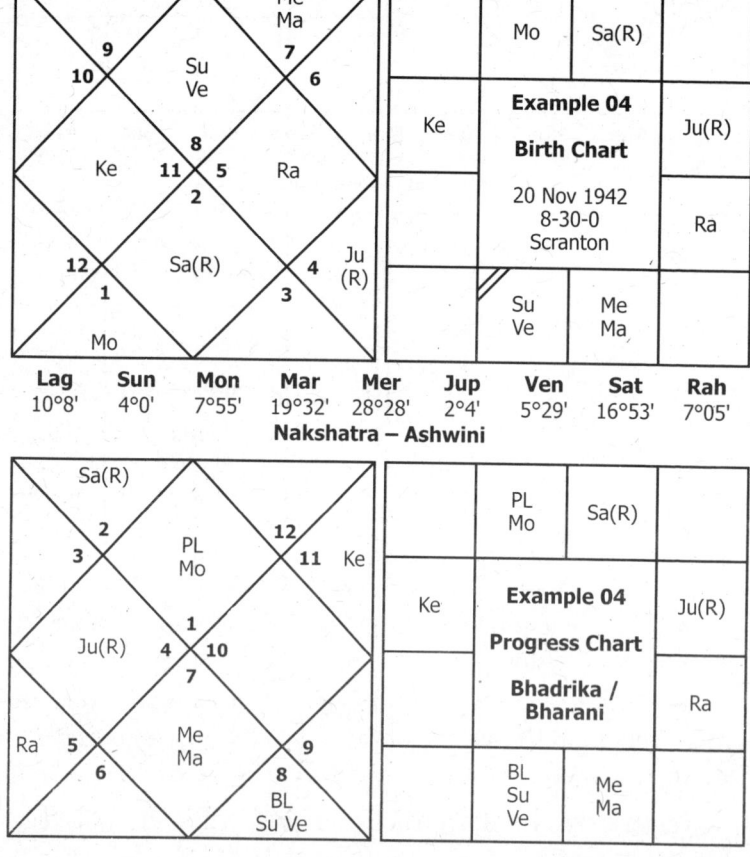

Lag	Sun	Mon	Mar	Mer	Jup	Ven	Sat	Rah
10°8'	4°0'	7°55'	19°32'	28°28'	2°4'	5°29'	16°53'	7°05'

Nakshatra – Ashwini

Venus is the lord of twelfth and seventh house in the birth chart. It is with Sun and aspected by Saturn and Jupiter.

In the progress chart, this Venus is in eighth house with Sun. Eighth house is the twelfth house of father. Sun is the karaka of father. Placement of Venus and Sun in eighth house indicate losses to father.

Bhadrika / Magha

Lord of nakshatra is Ketu and Ketu is not assigned any sign. Some scholars assign Scorpio as the sign of Ketu. Ketu itself is not in the eight Yoginis but its effects are felt. Normally Ketu acts its sign dispositor and also as the planet it is conjoined with.

Example: Maharaja Sri Nagendra Singh

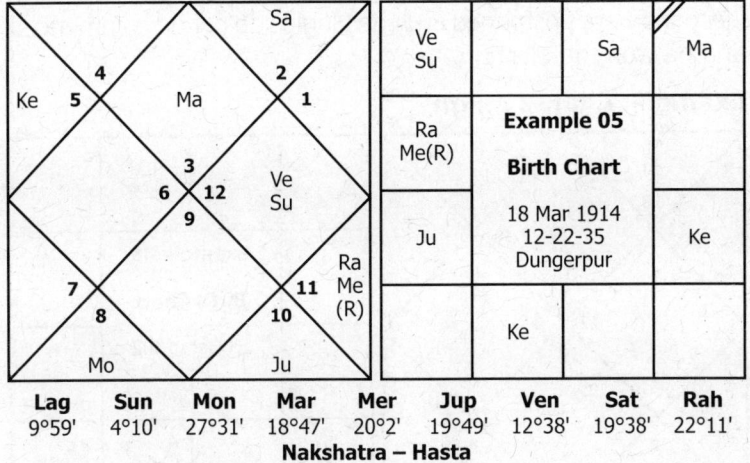

Lag	Sun	Mon	Mar	Mer	Jup	Ven	Sat	Rah
9°59'	4°10'	27°31'	18°47'	20°2'	19°49'	12°38'	19°38'	22°11'

Nakshatra – Hasta

He was elected as the President of International Court of Justice in 1985 November.

In the birth chart Ketu is in third house and acts as third lord. It is aspected by Mercury, the lagna lord.

Ketu is in the lagna of progress chart and the self efforts are highlighted. Ketu acts as Sun who is in eighth house and is

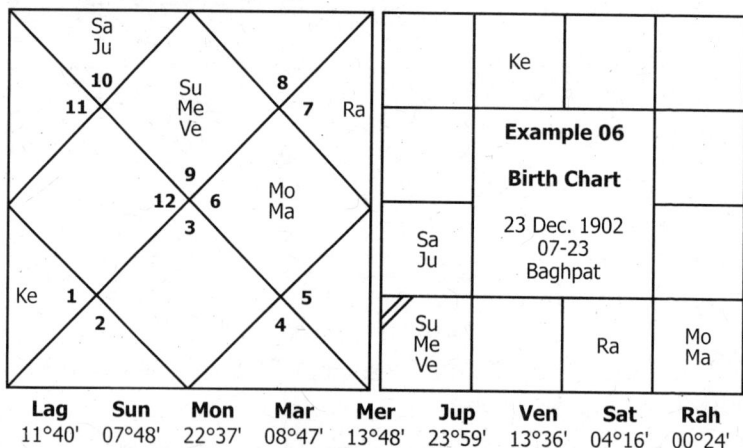

Ve Su		Sa	BL Ma
Ra Me(R)	**Example 05**		
	Progress Chart		
Ju	**Bhadrika / Magha**		PL Ke
		Ke	

with tenth lord Venus. Venus is also the third lord. The efforts are again seen.

The election for this post was to be held in September, 1985 when the sub was Mangla which is twelfth lord The elections were postponed and the Pingla sub period commenced and he won the election.

Example: Charan Singh

	Ke		
	Example 06		
	Birth Chart		
Sa Ju	23 Dec. 1902 07-23 Baghpat		
Su Me Ve		Ra	Mo Ma

Lag	Sun	Mon	Mar	Mer	Jup	Ven	Sat	Rah
11°40'	07°48'	22°37'	08°47'	13°48'	23°59'	13°36'	04°16'	00°24'

Nakshatra – Hasta

He expired on 23 May, 1987 in the Sub period of Siddha.

The maracas of birth chart are Mercury and Saturn. Moon is the lord of eighth house.

Both Mercury and Saturn are the maracas of the progress chart as well. Mercury is associated with lagna lord. The birth lagna lord is with Saturn.

Venus is associated with Lagna lord and Mercury. Therefore the relation with nakshatra lord and maracas is established.

Example: Bharti Taneja

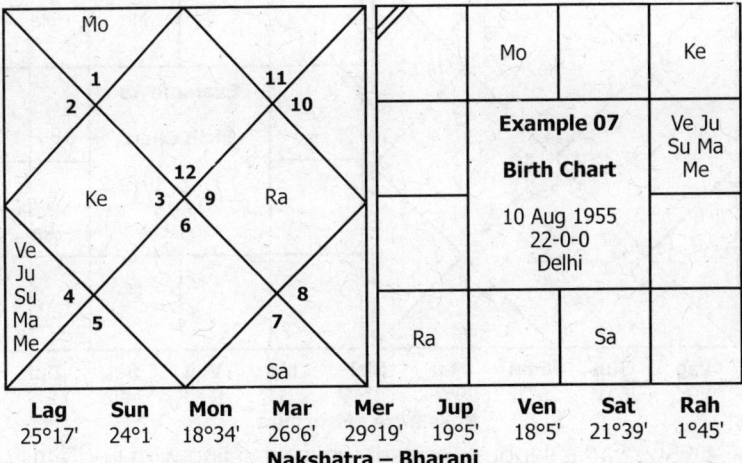

Lag	Sun	Mon	Mar	Mer	Jup	Ven	Sat	Rah
25°17'	24°1	18°34'	26°6'	29°19'	19°5'	18°5'	21°39'	1°45'

Nakshatra – Bharani

Ketu is the Nakshatra lord and is placed in eleventh house. Ketu acts as Mercury. Mercury is the lord of eleventh and is with both the trine Lords Mars and Jupiter. An excellent Raj Yoga and dhana Yoga is present.

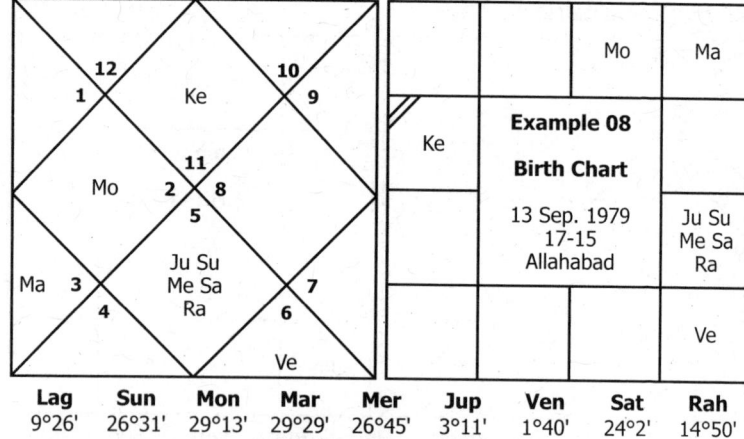

During the Sub period of Siddha, Lord of tenth house, She founded Alps academy and the business flourished.

In the sub period of Sankata she opened many branches in India and abroad.

Example: Serious Accident.

Lag	Sun	Mon	Mar	Mer	Jup	Ven	Sat	Rah
9°26'	26°31'	29°13'	29°29'	26°45'	3°11'	1°40'	24°2'	14°50'

Nakshatra –Mrigshira

She had a serious accident while traveling with her family. Father died and she along with sister injured. Mother was seriously injured.

In the birth chart Mars is the maraca for father. In the progress chart, Venus is the killer of father. Venus is aspected

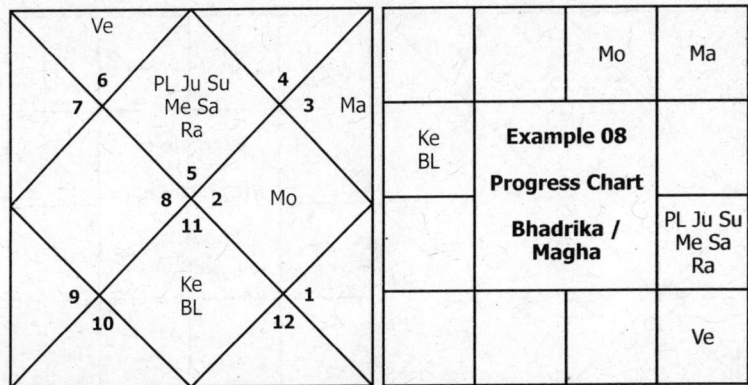

by Mars. The accident happened on 26 Oct. 1995. The sub period was of Venus.

For mother, Mars is in the eighth house from fourth. Mars is in second from Moon. Mars or Moon is not aspected by Jupiter and she was saved with serious injuries.

For her the maraca connections are present. Ketu is like Saturn. The progress lagna lord and birth lagna lord are with birth and progress maracas. Her safety in the accident is a miracle.

Example: Srimavo Bandaranaike

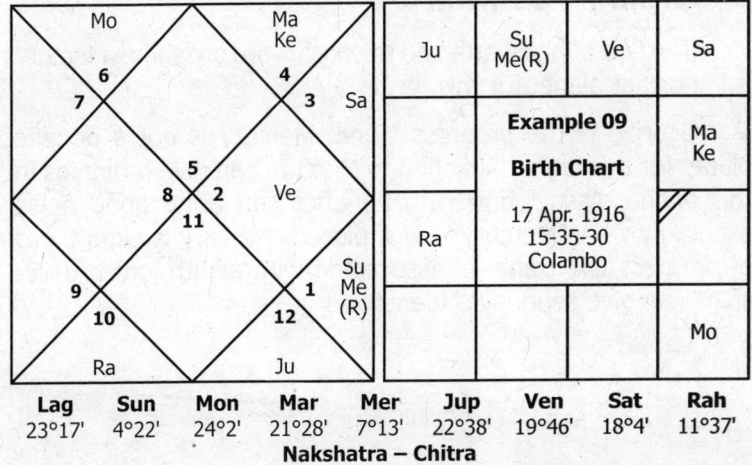

Lag	Sun	Mon	Mar	Mer	Jup	Ven	Sat	Rah
23°17'	4°22'	24°2'	21°28'	7°13'	22°38'	19°46'	18°4'	11°37'

Nakshatra – Chitra

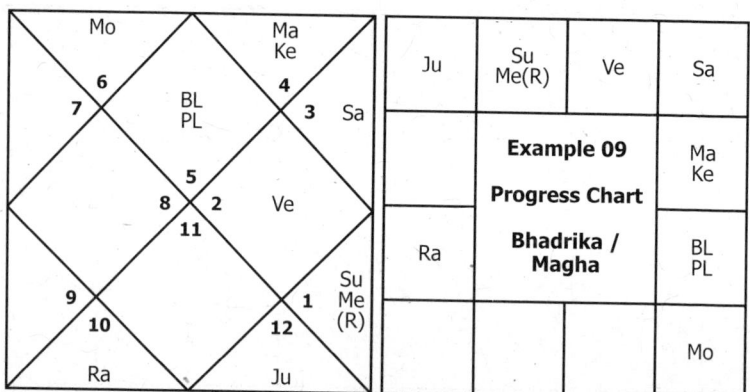

She died on 12 Oct. 2000 in the dasha of Bhadrika / Sankata.

The birth and the progress charts are same and the maracas are Mercury and Saturn.

Ketu is in twelfth house with debilitated Mars. The lord of lagna is with Mercury who stronger maraca being lord of Second house. Moon is in second house and thus nakshatra is connected to Maraca. Jupiter is the eighth lord an aspects Moon and Ketu. Jupiter is afflicted by maraca Saturn.

Bhadrika / Jyeshtha

The lord of nakshatra and the dasha lord are same. Mercury is important planet for this dasha.

Scorpio is the progress lagna. Mercury is not a benefic planet for this lagna. Affliction to Mercury can give problems in this dasha. Association with benefics can bring good news especially when Mercury is well placed. Mercury is eighth lord of progress chart and its association with eighth lord of birth chart can give serious accidents.

Example: Sanjay Gandhi

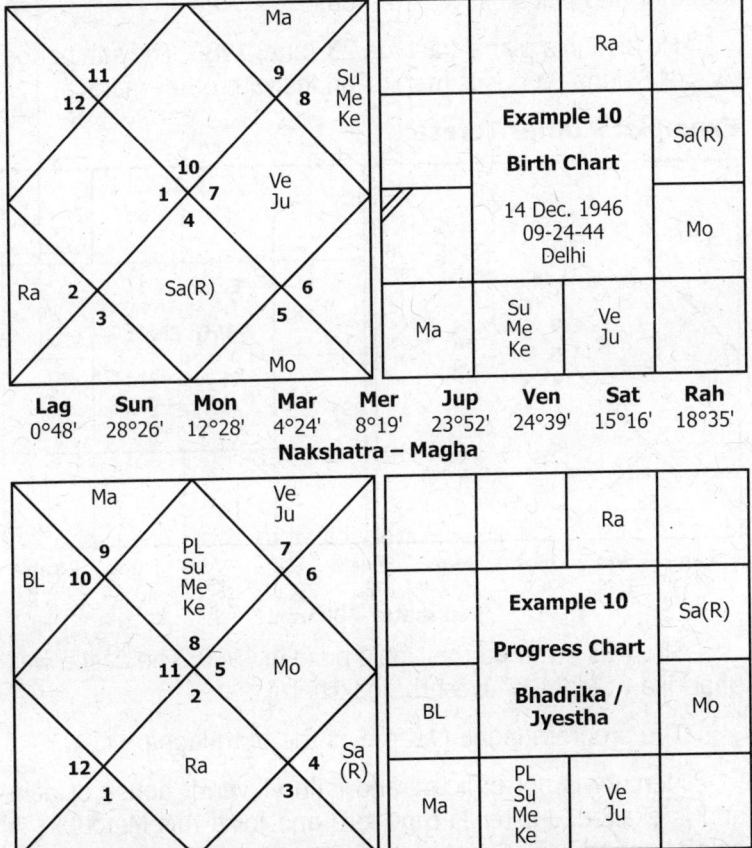

Lag	Sun	Mon	Mar	Mer	Jup	Ven	Sat	Rah
0°48'	28°26'	12°28'	4°24'	8°19'	23°52'	24°39'	15°16'	18°35'

Nakshatra – Magha

In the birth chart, Saturn is a maraca and lagna lord also. It is retrograde.

Mercury is the nakshatra lord. In the progress chart It is placed in lagna and afflicted by Ketu and the birth eighth lord Sun.

Venus and Jupiter are maraca in progress chart. Both are together and placed in twelfth house.

He died in a plane crash on 23 June, 1980. The sub period was of Siddha. Venus is maraca and is with other maraca.

Example: Mother Teresa

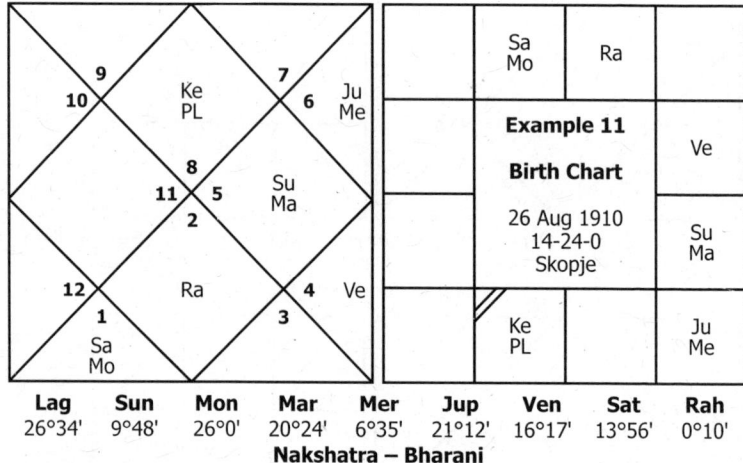

Lag	Sun	Mon	Mar	Mer	Jup	Ven	Sat	Rah
26°34'	9°48'	26°0'	20°24'	6°35'	21°12'	16°17'	13°56'	0°10'

Nakshatra – Bharani

She was awarded the Noble prize in 1980. The dasha was Bhadrika / Siddha of Jyeshtha nakshatra.

The progress lagna is same as the birth lagna.

Mercury is not afflicted and is in eleventh house of gain and is exalted. Jupiter is trine lord and joins this Mercury - A gainful period.

Venus is in ninth house ad is in eleventh from Mercury.

The honor is seen from tenth house. The lagna lord and tenth lord are together in tenth house.

Example: Jawaharlal Lal Nehru

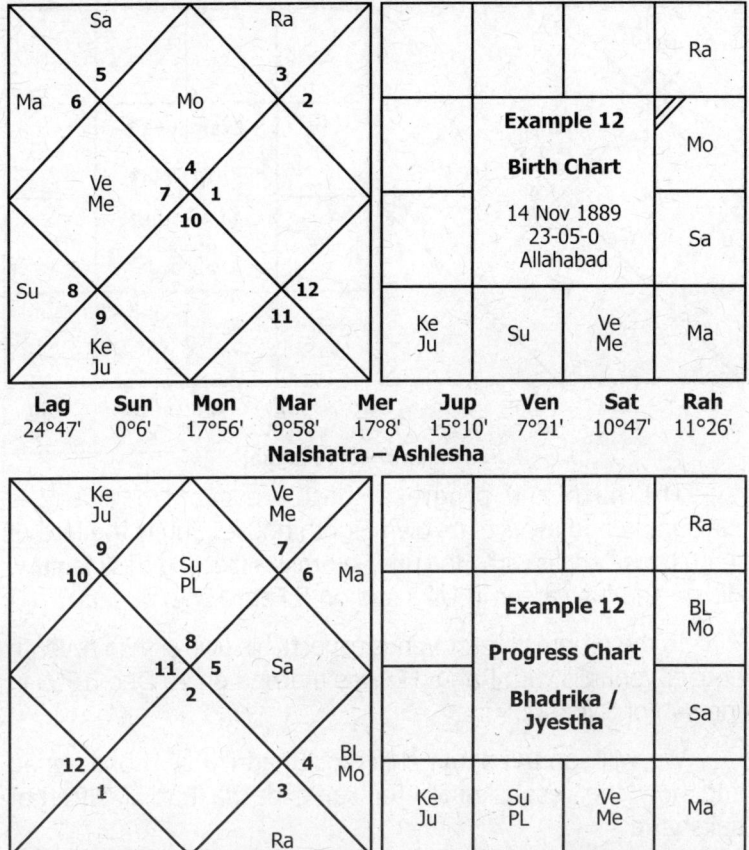

Lag	Sun	Mon	Mar	Mer	Jup	Ven	Sat	Rah
24°47'	0°6'	17°56'	9°58'	17°8'	15°10'	7°21'	10°47'	11°26'

Nalshatra – Ashlesha

In the birth chart, Mercury is maraca of father. Mercury is in fourth house which is eighth for father and is with Venus. Thus Mercury is a strong maraca for father.

In the progress chart, this combination has moved to twelfth house. His father expired on 6 Feb. 1931 in the Sub period of Siddha. Venus and Mercury are aspected by Saturn who is the lord of 7th and 8th for father.

Example: Job and Marriage

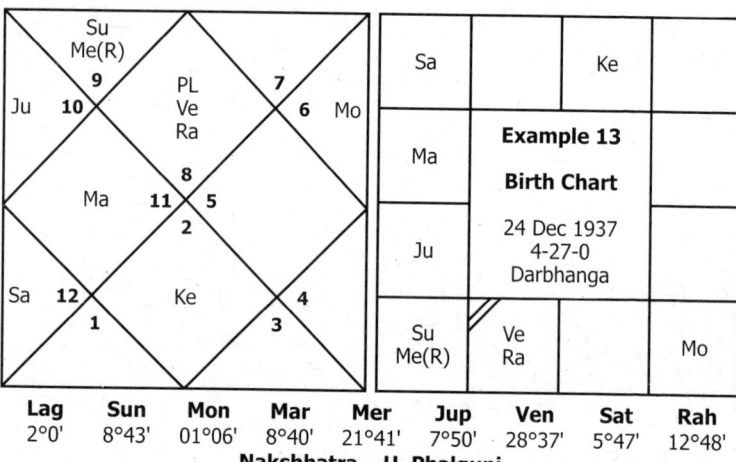

Lag	Sun	Mon	Mar	Mer	Jup	Ven	Sat	Rah
2°0'	8°43'	01°06'	8°40'	21°41'	7°50'	28°37'	5°47'	12°48'

Nakshhatra – U. Phalguni

The birth and progress chart are same. Mercury is retrograde and aspects its own eighth house. Sun is the lord of tenth house and is with Mercury. Saturn is aspecting this Mercury. He started his career in Ulka sub on 5 Feb. 1962.

In the progress chart Venus aspects his own sign in seventh house. Venus is with Rahu. He was married on 10 Dec. 1963 in the sub of Sankata.

We will see the same chart for Bhadrika of U.Bhadrapad and how the results differ for same dasha but of different nakshatra.

Example: Marriage and Child

Mercury is eleventh and second lord of the birth chart and is conjoined with lagna lord and the Yoga karaka Mars in the tenth house.

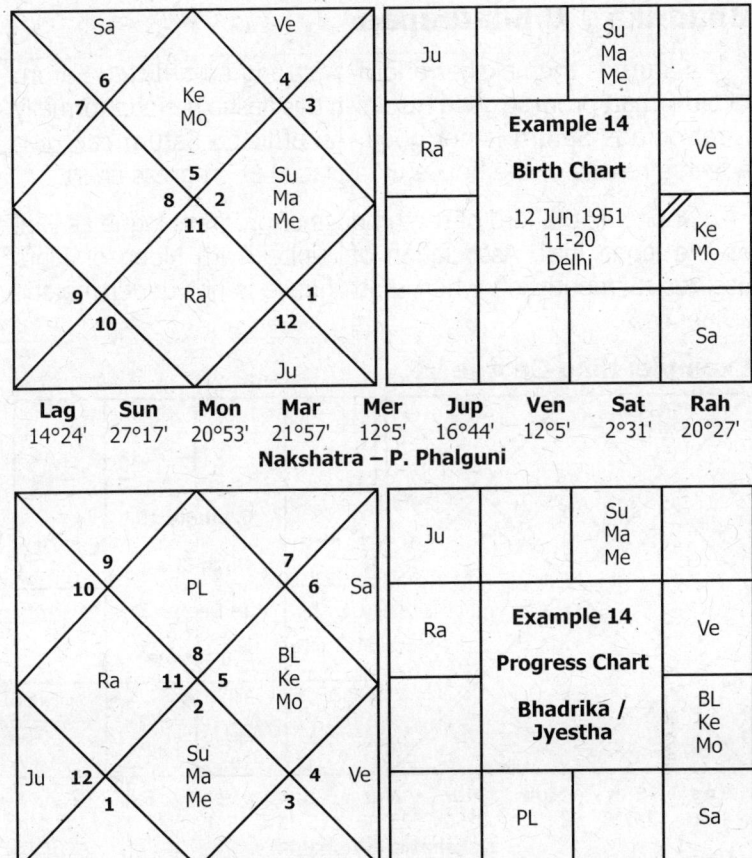

		Su Ma Me	
Ju			
Ra	Example 14 **Birth Chart** 12 Jun 1951 11-20 Delhi		Ve
			Ke Mo
			Sa

Lag	Sun	Mon	Mar	Mer	Jup	Ven	Sat	Rah
14°24'	27°17'	20°53'	21°57'	12°5'	16°44'	12°5'	2°31'	20°27'

Nakshatra – P. Phalguni

		Su Ma Me	
Ju			
Ra	Example 14 **Progress Chart** **Bhadrika / Jyestha**		Ve
			BL Ke Mo
		PL	Sa

We can expect good results during dasha of Mercury nakshatra.

In the progress chart, Mercury is now in seventh house and gives results of this house. He was married in May 1979 in the sub period of Bhadrika itself.

A son was born in March, 1980 in the sub of Ulka. Saturn is aspected by fifth lord Jupiter. Jupiter is strongly placed in own sign in fifth house.

Bhadrika / U.Bhadrapad

Saturn is the nakshatra lord. A strong un-afflicted Saturn of birth chart promise good results in this dasha period. Normally a retrograde Saturn is not good. An afflicted Saturn can give adverse results of the house, it is placed in progress chart.

Jupiter is the lord of tenth house of progress lagna as well as the lagna lord. Association of Jupiter with Moon or Mars assures a smooth job when tenth house is not under malefic influence.

Example: King George VI

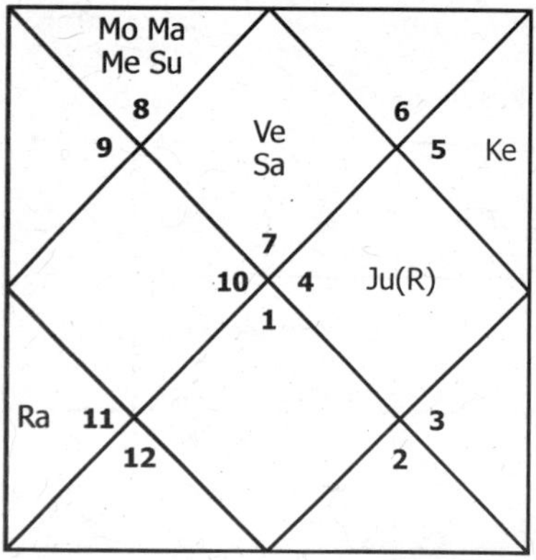

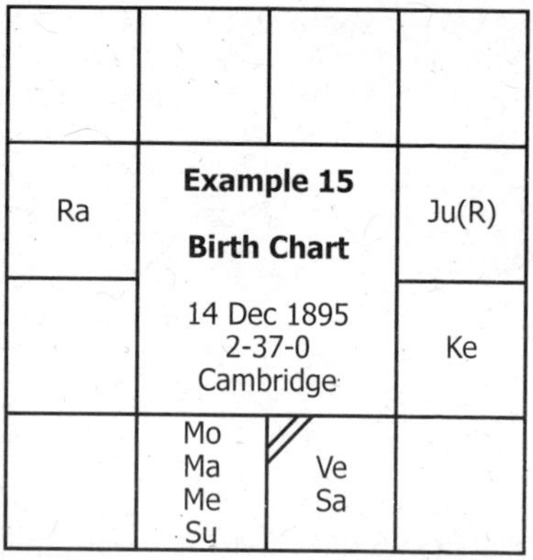

Lag	Sun	Mon	Mar	Mer	Jup	Ven	Sat	Rah
4°36'	29°29'	2°10'	8°56'	25°48'	16°11'	13°19'	22°21'	14°32'

Nakshatra – Vishakha

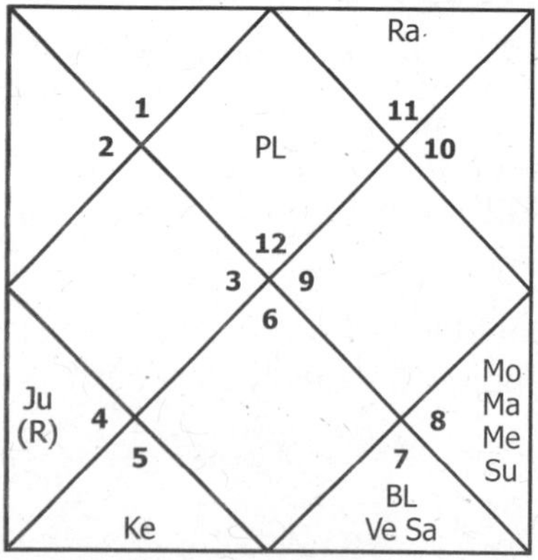

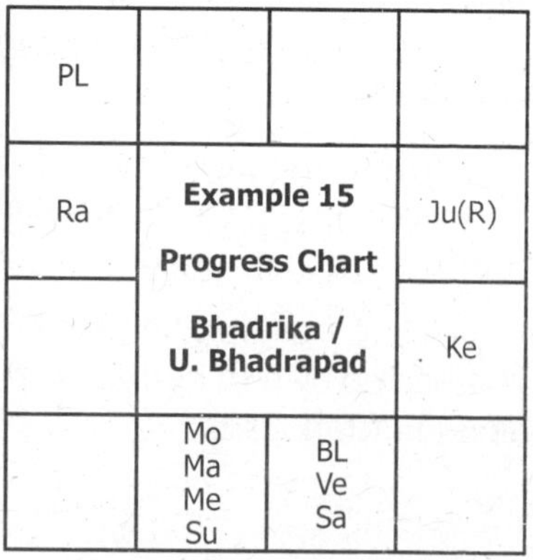

Saturn is powerfully placed and is yoga karaka of birth chart. It is exalted and with lagna lord. He is expected to give good results.

King George VI was not expected to be the king. His elder brother Edward ascended the throne as Edward VII. He desired to marry Walls Simpson, a divorcee. This was not permitted and he abdicated the throne to marry her.

King George was coroneted on 11 Dec., 1936 in the sub period of Ulka, the nakshatra lord. The Ulka period started on 27 November, 1936.

We have seen in birth chart that Saturn is strong to give good result. The progress chart is again strong. The lagna lord is exalted and aspects lagna. Ninth lord is with fourth and seventh lord in ninth house. The placement of eleventh lord in eighth house did harm the elder brother.

Example: Foreign

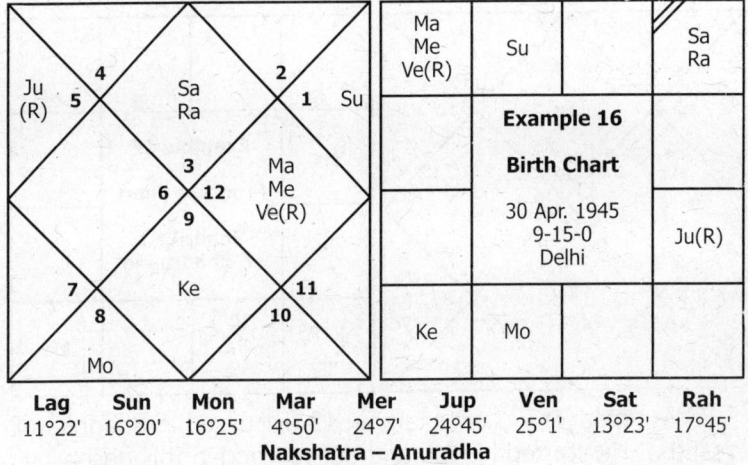

Lag	Sun	Mon	Mar	Mer	Jup	Ven	Sat	Rah
11°22'	16°20'	16°25'	4°50'	24°7'	24°45'	25°1'	13°23'	17°45'

Nakshatra – Anuradha

Saturn is the lord of eighth and ninth in the birth Chart. It is with Rahu and aspected by Malefic Mars. Saturn is expected to give average results.

Rasi Chart (Example 16): House 1/2, PL Ma Me Ve(R) in house 12; 11, 10; BL Sa Ra; Ke in 9; Mo in 8; Ju(R) in house 5.

PL Ma Me Ve(R)			BL Sa Ra
	Example 16 **Progress Chart**		
	Bhadrika / **U. Bhadrapad**		Ju(R)
Ke	Mo		

In the progress chart, Saturn is in fourth house. It is aspecting tenth house and tenth lord. He left the country in August, 1982 to take up a job in Nigeria. The stay abroad was not happy. He moved out of country in Ulka sub period and came back in Mangla sub period.

Example: Death

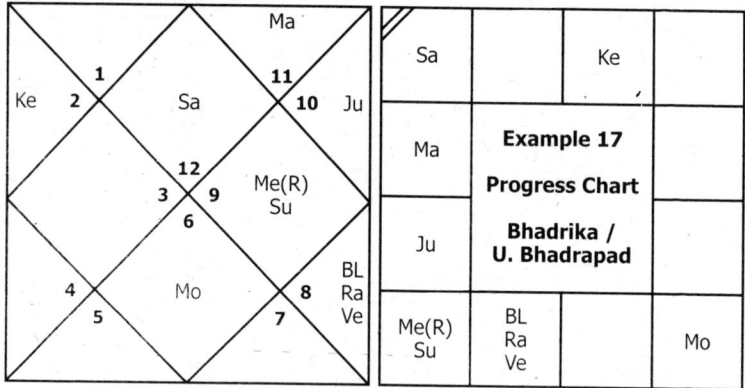

Sa		Ke	
Ma	**Example 17** **Progress Chart**		
Ju	**Bhadrika /** **U. Bhadrapad**		
Me(R) Su	BL Ra Ve		Mo

We repeat the chart example 13 discussed in Bhadrika of Jyeshtha. He started his job and got married in this dasha.

Next Bhadrika of U.Bhadrapad commenced on 24 Aug. 1996 up to 24 Aug., 2001. He died in July 2001.

The classical period was Bhadrika. For progress Yogini, the progress lagna is Ptsces and the nakshatra lords have changed. We give the progress chart for Bhadrika / U.Bhadrapad.

In the birth chart Saturn is in fifth house. Jupiter is maraca of birth chart. Jupiter and Saturn have exchanged places and thus Saturn is capable of giving maraca effects.

In the progress chart, Saturn is lord of twelfth and placed in lagna. Saturn influences Moon, Sun and Mercury. Sun is sixth lord and Karaka of heart.

He suffered a heart attack and died. The sub period was Bhramari.

Chapter 8

Ulka

Ulka period is of six years and in classics this period is not considered good since it is ruled by Saturn. Four nakshatras can generate this Ulka dasha. These are Kritika, P.Phalguni, Moola and Revati. The results are dependent on the strength of nakshatra lords.

Nakshatra	Nakshatra Lord	Sign	Remarks
Kritika	Sun	Aries / Taurus	For first one year six months, the progress lagna is Aries and for last four year six months it is Taurus.
P.Phalguni	Venus	Leo	Progress Lagna is Leo
Moola	Ketu	Sagittarius	Progress lagna is Sagittarius
Revati	Mercury	Pisces	Progress lagna is Pisces

Ulka / Kritika

Sun is the nakshatra lord and the progress lagna are Aries or Taurus.

This dasha period can operate up to a maximum age of 15 years in this scheme of progress yogini dasha.

When Aries is the progress lagna, Sun is the lord of fifth house. Depending upon status of Sun in birth chart, it will influence the education.

With Taurus progress lagna, Sun is fourth lord and thus is capable of giving fourth house effects like home, mother, accidents etc.

Example : L.K.Advani

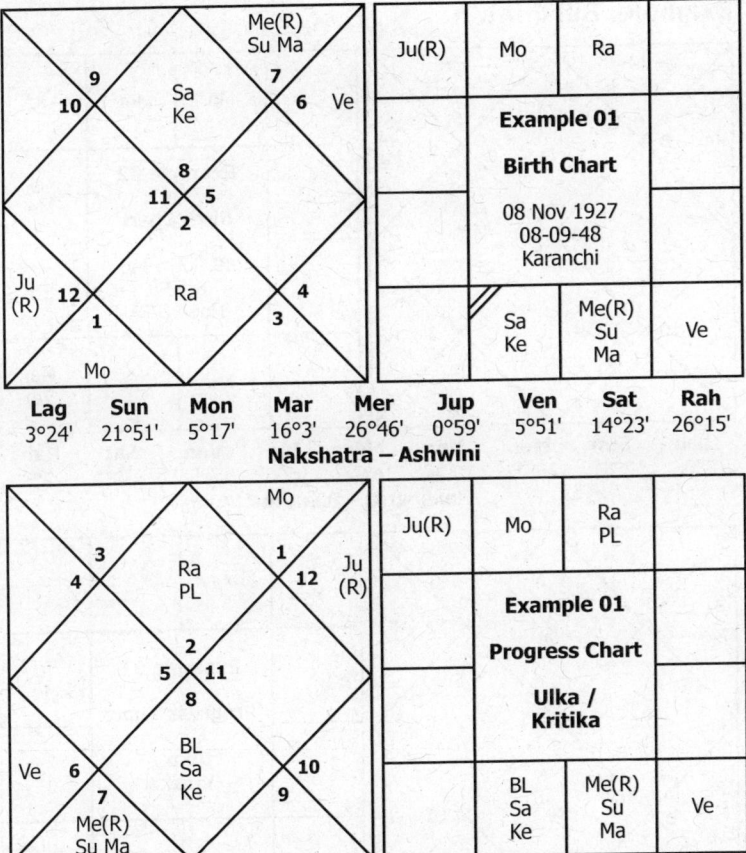

Lag	Sun	Mon	Mar	Mer	Jup	Ven	Sat	Rah
3°24'	21°51'	5°17'	16°3'	26°46'	0°59'	5°51'	14°23'	26°15'

Nakshatra – Ashwini

In the birth chart Sun is in twelfth house and is debilitated. It is afflicted by Mars.

Now see the progress chart. Sun is the fourth lord and placed in sixth house. The fourth house is aspected by Saturn. The fourth lord is with Mercury and Mars.

For fourth house, maracas are Saturn and Mercury. Both are making relation with fourth house and fourth lord.

His mother died when he was thirteen years of age and the sub period was of Bhadrika.

Example: Bill Clinton

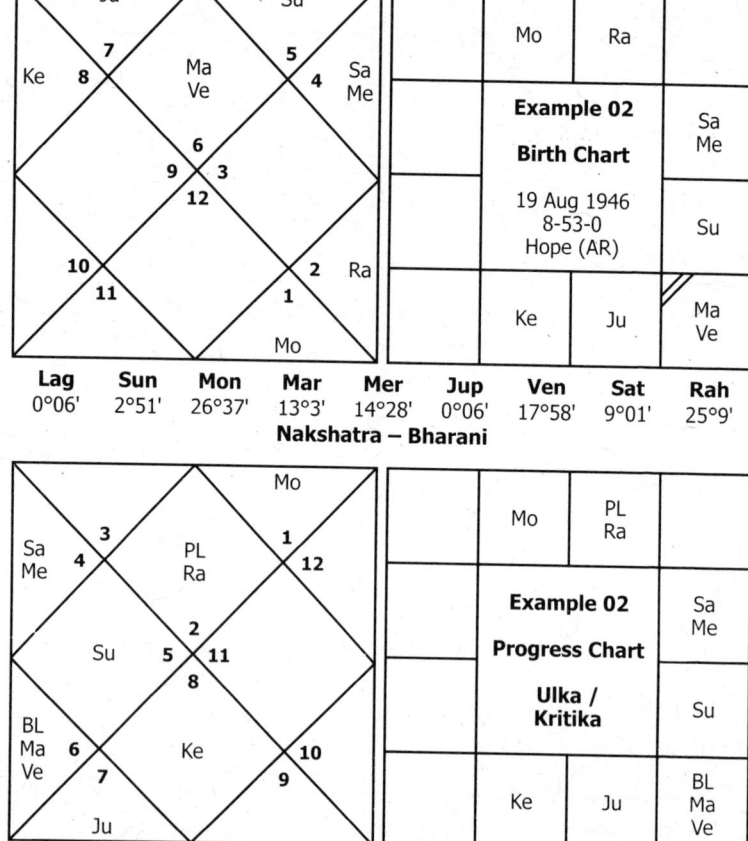

Lag	Sun	Mon	Mar	Mer	Jup	Ven	Sat	Rah
0°06'	2°51'	26°37'	13°3'	14°28'	0°06'	17°58'	9°01'	25°9'

Nakshatra – Bharani

Sun is twelfth lord and is placed in twelfth house of change in birth chart. It is in Kartari indicating dependence and external support.

Sun is placed in fourth house of progress chart and the events of home and mother are seen. He moved to hot springs when his mother married Roger Clinton who owned an automobile dealership.

Re marriage of mother is confirmed from fourth house. The seventh lord from fourth is Saturn in the progress chart and it is Mercury in birth chart. Both are together. The tenth house, i.e. seventh from fourth is aspected by seventh lord of birth chart.

Example: Joe Biden

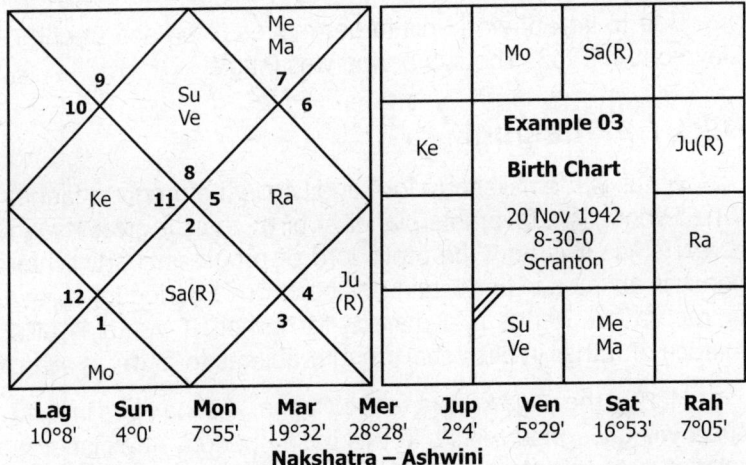

Lag	Sun	Mon	Mar	Mer	Jup	Ven	Sat	Rah
10°8'	4°0'	7°55'	19°32'	28°28'	2°4'	5°29'	16°53'	7°05'

Nakshatra – Ashwini

In the birth chart Sun is in lagna. It is with twelfth lord Venus. Retrograde Saturn and Jupiter aspects it. This aspect is of Kendra and trikona lords but retrograde. Sun given mixed results being tenth lord and related with yoga karakas.

In the progress chart fourth house has Rahu. Now Sun as fourth lord is in seventh house and aspected by eighth lord Jupiter.

Due to lack of work, his father moved to an apartment in Claymont in 1953. The sub period was Pingla

Ulka / P.Phalguni

Venus is the nakshatra lord and Leo is the progress lagna. When Venus is a favorable planet in birth chart it gives rise in career since it is now the tenth lord of progress chart. When Venus is afflicted in birth chart it is not a good period for career or reputation. Venus is a maraca for father. If Venus is also maraca of father in birth chart then problems to father is seen.

Mars is the yoga karaka for Leo lagna. A good Mars in birth chart will give good results in this dasha period. Any planet in relation with this Mars will have a say in its dasha period.

Example: Indira Gandhi

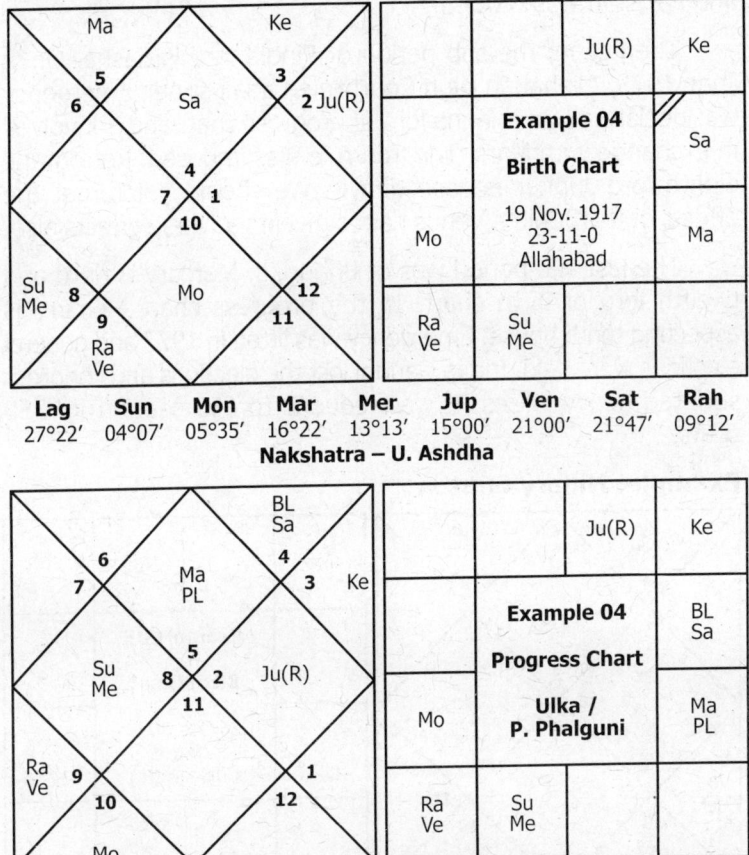

Lag	**Sun**	**Mon**	**Mar**	**Mer**	**Jup**	**Ven**	**Sat**	**Rah**
27°22′	04°07′	05°35′	16°22′	13°13′	15°00′	21°00′	21°47′	09°12′

Nakshatra – U. Ashdha

In the birth chart Venus is with Rahu in sixth house. It is not aspected by any planet. Venus is thus afflicted in birth chart.

In the progress chart, Venus is in fifth house which is eighth from tenth. The exchange of Jupiter and Venus is now the exchange of tenth and fifth lords and is Yoga karaka.

The Ulka dasha started on 13 July, 1971 and the situation in Bangladesh came up at the mind of nation.

She was hailed as durga when Bangladesh was created and Pakistan was divided.

Then came the sub period of Pingla in this dasha. On12 June 1975, Allahabad High Court ruled against her. Emergency was declared. Sun is lagna lord of progress chart and is involved in exchange with Mars. The iron rule was imposed. Retrograde eighth lord Jupiter is aspecting it. We should not forget the effects of this Jupiter. Venus has to give its adverse effects also.

The last sub period was of Bhadrika. Mercury is third and twelfth lord of birth chart. In the progress chart Mercury is aspecting tenth house. Emergency was lifted in 1977 and general elections were held. Indira Gandhi lost the elections and congress suffered heavy losses. It was reduced to 153 seats from 350 seats.

Example: Hillary Clinton

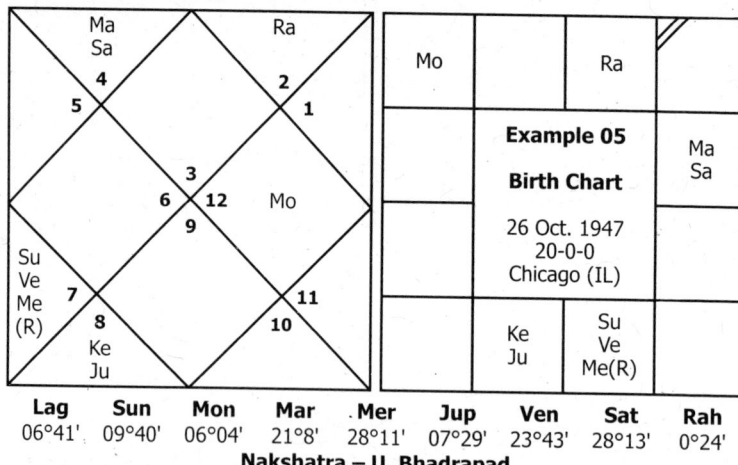

Lag	Sun	Mon	Mar	Mer	Jup	Ven	Sat	Rah
06°41'	09°40'	06°04'	21°8'	28°11'	07°29'	23°43'	28°13'	0°24'

Nakshatra – U. Bhadrapad

Venus is yoga karaka of birth chart. It is in own sign in fifth house and its placement with fourth lord Mercury is a great Raj yoga.

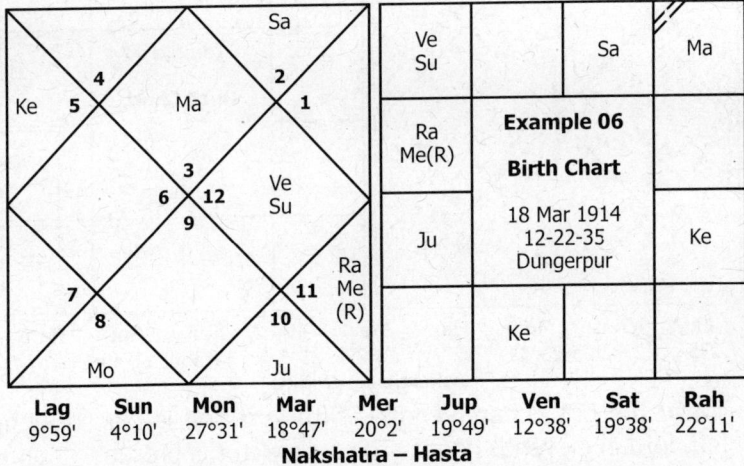

In the progress chart it is well placed. Mars is the Yoga karaka of progress chart. It is with Saturn who is seventh lord. Mars aspects Mercury. Mercury is with Venus. Her husband became President of USA on 20 Jan 1993 and she became the first lady.

Example: Maharaja Sri Nagendra Singh

Lag	Sun	Mon	Mar	Mer	Jup	Ven	Sat	Rah
9°59'	4°10'	27°31'	18°47'	20°2'	19°49'	12°38'	19°38'	22°11'

Nakshatra – Hasta

In the progress chart, Venus is placed in eighth house with lagna Lord Sun. No planet is aspecting this combination. Lagna is afflicted by Ketu and aspected by maraca Mercury. Mercury is aspected by Saturn.

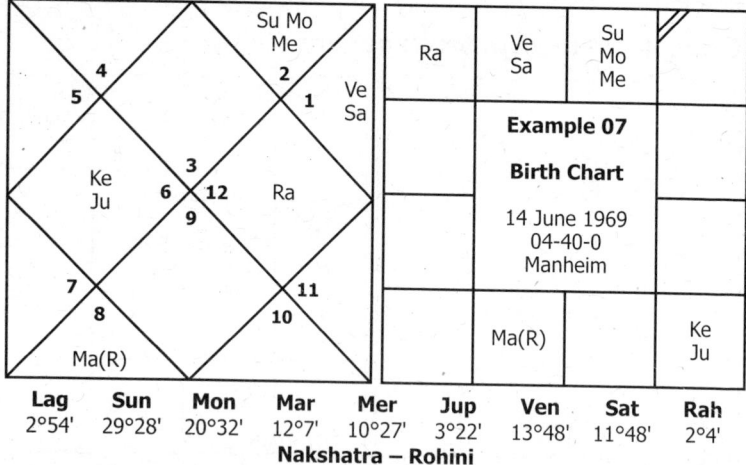

He left this world on 11 Dec. 1988 in the sub period of Siddha, the nakshatra lord. The pratyantra was Bhadrika which commenced on 11 December, 1988.

Example: Steffi Graph

Lag	Sun	Mon	Mar	Mer	Jup	Ven	Sat	Rah
2°54'	29°28'	20°32'	12°7'	10°27'	3°22'	13°48'	11°48'	2°4'

Nakshatra – Rohini

In the birth chart Venus is fifth lord and is placed with ninth lord in eleventh house. The luck factor is present.

In the progress chart Venus is in ninth house. There are four planets in four – ten axes. Now the ninth lord is aspecting tenth house and tenth lord is in ninth house. Mars is yoga karaka and gives great strength to professional matters.

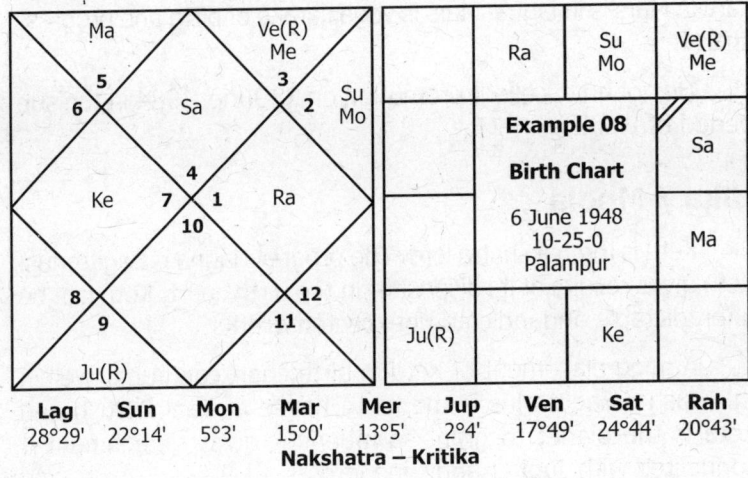

Ra	Ve Sa	Su Mo Me	BL
	Example 07		
	Progress Chart		
	Ulka / P. Phalguni		PL
	Ma(R)		Ke Ju

She remained on top during this Ulka period which lasted till 1999. Soon when Siddha of U Phalguni commenced she retired from active game. Sun is third lord of birth, placed in twelfth and aspected by Mars.

Example: Promotion

	Ra	Su Mo	Ve(R) Me
			Sa
	Example 08		
	Birth Chart		
	6 June 1948 10-25-0 Palampur		Ma
Ju(R)		Ke	

Lag	Sun	Mon	Mar	Mer	Jup	Ven	Sat	Rah
28°29'	22°14'	5°3'	15°0'	13°5'	2°4'	17°49'	24°44'	20°43'

Nakshatra – Kritika

Ra	Su Mo	Ve(R) Me	
	Example 08 Progress Chart		BL Sa
	Ulka / P. Phalguni		Ma PL
Ju(R)		Ke	

(Birth chart — North Indian diamond chart)
House 6/7: Ke; House 4: BL Sa; House 3: Ve(R) Me; Center: Ma PL; House 5/8/11/2: Su Mo; House 9/10: Ju(R); House 1/12: Ra

Venus is fourth and eleventh lord of birth chart. Venus cannot be termed as a good planet itself. The mutual aspect of fourth and ninth lord makes it participate in yoga.

The progress chart is having strength. The tenth house contains lagna lord Sun which is with exalted Moon. The Yoga karaka Mars is in lagna. Mars is yoga karaka of birth and progress chart.

He got an excellent promotion on 28 June, 1984 in the sub period of Pingla.

Ulka / Moola

Ketu is the nakshatra lord. The progress lagna is Sagittarius. Ketu gives results of its dispositor in the birth chart. Ketu can be unpredictable and indicate unexpected events.

A good placement of Ketu in birth chart can auger well in this dasha. Sagittarius is the ninth house of Kaal Purush and Ketu is the planet to grant salvation. It gives detachment if connected with Jupiter and trine lords.

Example: S.L.Shakdhar

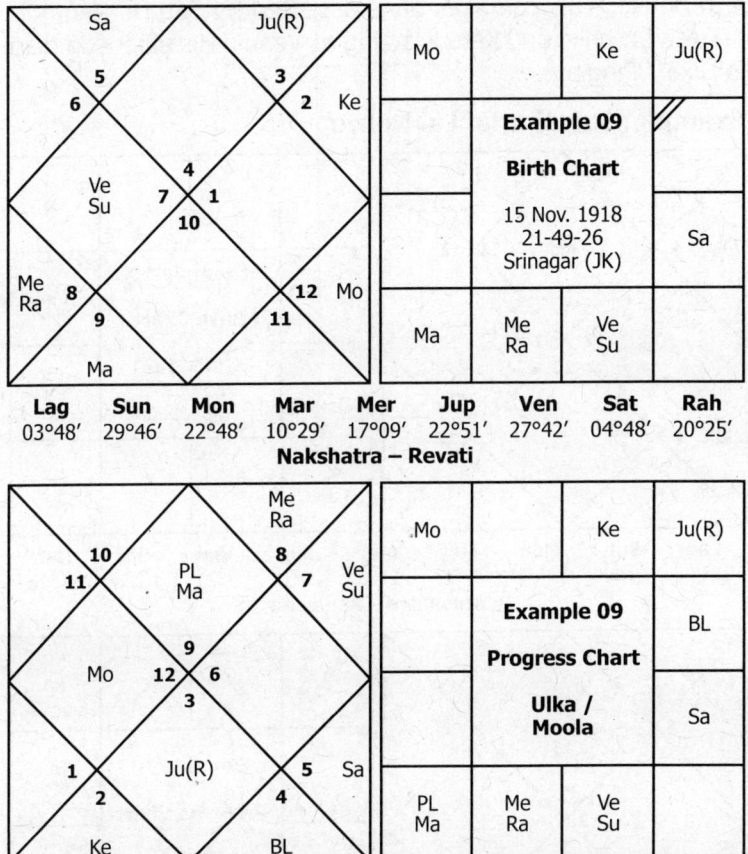

Mo		Ke	Ju(R)
	Example 09		
	Birth Chart		
	15 Nov. 1918		Sa
	21-49-26		
	Srinagar (JK)		
	Ma	Me Ra	Ve Su

Lag	Sun	Mon	Mar	Mer	Jup	Ven	Sat	Rah
03°48'	29°46'	22°48'	10°29'	17°09'	22°51'	27°42'	04°48'	20°25'

Nakshatra − Revati

Mo		Ke	Ju(R)
	Example 09		BL
	Progress Chart		
	Ulka /		Sa
	Moola		
	PL Ma	Me Ra	Ve Su

In the birth chart, Ketu is in eleventh house and is aspected by Saturn. Saturn is lord of eighth and is a maraca for wife. The axis of Rahu/Ketu is five / eleven.

Ketu is in sixth house of progress chart and Saturn is again eighth lord from seventh house. His wife died in Ulka / Ulka.

From birth chart, Ketu is capable of giving results of fifth house also. It is with Mercury who is eighth lord from fifth.

In the progress chart Sun and Venus are aspecting the fifth house. This combination is aspected by Saturn. Venus is maraca for child and Ketu is acting as Venus. His elder son died in Ulka / Pingla.

Example: Jawaharlal Lal Nehru

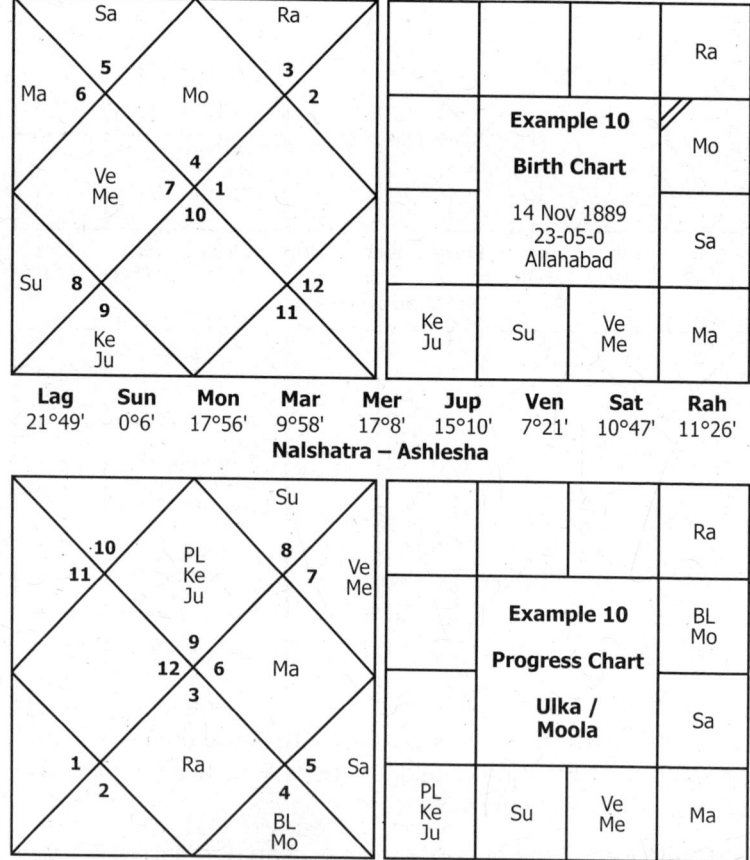

Lag	Sun	Mon	Mar	Mer	Jup	Ven	Sat	Rah
21°49'	0°6'	17°56'	9°58'	17°8'	15°10'	7°21'	10°47'	11°26'

Nalshatra – Ashlesha

Ketu is in sixth house of birth chart. The sixth lord Jupiter joins it. Thus Ketu is capable of giving illness.

In the progress chart Ketu is in lagna and afflicts one seven axis. Jupiter and Ketu are maraca for wife. The eighth lord of wife is Saturn. Saturn aspects Venus and Mercury.

Kamala Nehru expired on 28 Feb. 1936 in a T.B.Sanitorium in Switzerland. The dasha was Ulka / Siddha/ Dhanya.

Example: Rajesh Khanna

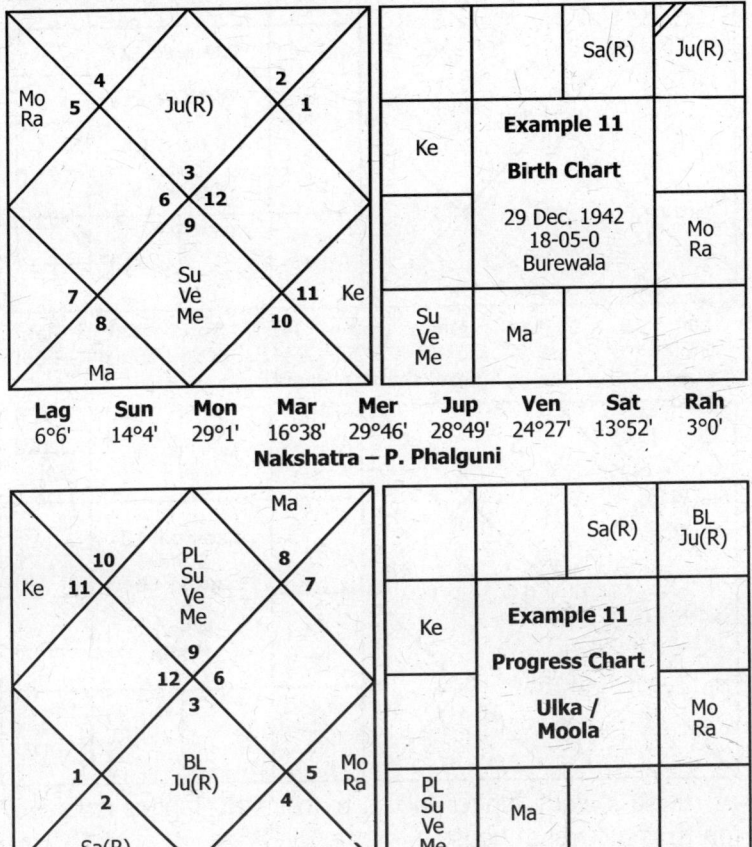

	Sa(R)	Ju(R)
Ke	Example 11 Birth Chart	
	29 Dec. 1942 18-05-0 Burewala	Mo Ra
Su Ve Me	Ma	

Lag	Sun	Mon	Mar	Mer	Jup	Ven	Sat	Rah
6°6'	14°4'	29°1'	16°38'	29°46'	28°49'	24°27'	13°52'	3°0'

Nakshatra – P. Phalguni

	Sa(R)	BL Ju(R)
Ke	Example 11 Progress Chart	
	Ulka / Moola	Mo Ra
PL Su Ve Me	Ma	

The Rahu / Ketu axis is in three / nine axis in both the charts.

With Sagittarius progress lagna, the seventh and lagna lords are in mutual aspect. He married Dimple Kapadia in March 1973 in the dasha of Ulka / Siddha.

The three nine axis indicate the arrival of child also. His daughter was born in Ulka / Sankata.

Example: Marriage

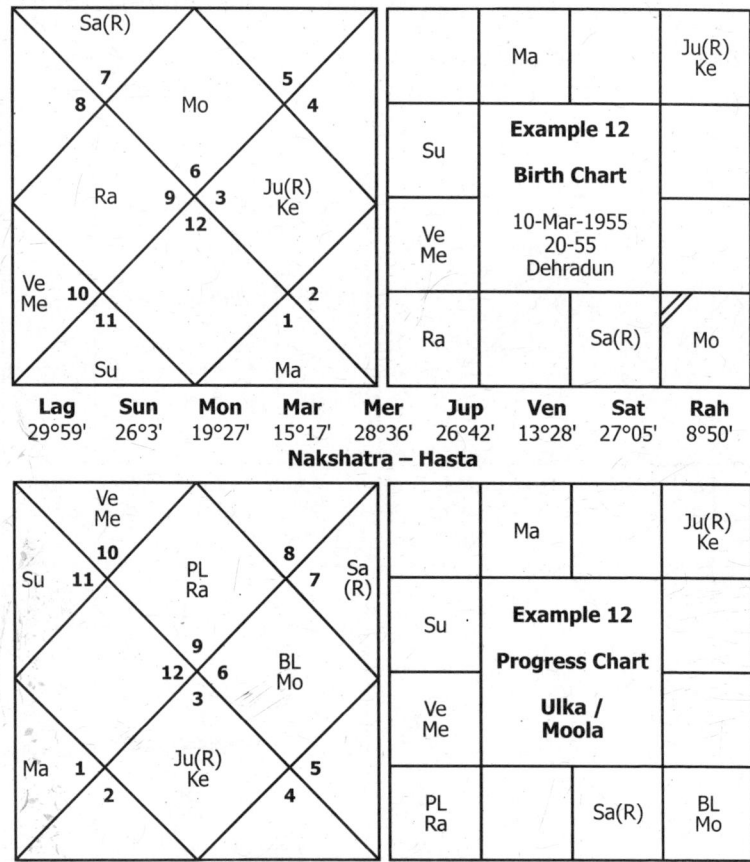

Lag	Sun	Mon	Mar	Mer	Jup	Ven	Sat	Rah
29°59'	26°3'	19°27'	15°17'	28°36'	26°42'	13°28'	27°05'	8°50'

Nakshatra – Hasta

Ketu is with Jupiter in the birth chart. Jupiter is lord of fourth and seventh house.

Now Ketu is moved to seventh house and with lagna and fourth lord. The promise of seventh and fourth house is highlighted. He married on 30 Jan. 1975 in the dasha of Ulka / Sankata.

Is the dasha of Ulka / Sankata is bad?

Example; Scorpion bite

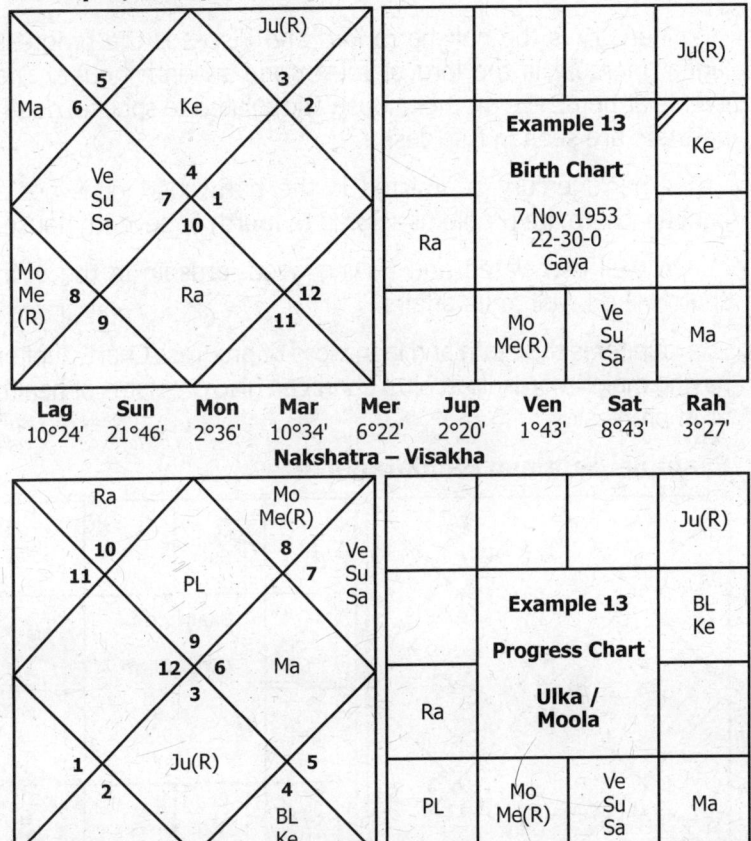

Lag	Sun	Mon	Mar	Mer	Jup	Ven	Sat	Rah
10°24'	21°46'	2°36'	10°34'	6°22'	2°20'	1°43'	8°43'	3°27'

Nakshatra – Visakha

In the birth chart Ketu is in Lagna and aspected by Saturn. Saturn is lord of eighth and seventh house of birth. The Position of Ketu is not good for the body.

This Ketu has moved to eighth house of progress chart. A serious condition and to make matters worse, it is now aspected by second and third lord Saturn.

A Scorpion bit him in December 1964 in the sub period of Siddha. Siddha is with Saturn and is a malefic planet for Sagittarius lagna. He survived. Lagna lord Jupiter is aspecting lagna.

Ulka / Revati

Mercury is the nakshatra lord and Pisces is the progress lagna. Mercury is the lord of fourth and seventh house. The events at home like mother, house and related to spouse, death partners are seen in this dasha.

When Mercury is afflicted in the birth chart or is not a benefic, there are problems related to fourth or seventh house.

A well associated and having good lordship in the birth chart will do well to its affairs.

Jupiter is the tenth and lagna lord of progress Chart. Jupiter having malefic lordship in birth chart can give problems of health or in profession.

Example: Srimavo Bandaranaike

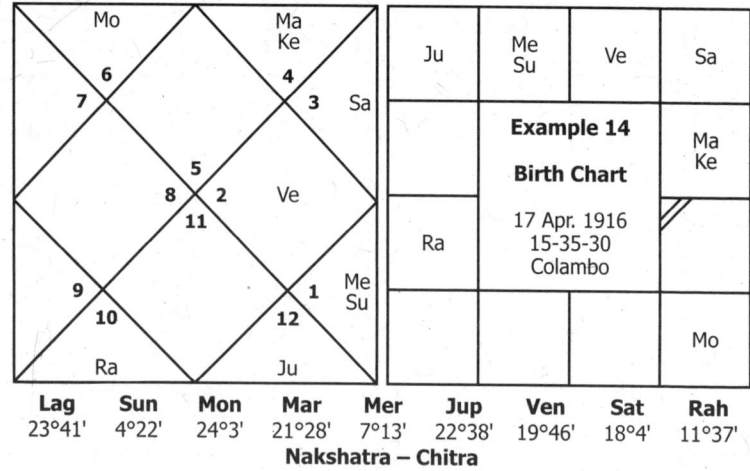

Lag	Sun	Mon	Mar	Mer	Jup	Ven	Sat	Rah
23°41'	4°22'	24°3'	21°28'	7°13'	22°38'	19°46'	18°4'	11°37'

Nakshatra – Chitra

Mercury is the lord of second and eleventh lord in birth chart. It is with exalted lagna lord causing dhana yoga and also a maraca.

In the progress chart, lagna lord is in lagna. Jupiter is also tenth lord. Mercury is in second house with exalted sixth lord. Sun is birth lagna lord. She was elected Prime Minister in Ulka /

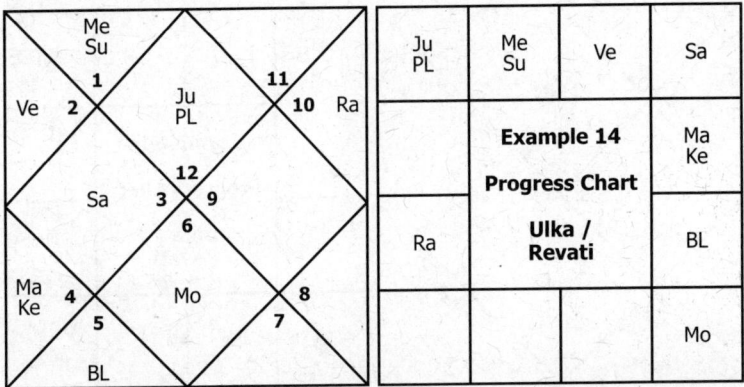

Sankata. Rahu is in eleventh from Progress lagna and in tenth from Mercury.

Sri Lanka became a republic on 22 May, 1972. The sub period was Bhadrika and she was again elected P.M. for second term.

Example: K.R. Bhatnagar

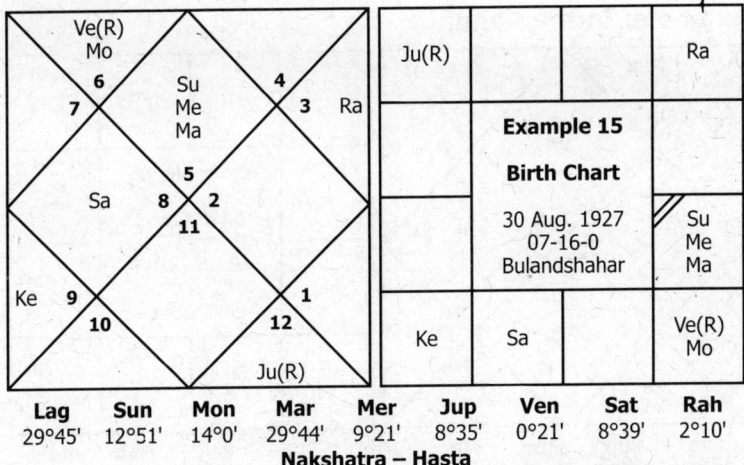

Lag	Sun	Mon	Mar	Mer	Jup	Ven	Sat	Rah
29°45'	12°51'	14°0'	29°44'	9°21'	8°35'	0°21'	8°39'	2°10'

Nakshatra – Hasta

Compare this with previous example. Both charts have Leo as birth lagna. The association of Jupiter and placement of Mercury in progress chart have made the difference.

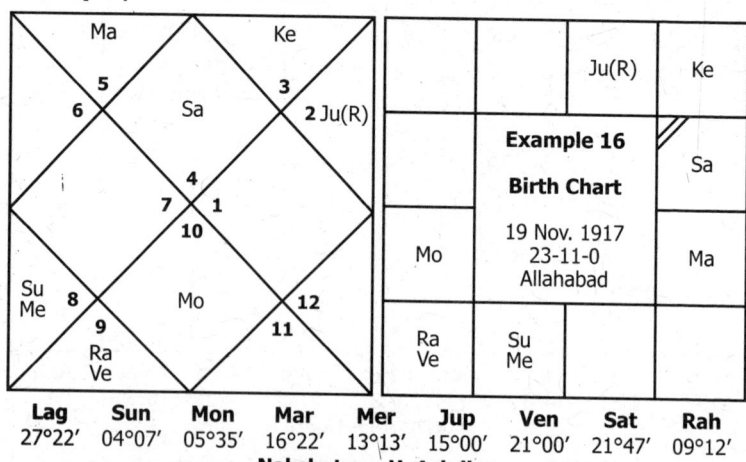

In the progress chart, Mercury is in sixth house with sixth lord. The maracas of progress chart are Mercury and Mars. Mercury is maraca of birth chart as well.

The eighth lord Venus and the second lord Mars are now aspecting lagna and lagna lord Jupiter. Rahu acts as Mercury.

He died on 26 Aug. 1986 in the sub period of Sankata.

Example; Indira Gandhi

Lag	Sun	Mon	Mar	Mer	Jup	Ven	Sat	Rah
27°22'	04°07'	05°35'	16°22'	13°13'	15°00'	21°00'	21°47'	09°12'

Nakshatra – U. Ashdha

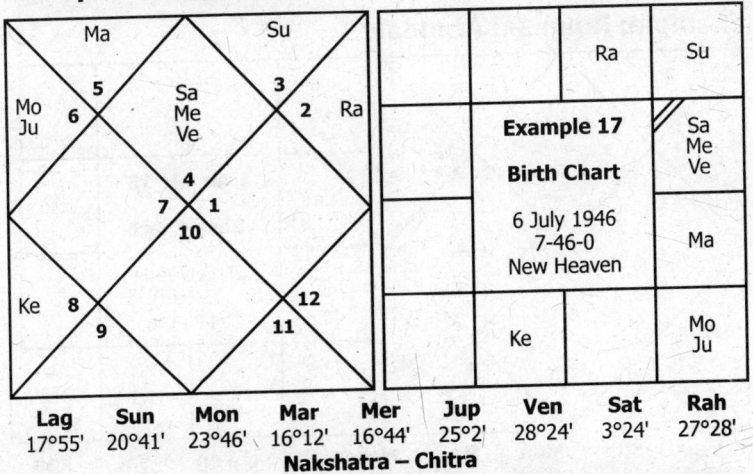

Mercury is with Sun and aspected by ninth lord Jupiter. Mercury is lord of third and twelfth house. It promises mixed results in the birth chart.

In the progress chart, Mercury is in ninth house of father and aspected by maraca of mother and father Jupiter. Saturn is placed in fifth house. For mother it is maraca house and is aspected by maraca lord Moon. Her mother expired on 22 June, 1936 in the sub period of Ulka.

Example: George Bush

Lag	Sun	Mon	Mar	Mer	Jup	Ven	Sat	Rah
17°55'	20°41'	23°46'	16°12'	16°44'	25°2'	28°24'	3°24'	27°28'

Nakshatra – Chitra

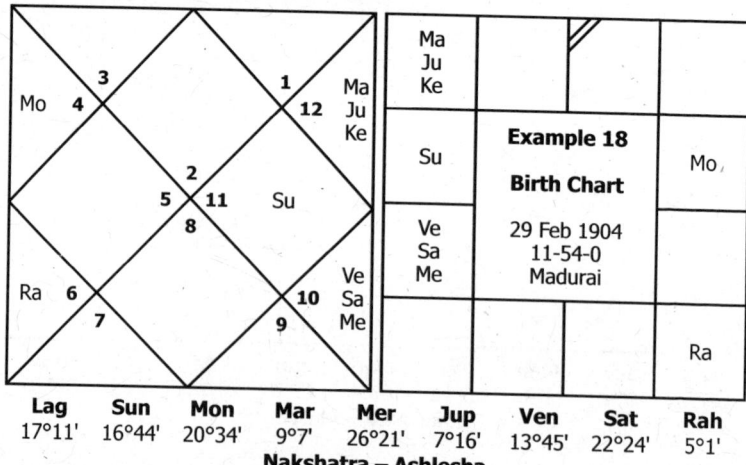

Ra 2	1	PL	11	10
Su 3	12	9
BL Sa Me Ve 4	5	Mo Ju 6	7	8 Ke
	Ma		

PL		Ra	Su
	Example 17 **Progress Chart** **Ulka / Revati**		BL Sa Me Ve
			Ma
Ke			Mo Ju

Mercury is in the lagna in birth chart. It is involved in exchange with lagna lord. The ninth house is aspected by lagna lord, ninth lord and the tenth lord.

The position in progress chart improves. Now Mercury is in exchange with fifth lord, Kendra trikona yoga. The tenth and lagna lord aspects lagna.

He assumed office of president of USA on 20 Jan. 2001. The sub period was of Mangla. Moon is with tenth lord and involved in exchange with dasha nakshatra lord.

Example: Rukmani Arundale

Mo 4	3	1	12 Ma Ju Ke
5 11	2	Su	8
Ra 6	7	9	10 Ve Sa Me

Ma Ju Ke			
Su	**Example 18** **Birth Chart** **29 Feb 1904 11-54-0 Madurai**		Mo
Ve Sa Me			
			Ra

Lag	Sun	Mon	Mar	Mer	Jup	Ven	Sat	Rah
17°11'	16°44'	20°34'	9°7'	26°21'	7°16'	13°45'	22°24'	5°1'

Nakshatra – Ashlesha

PL Ma Ju Ke		BL	
Su	**Example 18** **Progress Chart**		Mo
Ve Sa Me	**Ulka /** **Revati**		
			Ra

Mercury is lord of second house of birth chart. It is also fifth lord but Rahu is in fifth house. Jupiter is the eighth lord.

In the progress chart also, Mercury and Mars are the maracas as in the birth chart. Mars is now in lagna with Ketu and eighth lord of birth chart. Jupiter is now the lagna lord.

The lagna and lagna lord are badly afflicted. It is aspected by Saturn. Venus is with dasha and nakshatra lord.

She died on 24 Feb. 1986. The Sankata sub started on the same day.

Chapter 9

Siddha

Siddha dasha is considered as giver of all desired results. We cannot generalize the results of a dasha in this way. It depends on the total horoscope and dasha is the dynamic unfolding of events.

Siddha is generated by three nakshatra

Nakshatra	Nakshatra Lord	Sign	Remarks
Rohini	Moon	Taurus	Taurus is the progress lagna
U.Phalguni	Sun	Leo/ Virgo	First one year nine months Leo is progress lagna. For last five year three months progress lagna is Virgo.
P.Ashadha	Venus	Sagittarius	Sagittarius is the progress lagna

Siddha / Rohini

We must note that after Revati we jump to Rohini in this scheme of progress yogini dasha.

Moon is the nakshatra lord and Taurus is the progress lagna. Moon is lord of third house and gets exalted in lagna. Moon is easily influenced by other planets and the results will depend on its and placement and strength.

For this progress lagna, Mercury and Mars are Maraca. Saturn is Yoga karaka. Jupiter is a malefic planet being lord of eighth and eleventh house.

Example: King George VI

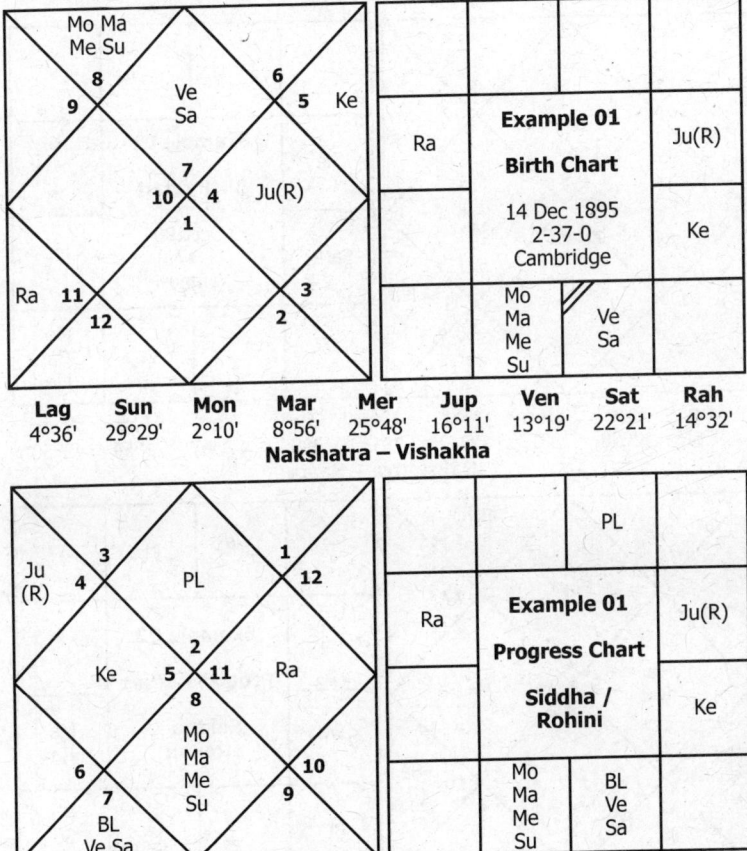

Lag	Sun	Mon	Mar	Mer	Jup	Ven	Sat	Rah
4°36'	29°29'	2°10'	8°56'	25°48'	16°11'	13°19'	22°21'	14°32'

Nakshatra – Vishakha

Moon is the tenth lord of Birth Chart and is placed in second house with three planets and aspected by Jupiter. Lagna is having Yoga Karaka Saturn with lagna lord.

The progress lagna is Taurus. Moon is now in seventh house with seventh, fourth and fifth lord. Mars also join it. Mars is the strong maraca of birth Chart. Mars and Mercury are maraca of progress chart. Both of them join Moon. It was a period of glory but the maraca effects are also present.

He died in sleep in May 1952 in the sub period of Bhadrika.

Example: Lal Bahadur Shastri

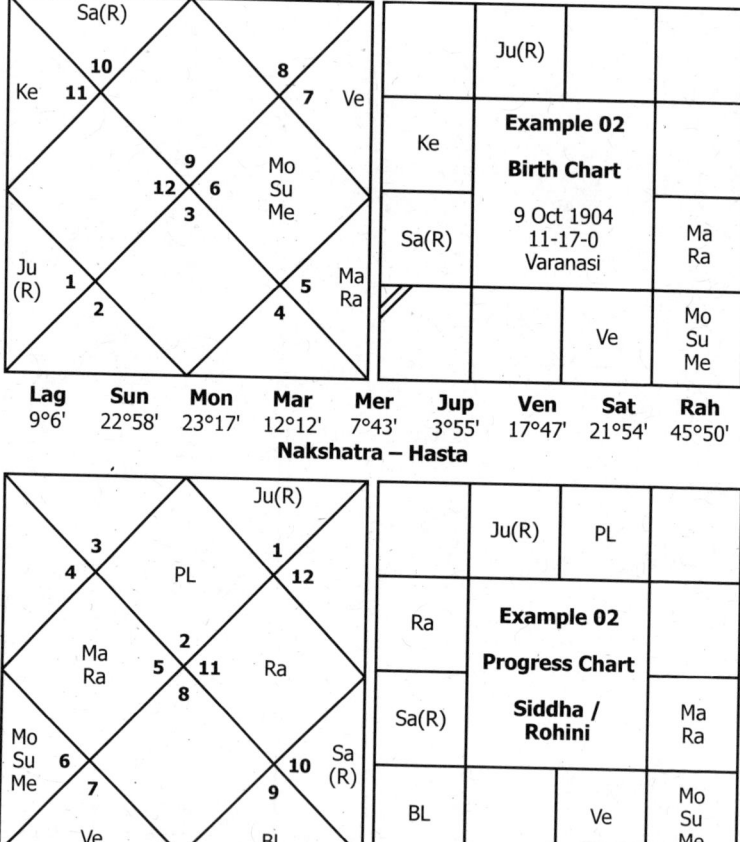

Lag	Sun	Mon	Mar	Mer	Jup	Ven	Sat	Rah
9°6'	22°58'	23°17'	12°12'	7°43'	3°55'	17°47'	21°54'	45°50'

Nakshatra – Hasta

Moon is in the tenth house of Birth chart. It is joined by Sun and Mercury which are tenth and ninth lords. Moon is in Yoga. Remember Moon is eighth lord. The dasha of Moon nakshatra will give Yoga effects beside effect of eighth house.

Moon is in fifth house of progress chart and in again with Kendra trikona lords. Rahu / Ketu are in four ten axis.

He became Prime Minister after death of Jawaharlal Lal Nehru. He took office in 9 June 1964 in sub Of Sankata.

The sinister role of Moon was to unfold in dasha of maraca Mars. He died in mysterious circumstances on 10 Jan. 1966 in the sub of Mars.

Example: Indira Gandhi

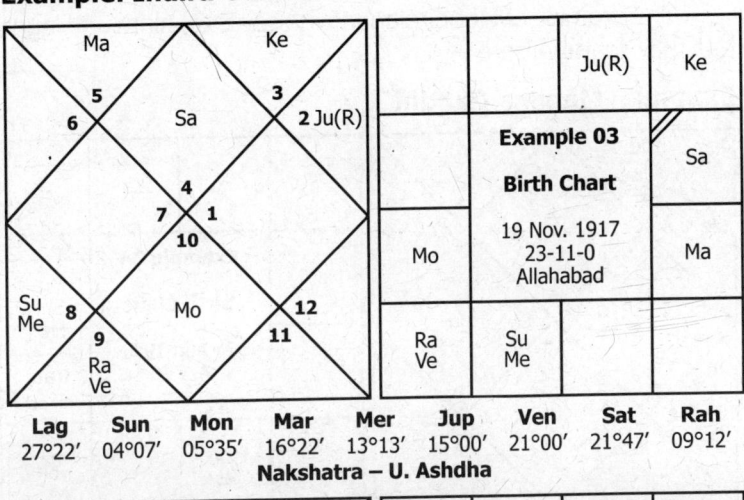

Lag	Sun	Mon	Mar	Mer	Jup	Ven	Sat	Rah
27°22′	04°07′	05°35′	16°22′	13°13′	15°00′	21°00′	21°47′	09°12′

Nakshatra – U. Ashdha

Many personal events took place in this Siddha dasha. In the birth chart Moon is the lagna lord and placed in seventh. Being lagna lord it announces the personnel matters. It is aspected by Saturn, lord of seventh and eighth house.

In the progress chart, seventh house is aspected by seventh lord Mars and eighth lord Jupiter. Venus is lagna lord. She married Feroze Gandhi on 26 March 1942 in the sub Of Siddha.

Moon is in the ninth house and aspected by Jupiter. Rajiv was born on 14 Dec. 1946 in the sub of Bhadrika. Mercury is fifth lord.

The promise of Moon relation with seventh, ninth and lagna has fully materialized.

Example: Menaka Gandhi

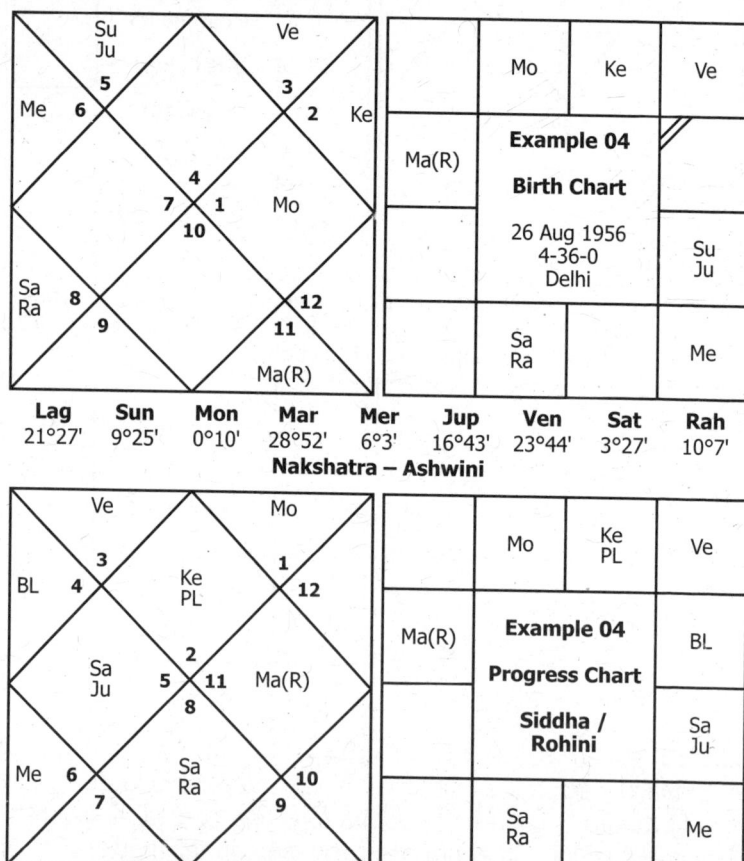

Lag	Sun	Mon	Mar	Mer	Jup	Ven	Sat	Rah
21°27'	9°25'	0°10'	28°52'	6°3'	16°43'	23°44'	3°27'	10°7'

Nakshatra – Ashwini

In the birth chart Moon is the lagna lord. The personal matters are important. It is aspected by Jupiter.

Moon moves to twelfth house of progress chart.

Seventh lord of birth chart aspects lagna. The seventh lord of progress chart also aspects lagna. Mars is influencing Sun and Jupiter and Mercury.

She was married to Sanjay Gandhi on 23 Dec. 1974 in the sub of Pingla. The aspect of eighth lord Jupiter on the seventh lord Mars is not welcomed.

Example: Death of husband

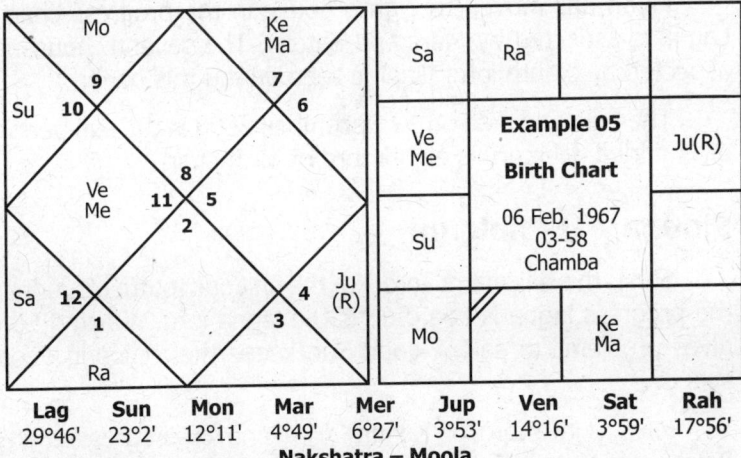

Lag	Sun	Mon	Mar	Mer	Jup	Ven	Sat	Rah
29°46'	23°2'	12°11'	4°49'	6°27'	3°53'	14°16'	3°59'	17°56'

Nakshatra – Moola

In the birth chart Moon is placed in the second house which is eighth for husband. Moon is aspected by Saturn. Moon is lord of ninth house. The Siddha of Rohini gives results of ninth, second and that of Saturn.

Sa	Ra	PL	
Ve Me	**Example 05**		Ju(R)
Su	Progress Chart Siddha / Rohini		
Mo	BL	Ke Ma	

Moon has moved to eighth house in the progress chart. Lagna is aspected by Mars and Saturn. The seventh house is aspected by eighth lord. Grief is seen during this period.

The husband died on 19 December, 2008 in the sub period of Bhadrika. Mercury is eighth lord of birth chart.

Siddha / U.Phalguni

Sun is the Nakshatra Lord. For the first one fourth of Siddha, the progress lagna is Leo. Sun is the lagna lord. Afflicted Sun gives problems to self. A good Sun keeps the things in good shape.

Mars is the lord of Kendra / Trikona of progress chart. Relation of Mars with Venus, tenth lord, can give good position in this progress lagna.

The progress lagna moves to Virgo after one year nine months of Siddha. The change comes in Sankata sub period. The events can take big change towards good or bad. Sun is now twelfth lord.

Example: Indira Gandhi

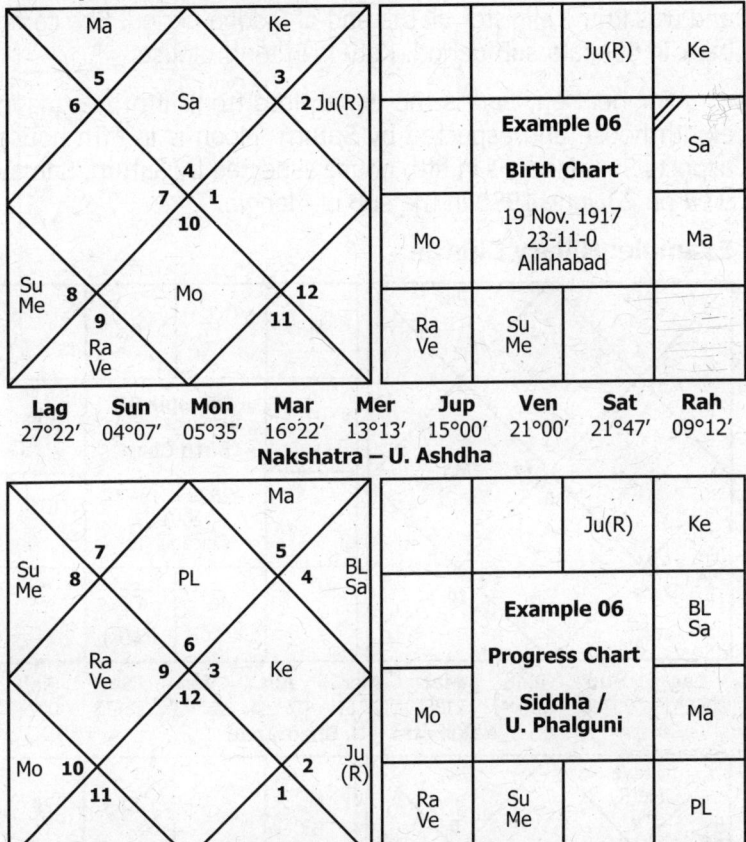

Lag	Sun	Mon	Mar	Mer	Jup	Ven	Sat	Rah
27°22'	04°07'	05°35'	16°22'	13°13'	15°00'	21°00'	21°47'	09°12'

Nakshatra – U. Ashdha

Sun is the lord of second house and placed in fifth house with Mercury in the birth chart. Jupiter is aspecting this Sun.

For Leo Progress Lagna, Sun is in fourth house and aspects tenth house. The tenth house is not making any relation with tenth house or tenth lord. It is afflicted by Rahu. Sun is in twelfth from Venus. She was rather humiliated and was out of power.

The progress lagna changes to Virgo on 12th April 1979. The things looked up. Now Sun is with tenth lord Mercury. Ninth lord is aspecting tenth lord and tenth lord is aspecting ninth house. This is RAJ yoga situation.

She fought back and came back to power on 14 Jan. 1980 and was Prime Minister till the end of Siddha period. She came back in Sankata sub period. Ketu is in tenth house.

For her son, Sun is the eighth lord from fifth. Mars is in eighth house and aspected by Saturn. Moon is in fifth house aspects Sun. Moon is in fifth house aspected by Saturn. Sanjay died on 23 June 1980 in the sub of Mangla.

Example: Hillary Clinton

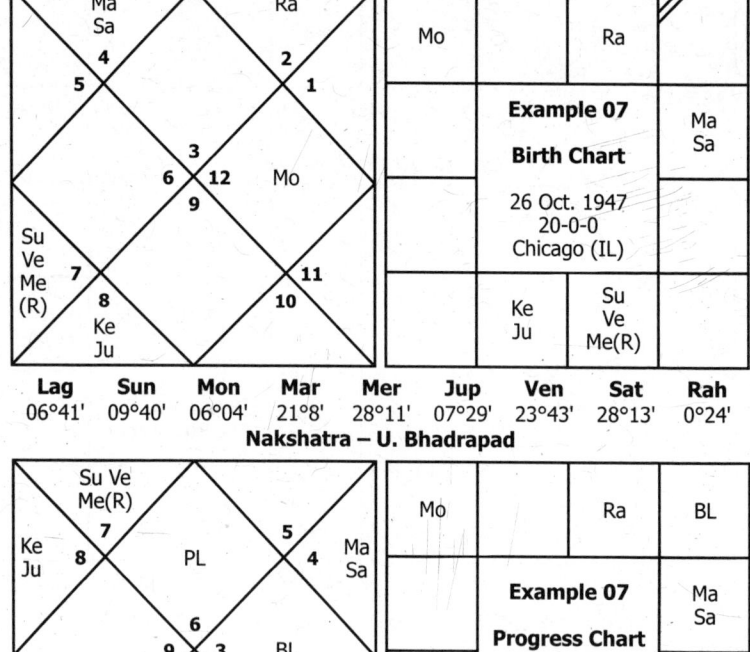

Lag	Sun	Mon	Mar	Mer	Jup	Ven	Sat	Rah
06°41'	09°40'	06°04'	21°8'	28°11'	07°29'	23°43'	28°13'	0°24'

Nakshatra – U. Bhadrapad

In the birth chart Sun is debilitated with cancellation of debilitation. It is participating in Raj yoga with Venus and Mercury.

Aspect of sixth lord Mars is not welcome even though Mars debilitated is Yoga Karaka.

In the progress chart, we examine the husband. The lord of seventh house is with Ketu giving secret affairs. Sun is placed in eighth house from the seventh and with seventh and eighth lord. Worst is the aspect of debilitated Mars on this combination.

Her husband was involved in an affair with a girl and it became public. He was holding the post of President of USA. For husband we see the seventh house of progress chart. Placement of Moon, fifth lord and aspect of lagna lord and tenth lord saved him.

Example: Marriage

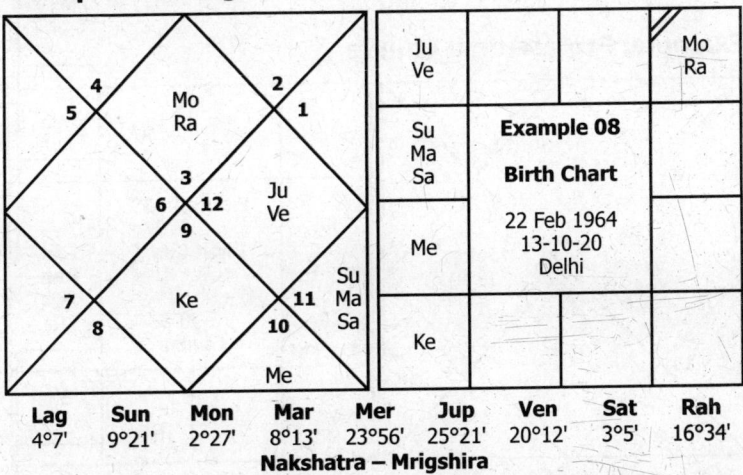

Lag	Sun	Mon	Mar	Mer	Jup	Ven	Sat	Rah
4°7'	9°21'	2°27'	8°13'	23°56'	25°21'	20°12'	3°5'	16°34'

Nakshatra – Mrigshira

Sun is the third lord of birth chart. It is placed in ninth house with ninth lord.

With progress lagna as Leo, Sun moves to seventh house as lagna lord. It is conjoined with Saturn, the seventh lord. Mars is now the fourth and ninth lord.

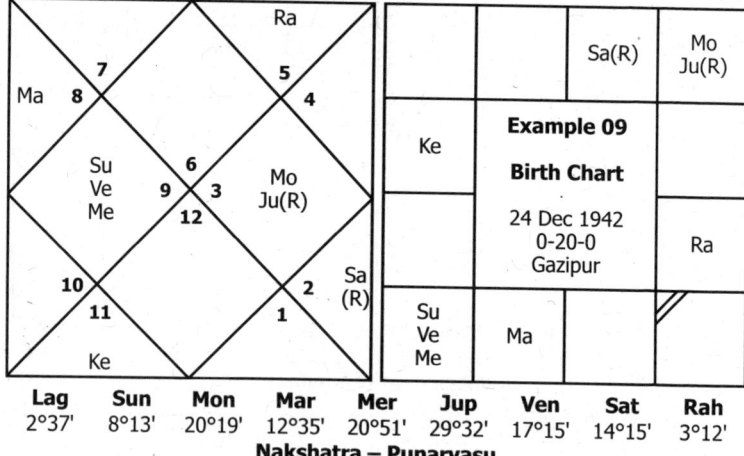

She got married in the sub period of Sankata before the progress lagna changes to Virgo.

Example: Professional Course

Ra

		Sa(R)	Mo Ju(R)
Ke	**Example 09**		
	Birth Chart		
	24 Dec 1942 0-20-0 Gazipur		Ra
Su Ve Me	Ma		

Lag	Sun	Mon	Mar	Mer	Jup	Ven	Sat	Rah
2°37'	8°13'	20°19'	12°35'	20°51'	29°32'	17°15'	14°15'	3°12'

Nakshatra – Punarvasu

Sun is twelfth lord of birth chart. It is placed in fourth house. Lord of twelfth in fourth can give shift from home. It is with ninth and tenth lord. Sun is thus participating in Yoga.

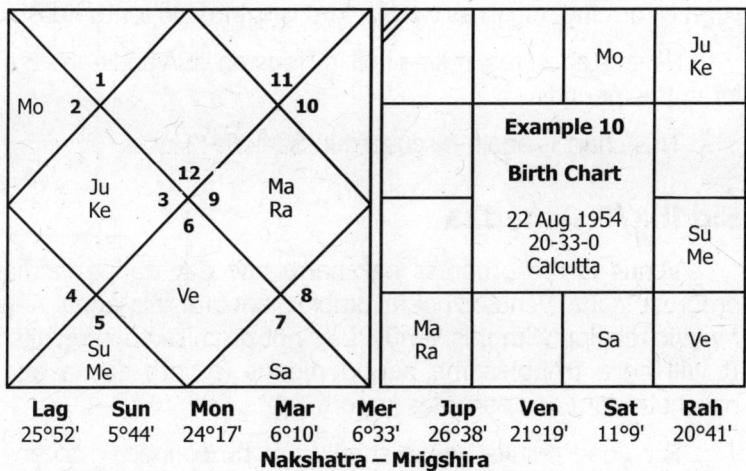

		Sa(R)	Mo Ju(R)
Ke	Example 09 Progress Chart		PL Ra
	Siddha / U. Phalguni		
Su Ve Me	Ma		BL

In the progress chart, Sun is in fifth with third and tenth lord. Fifth house is of higher education. He got admission in engineering college and moved to hostel in Siddha sub period.

Example- Wealth

		Mo	Ju Ke
	Example 10 Birth Chart		
	22 Aug 1954 20-33-0 Calcutta		Su Me
Ma Ra	Sa		Ve

Lag	Sun	Mon	Mar	Mer	Jup	Ven	Sat	Rah
25°52'	5°44'	24°17'	6°10'	6°33'	26°38'	21°19'	11°9'	20°41'

Nakshatra – Mrigshira

This chart was discussed in the research class of Bhartiya Vidya Bhavan. We were to assess the event in Jan1983 of this chart.

The progress yogini dasha was used and the reading was correct.

Ve
6
Sa 7
Su
Me
PL
4
3
Ju
Ke
5
8 2 Mo
11
Ma
Ra 9
10
1
12
BL

BL		Mo	Ju Ke
	Example 10		
	Progress Chart		Su Me PL
	Siddha / U. Phalguni		
Ma Ra		Sa	Ve

In the birth chart Sun is the sixth lord and is in own sign with Kendra lord Mercury.

In the progress chart the picture is clear. Now Sun is lagna lord in Lagna and with eleventh and second lord. Great dhana yoga is forming. Moon as twelfth lord is exalted in tenth house.

He started a steel rolling mill in Houston USA and earned a lot in this period.

This chart is again discussed in Sankata/ Hasta.

Siddha/P Ashadha

Venus is the progress nakshatra and Sagittarius in the progress lagna. Venus is not favorable planet for this lagna. Any malefic relation with this Venus does not promise good results. It will be a troublesome period. Venus is both dasha and nakshatra lord and assumes importance.

For good results Venus should not be connected to any planet.

This dasha period needs careful examination as troubles are expected.

Example- Rajiv Gandhi

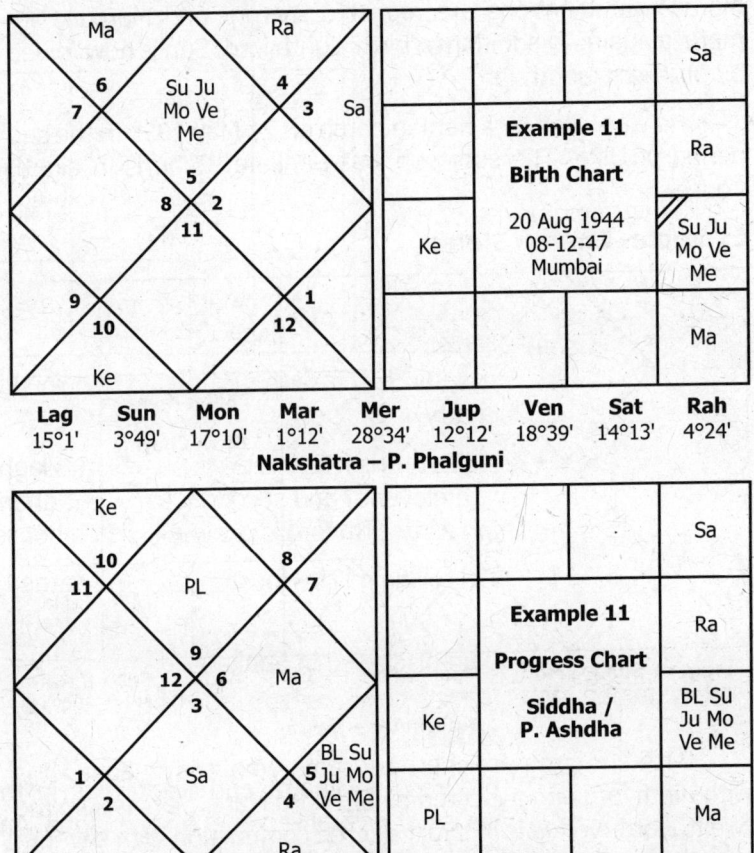

Lag	Sun	Mon	Mar	Mer	Jup	Ven	Sat	Rah
15°1'	3°49'	17°10'	1°12'	28°34'	12°12'	18°39'	14°13'	4°24'

Nakshatra – P. Phalguni

The birth lagna is Leo. Venus is not friendly to the lagna lord. It is with second and eighth lord and aspected by seventh lord Saturn. These planets have other lordship also and have given their due results.

The condition is not improved in progress chart. All the maraca combinations are repeated. Saturn and Mercury are maraca again. In addition to birth eighth lord, Sun is now joined by progress eighth lord.

He was killed by a human bomb on 21 May 1991 in the sub period of Ulka. The sub- sub was Sankata. Rahu is in eighth house.

Example- Charan Singh

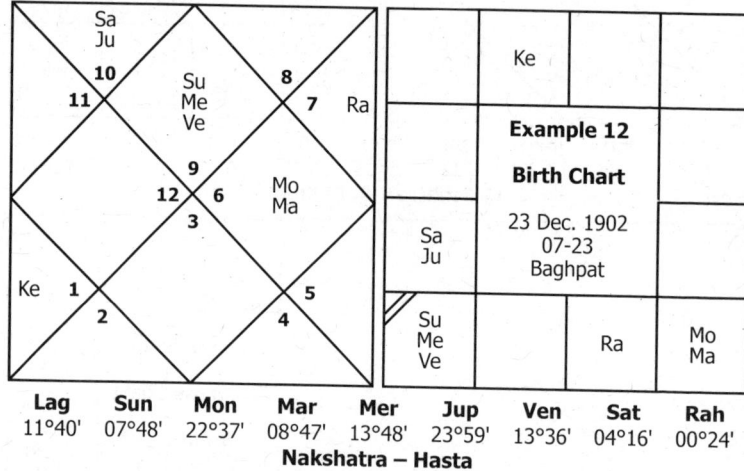

Lag	Sun	Mon	Mar	Mer	Jup	Ven	Sat	Rah
11°40'	07°48'	22°37'	08°47'	13°48'	23°59'	13°36'	04°16'	00°24'

Nakshatra – Hasta

Birth and progress chart are same. Venus is in lagna. It is with ninth lord and aspected by fifth lord Mars. Mars is also the twelfth lord. Venus is in exact degree conjunction with seventh lord Mercury. He got married in Siddha sub period.

Mars is with eighth lord Moon and not favorable.

A daughter was born in Pingla sub period but could not survive

Example - Rajendra Prasad

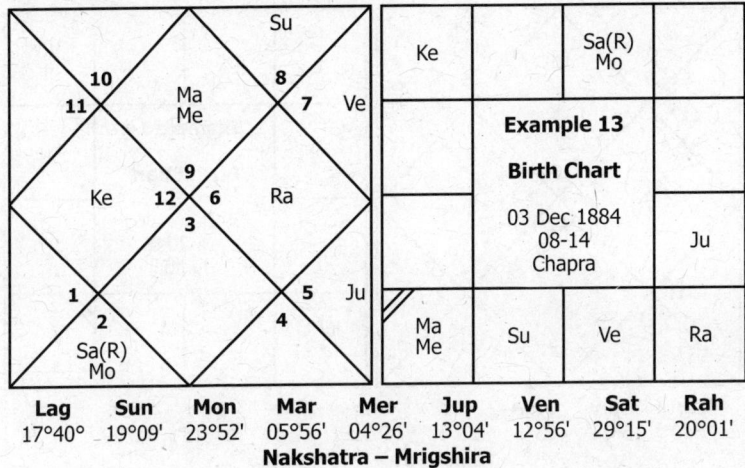

Lag	Sun	Mon	Mar	Mer	Jup	Ven	Sat	Rah
17°40°	19°09'	23°52'	05°56'	04°26'	13°04'	12°56'	29°15'	20°01'

Nakshatra – Mrigshira

The birth lagna and the progress lagna are same.

Venus is eleventh lord and placed in eleventh house. Venus is not having any aspect or association.

The lord of tenth house is in lagna and aspected by lagna lord from ninth house. A very good tenth house and tenth lord.

He was elected first president of republic of India in the Sankata sub period. Rahu is in tenth house and Venus in eleventh.

Example: Closure of business

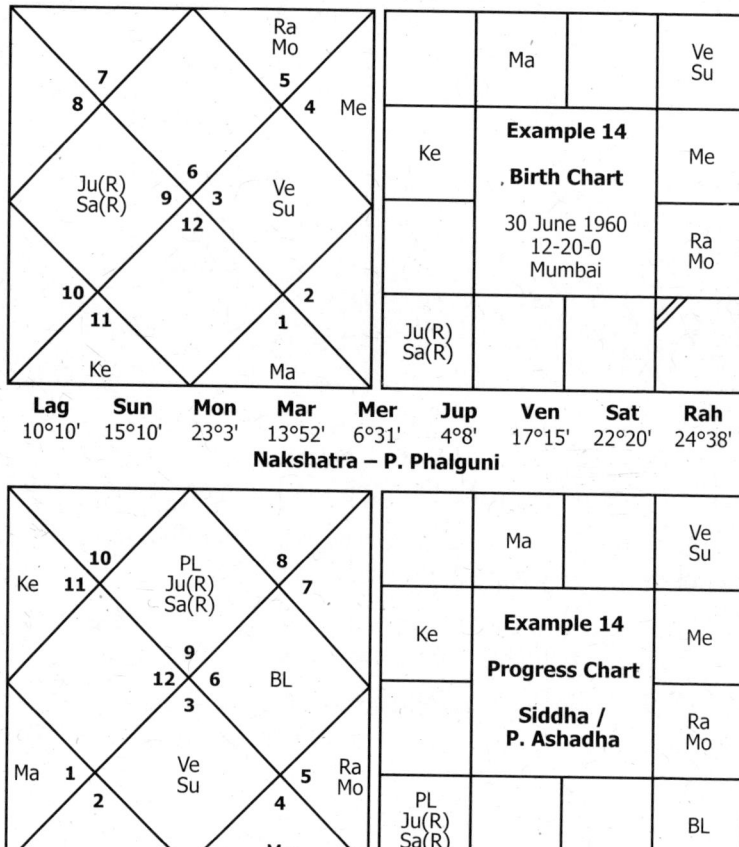

Lag	Sun	Mon	Mar	Mer	Jup	Ven	Sat	Rah
10°10'	15°10'	23°3'	13°52'	6°31'	4°8'	17°15'	22°20'	24°38'

Nakshatra – P. Phalguni

Venus is the ninth lord of birth chart. It is with twelfth lord Sun and is aspected by retrograde lords of fourth and fifth house. This gives yoga. The other lordship of Jupiter and Saturn is not good and they are retrograde.

Now see the progress chart. Venus is with ninth lord Sun and is in seventh house. Jupiter and Saturn are not so powerful now.

The lord of tenth house has moved to eighth house with an aspect of twelfth lord Mars. The ninth house is spoiled with the placement of Rahu and eighth lord.

The luck has run out. He had to close down his business in July 2002 in the sub period of Bhramari

Example: Up and down in Profession

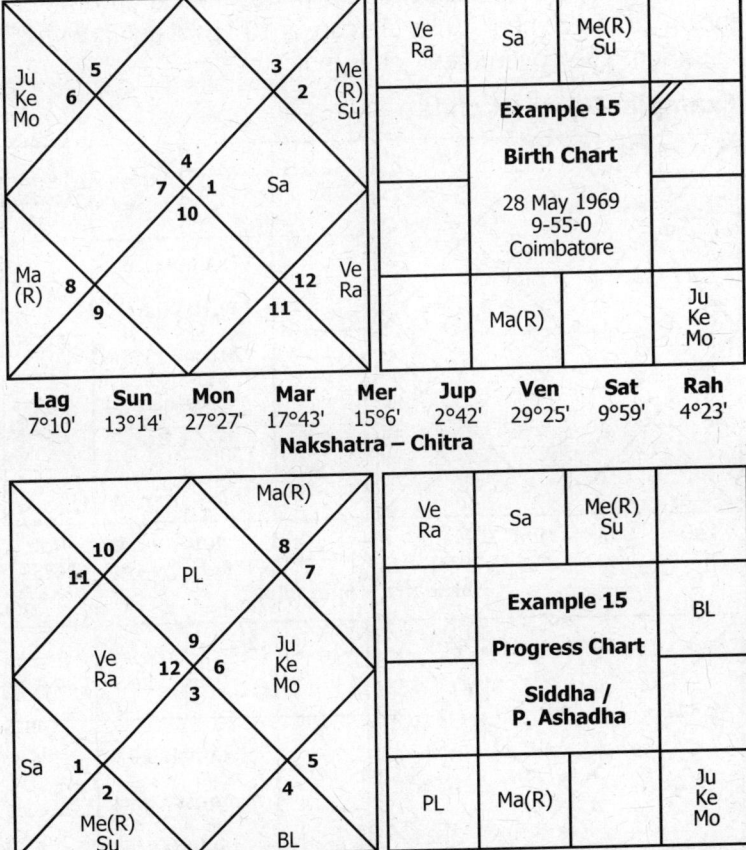

Lag	Sun	Mon	Mar	Mer	Jup	Ven	Sat	Rah
7°10'	13°14'	27°27'	17°43'	15°6'	2°42'	29°25'	9°59'	4°23'

Nakshatra – Chitra

Venus is exalted in birth chart. It is with Rahu and aspected by ninth lord and the lagna lord. Not a bad position.

In the progress chart Venus moves to fourth house along with Rahu. The eighth lord Moon is in tenth house. Moon was lagna lord of birth chart and now it is eighth lord in tenth. It gives problems and dissatisfaction in profession.

He started work in October 1992 in the sub of Sankata. Ketu is in tenth house. By the time Mangla sub period commenced the trouble started and he begin to look for other work.

In the Bhadrika sub period he landed a good government job on 16th December 1994. Mercury is 10th Lord and is with 9th Lord Sun. The government job is indicated.

Example: Death of child

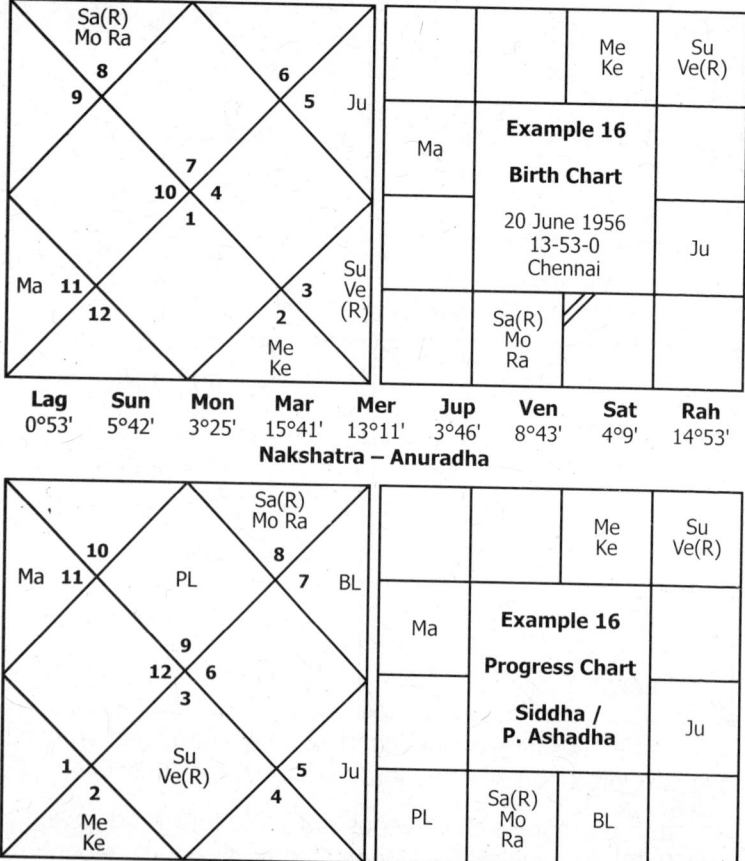

Lag	Sun	Mon	Mar	Mer	Jup	Ven	Sat	Rah
0°53'	5°42'	3°25'	15°41'	13°11'	3°46'	8°43'	4°9'	14°53'

Nakshatra – Anuradha

This case was also a test case for verification of yogini dasha. The case was also put up in the research class of Bharti Vidya Bhavan.

Venus is Lagna Lord of birth chart and is with Sun. It is placed in 9th house. There is an exchange of 9th and 8th Lord. Venus is retrograde.

This chart is examined for events related to her 1 year old child. The event took place in December 1974. In the progress chart, Venus is the Lord of second and seventh house from fifth house. It is a maraca for child. The fifth lord of birth chart is now in twelfth house. It is with eighth Lord and Rahu.

Her one year old child fell down from chair and could not survive. The sub period was Dhanya.

Chapter 10

Sankata

Sankata is the longest dasha period in yogini. Rahu is the mother yogini of Sankata. Ketu is not assigned any dasha period. Rahu and Ketu are always forming an axis. We can thus take Ketu also in this axis.

In our scheme of progressive Yogini, it is the nakshatra lord which is given importance along with the progress lagna. Therefore, Rahu / Ketu axis is not very important consideration.

Sankata is generated by three nakshatra. These are Mrigshira, Hasta and U.Ashadha. These three nakshatra lords are Mars, Moon and Sun. Sun and Moon are enemies of Rahu. It may be a reason that this dasha of Sankata is not welcomed in classics. However we have witnessed many important events in every one's life in Sankata period.

Nakshatra	Nakshatra Lord	Sign of Progress Lagna	Remarks
Mrigshira	Mars	Taurus/ Gemini	For first four years, progress lagna is Taurus. For last four years it is Gemini.
Hasta	Moon	Virgo	Virgo is progress lagna

U.Ashadha	Sun	Sagittarius / Capricorn	For first two years, progress lagna is Sagittarius. For last six years it is Capricorn.

Sankata / Mrigshira

For Taurus lagna, Mars is the lord of seventh and twelfth. It can give marriage, death, long travels, expenditure illness etc. when Mars is related to these houses in the birth chart. For Taurus lagna, Saturn is a good planet as it is lord of ninth and tenth house. Venus is the lagna lord and sixth lord.

When Gemini is the progress lagna, Mars is the sixth and eleventh lord. It is capable of giving illness and gain also. When afflicted it gives expenditure etc.

This dasha period gives sudden events.

Example: Chandra Shekhar

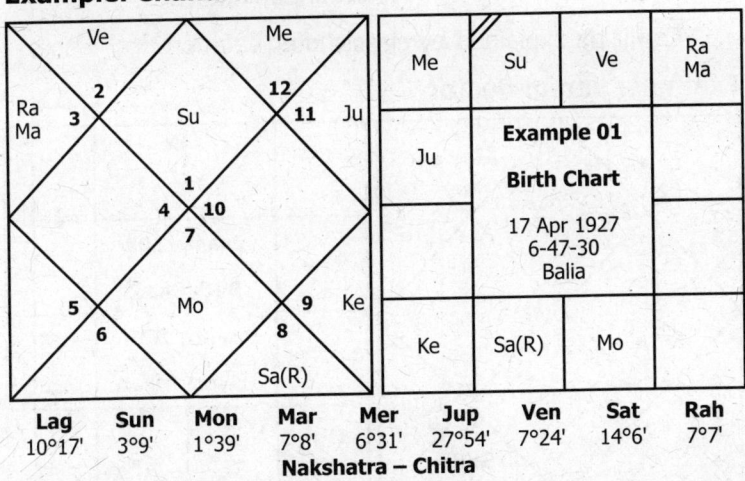

Lag	Sun	Mon	Mar	Mer	Jup	Ven	Sat	Rah
10°17'	3°9'	1°39'	7°8'	6°31'	27°54'	7°24'	14°6'	7°7'

Nakshatra – Chitra

Mars is the lagna lord and eighth lord of birth chart. Mars is aspected by ninth lord Jupiter. Mars influences tenth house of birth chart. It is with Rahu.

Me	BL Su	PL Ve	Ra Ma
Ju	**Example 01** **Progress Chart** **Sankata / Mrigshira**		
Ke	Sa(R)	Mo	

Now the progress chart with Taurus lagna. Lagna lord and tenth lords are in mutual aspect in one seven axis. Jupiter is in tenth house as eighth and eleventh lord. Eighth lord is good in tenth for politicians.

Association of Rahu with nakshatra lord Mars gives the promise of the chart.

He became Prime Minister of India on 27 November 1990 to 21 June 1991 in the sub period of Sankata itself.

Can it be explained by classic interpretation?

Example: Senior doctor

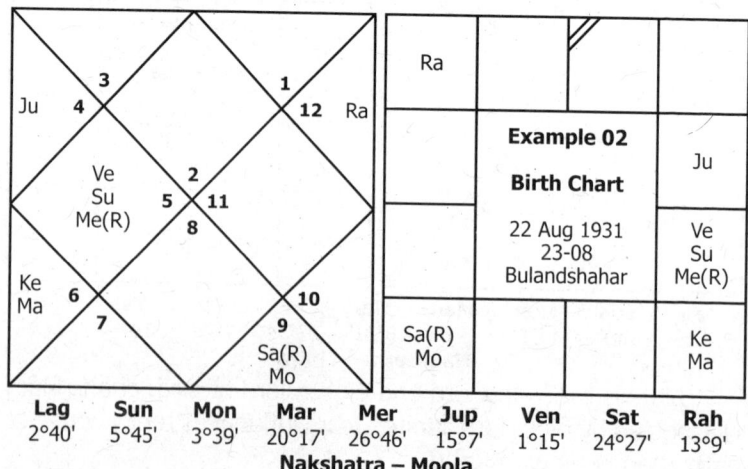

Lag	Sun	Mon	Mar	Mer	Jup	Ven	Sat	Rah
2°40'	5°45'	3°39'	20°17'	26°46'	15°7'	1°15'	24°27'	13°9'

Nakshatra – Moola

	3 BL PL	**1**	
Ju **4**		**12** Ra	
	Ve Su Me(R) **5** **2** **11** **8**		
Ke Ma **6** **7**		**10** **9** Sa(R) Mo	

Ra		BL PL	
	Example 02 **Progress Chart** **Sankata / Mrigshira**		Ju
			Ve Su Me(R)
Sa(R) Mo			Ke Ma

The birth chart and the progress chart are same.

Mars is in fifth house which is eighth from tenth. It is with Ketu and aspected by retrograde Saturn from eighth house. Saturn is tenth lord and its retrogration indicate reversal.

In 1980 he was forced to resign his job as a very senior doctor in a well known Government hospital. He is honored by Padam Vibhushan for his good work.

He resigned in the sub period of Mangla. Moon is in eighth house with tenth lord and aspected by nakshatra lord Mars.

Example: Menaka Gandhi

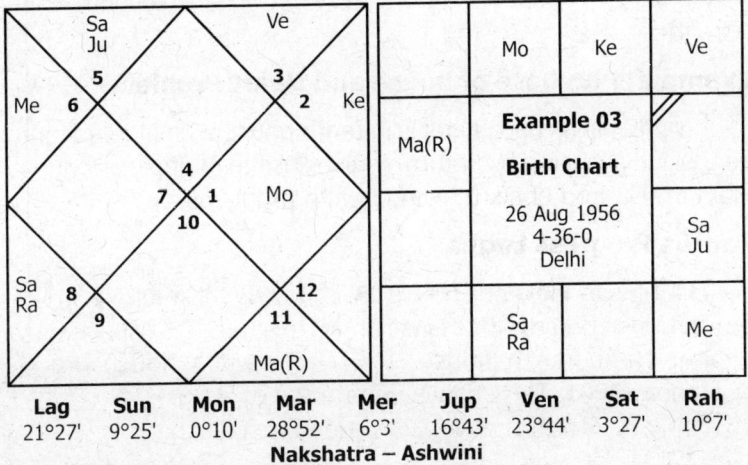

Lag	Sun	Mon	Mar	Mer	Jup	Ven	Sat	Rah
21°27'	9°25'	0°10'	28°52'	6°3'	16°43'	23°44'	3°27'	10°7'

Nakshatra – Ashwini

In the birth chart, Mars is the lord of fifth and tenth. It is placed in eighth house which is the maraca house for husband.

The progress lagna is Taurus and Mars moves to tenth house. It is aspecting fifth house and fifth lord Mercury. Her son Varun was born on 13 March, 1980 in the sub of Sankata.

From tenth house it is aspecting lagna which is maraca house for husband. The lagna is also aspected by Saturn. Saturn is birth seventh and eighth lord. The aspect of Jupiter is no good as it is eighth lord. Eighth house is Mangalya house.

Sanjay died in an air crash on 23 June 1980 in the sub period of Moon. Moon is lagna lord of birth chart (seventh from seventh).

Example: Purchase of house and Heart Problem

In the birth chart, Mars is in tenth house with Mercury and Venus and aspected by Saturn. It gives rise to multiple activities. Mars is also lord of sixth giving health problems.

Taurus Progress Lagna

Mars is in eleventh house. It is now twelfth lord. Lord of fourth house is in twelfth house and is exalted. It is aspected by Jupiter from fourth house. He purchased a house on 21 November, 2001. The Dhanya Sub started on 4 November, 2001. Fourth lord is twelfth gave a change of residence.

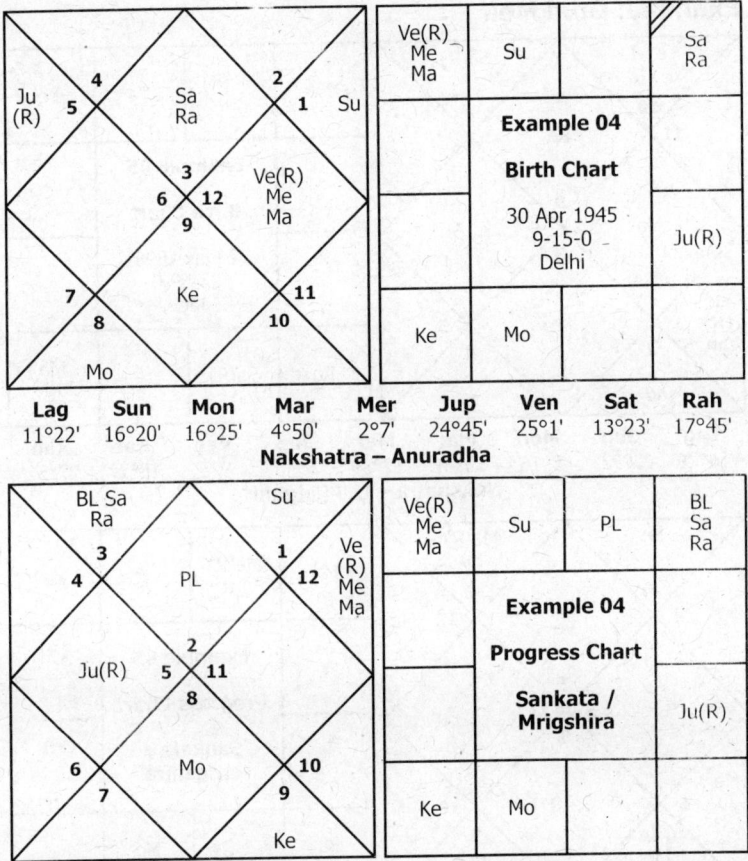

Ve(R) Me Ma	Su		Sa Ra
	Example 04		
	Birth Chart		
	30 Apr 1945 9-15-0 Delhi		Ju(R)
Ke	Mo		

Lag 11°22'	**Sun** 16°20'	**Mon** 16°25'	**Mar** 4°50'	**Mer** 2°7'	**Jup** 24°45'	**Ven** 25°1'	**Sat** 13°23'	**Rah** 17°45'

Nakshatra – Anuradha

Ve(R) Me Ma	Su	PL	BL Sa Ra
	Example 04		
	Progress Chart		
	Sankata / Mrigshira		Ju(R)
Ke	Mo		

Mars is aspecting fifth house along with fifth lord. The fifth lord of birth chart is also with it. In July 2003 he was asked to join the teaching facility of institute of astrology.

Gemini Progress lagna

The progress chart is same as birth chart. Now Mars is sixth lord. It is with fifth and twelfth lord Venus. Both Venus and Mars are aspected by eighth lord Saturn. The Siddha period started on 4 November, 2005. On 27 November, 2005 he suffered a stroke and was rushed to hospital. He was advised immediate surgery. On the astrological considered he has not undergone surgery till date.

Example: Gold Meir

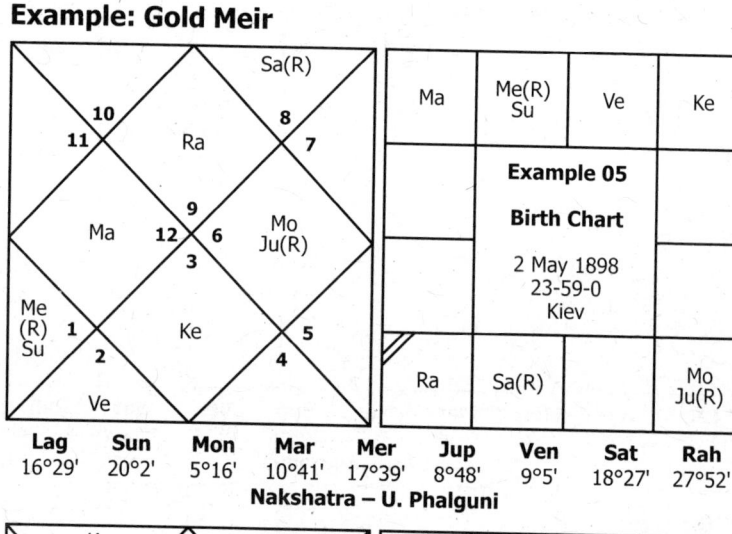

Ma	Me(R) Su	Ve	Ke
	Example 05		
	Birth Chart		
	2 May 1898 23-59-0 Kiev		
Ra	Sa(R)		Mo Ju(R)

Lag	Sun	Mon	Mar	Mer	Jup	Ven	Sat	Rah
16°29'	20°2'	5°16'	10°41'	17°39'	8°48'	9°5'	18°27'	27°52'

Nakshatra – U. Phalguni

Ma	Me(R) Su	PL Ve	Ke
	Example 05		
	Progress Chart		
	Sankata / Mrigshira		
BL Ra	Sa(R)	Mo Ju(R)	Mo Ju(R)

Mars is fifth and twelfth lord of birth chart. It is aspected by lagna and fourth lord Jupiter. This way Mars is yoga karaka. It is aspected by eighth lord Moon. This is a relation of separation.

Taurus lagna

Mars is in eleventh house and aspected by eighth and eleventh lord Jupiter. The lord of tenth house of birth has moved to twelfth house and is in six eight with progress tenth lord. Moon was eighth lord of birth chart and now it is in fifth house.

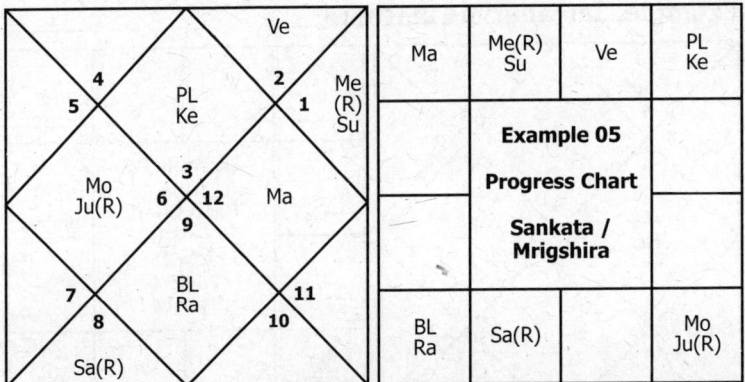

Ma	Me(R) Su	Ve	PL Ke
	Example 05		
	Progress Chart		
	Sankata / Mrigshira		
BL Ra	Sa(R)		Mo Ju(R)

She resigned from the post of Prime Minister of Israel on 3 June, 1974 in the sub period of Mangla.

Gemini Lagna

Now Mars is in tenth house. It is aspected by progress lagna maracas Moon and Jupiter. Venus is in twelfth house and aspected by eighth lord Saturn. She died of lymphoma on 8 Dec. 1978 in the sub of Ulka.

Sankata / Hasta

Moon is the nakshatra lord and Virgo is the progress lagna. The relation of Moon in birth chart and its placement in progress chart is important.

The paksha bala of Moon in the birth chart is important. A waxing Moon tends to give favorable results. A waning Moon will tend to give adverse result.

Mercury and Jupiter are the lords of Kendra's or the **sukh sthan** Their relation with Moon in a good house and having benefic association will provide happiness. Adverse relation can give disappointment in these affairs.

When Moon is maraca or lagna lord in birth chart and is related to malefic, it can give physical or mental problems. Even death can occur.

Example: Jawaharlal Lal Nehru

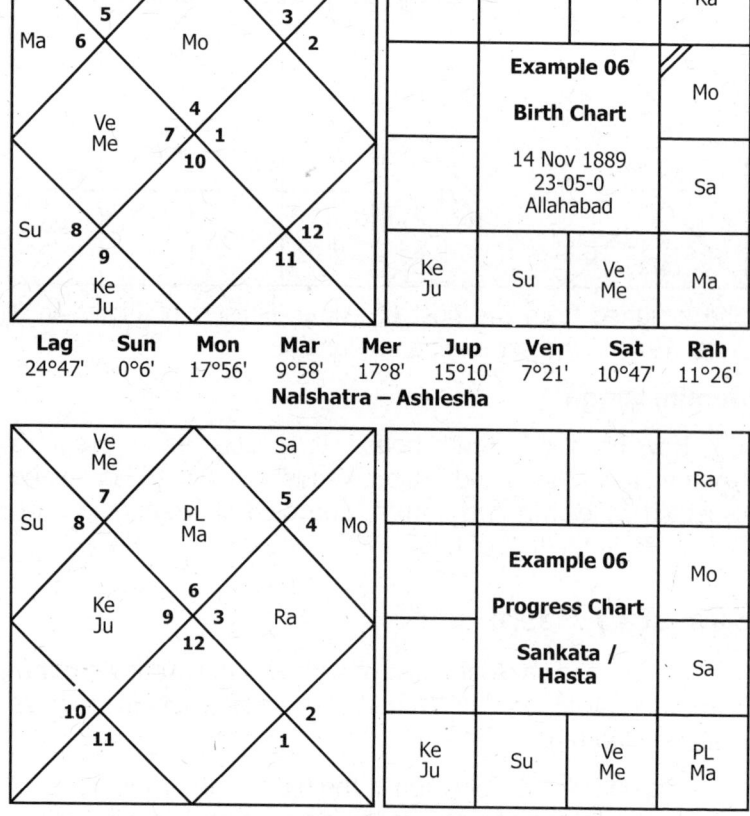

Lag	Sun	Mon	Mar	Mer	Jup	Ven	Sat	Rah
24°47'	0°6'	17°56'	9°58'	17°8'	15°10'	7°21'	10°47'	11°26'

Naishatra – Ashlesha

Moon is the lagna lord of birth chart and is in lagna. It is not aspected by any planet.

In the progress chart Moon is in eleventh house. The birth seventh lord has moved to twelfth house and aspects progress lagna lord.

Jupiter is progress seventh lord an aspects birth seventh lord.

He married on 7 Feb., 1916 in the sub of Bhadrika.

Saturn is also aspecting Venus. Venus is the ninth lord of progress chart. For even Lagna, ninth is the house of child.

Daughter Indira Gandhi was born on 19 Nov., 1917 in the sub period of Siddha.

Example: Indira Gandhi

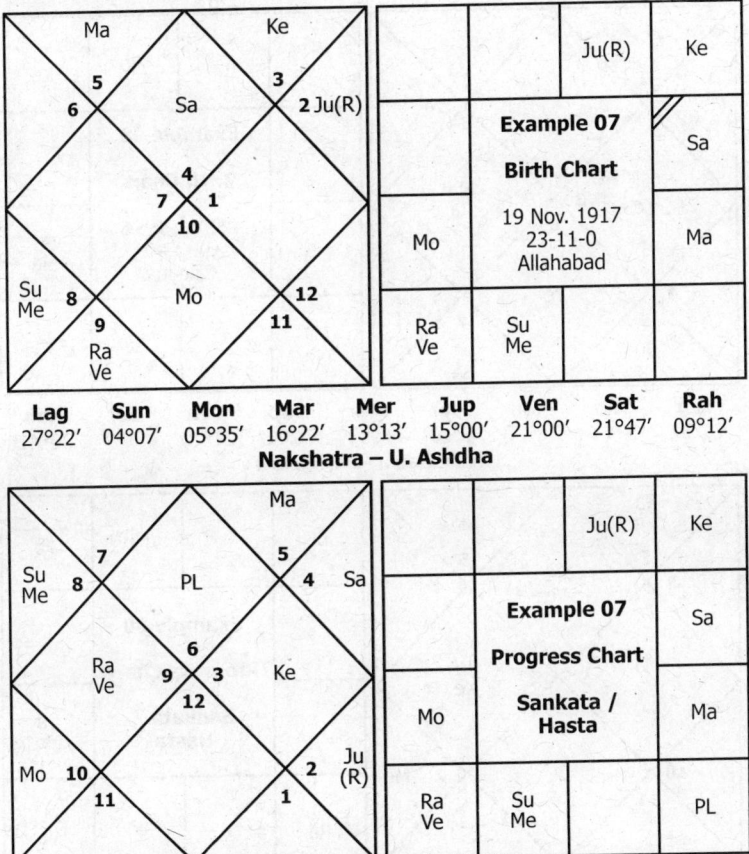

Lag	Sun	Mon	Mar	Mer	Jup	Ven	Sat	Rah
27°22'	04°07'	05°35'	16°22'	13°13'	15°00'	21°00'	21°47'	09°12'

Nakshatra – U. Ashdha

Moon is the lagna lord of birth chart and aspects lagna. It is fully connected with lagna. It is aspected by Saturn, who is maraca and lord of eighth house.

With the progress lagna moving to Virgo and Moon as nakshatra lord and Jupiter becomes maraca along with Venus.

Now Moon is influenced by birth maraca and progress maraca. Rahu is with Venus.

She was shot by her security guard on 31 Oct 1984 and was killed.

Example: Suicide by wife

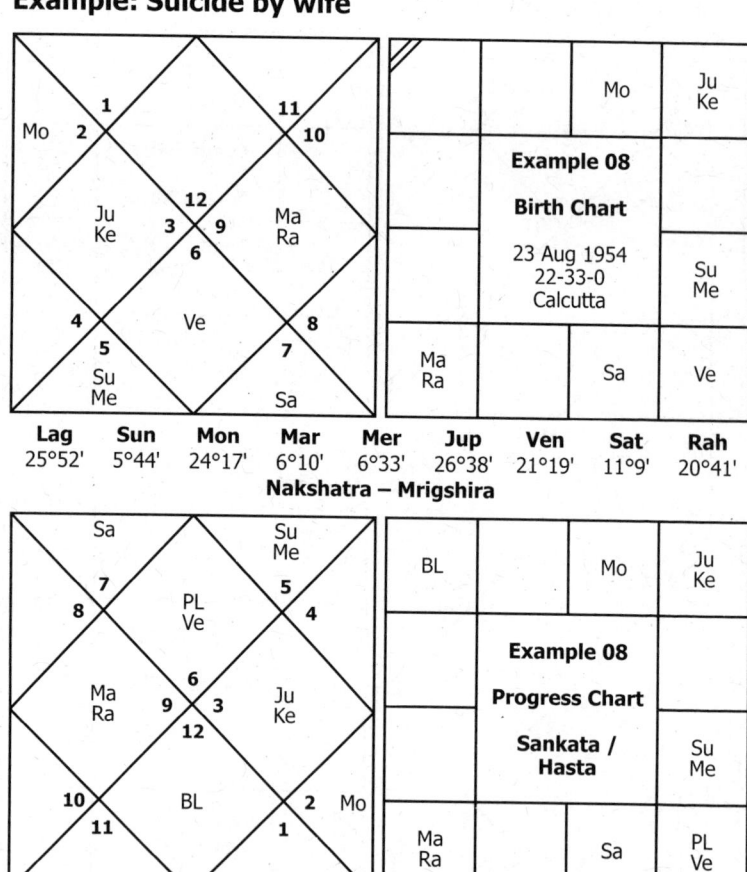

Lag	Sun	Mon	Mar	Mer	Jup	Ven	Sat	Rah
25°52'	5°44'	24°17'	6°10'	6°33'	26°38'	21°19'	11°9'	20°41'

Nakshatra – Mrigshira

This chart has been discussed in Siddha / U.Phalguni. In the dasha of Siddha in 1983, he was earning very well in USA.

We now discuss his Sankata / Hasta. With this progress chart, the fourth house is badly afflicted. The eighth lord Mars is placed in fourth with Rahu. It aspects seventh house and seventh lord. It is aspected by Saturn.

It gives a clear indication that there is trouble in the domestic front.

His wife committed suicide due to outside influence in her married life. His business was ruined and he faced lots of problems.

Example: Pranab Mukherjee

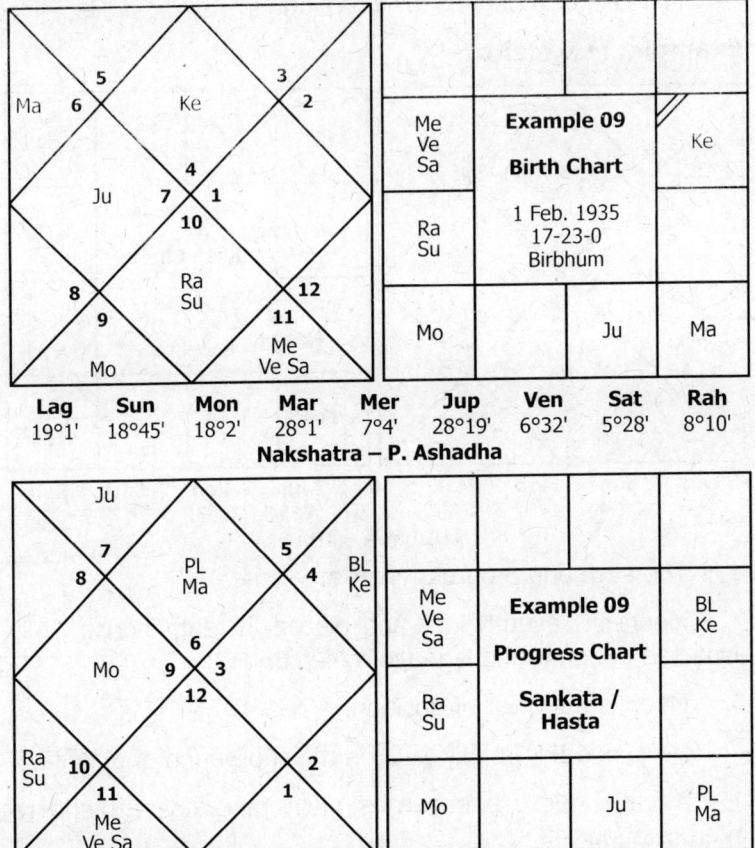

Lag	Sun	Mon	Mar	Mer	Jup	Ven	Sat	Rah
19°1'	18°45'	18°2'	28°1'	7°4'	28°19'	6°32'	5°28'	8°10'

Nakshatra – P. Ashadha

Moon is lagna lord of birth chart. It is aspected by Yoga karaka Mars. Moon can give yoga karaka effect as well events relating to body and self.

In the progress chart, this Moon is eleventh lord and aspects tenth house. The tenth lord, ninth lord and lagna lord are joined together forming a Raj Yoga in sixth house of competition.

He was elected President of India and took oath of office on 25 July, 2013 in the sub period of Mangla.

Mars is not a benefic for Virgo lagna.

Example: M.S.Mehta

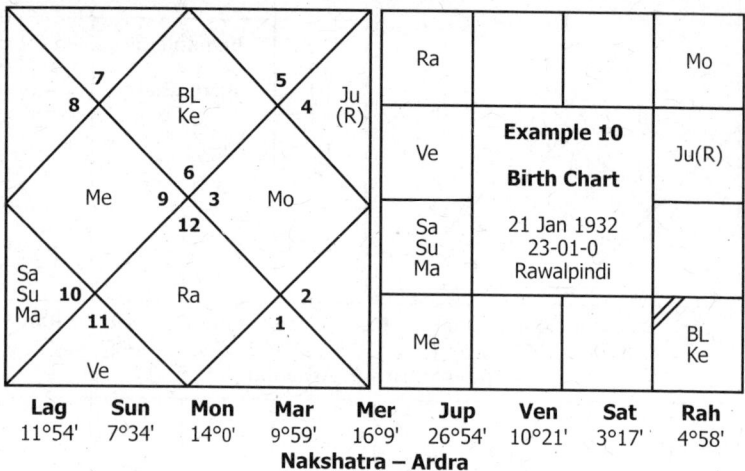

Lag	Sun	Mon	Mar	Mer	Jup	Ven	Sat	Rah
11°54'	7°34'	14°0'	9°59'	16°9'	26°54'	10°21'	3°17'	4°58'

Nakshatra – Ardra

The birth and progress chart are same.

Moon is eleventh lord and placed in tenth house. It is aspected by tenth and lagna lord Mercury.

Moon is the giver of position.

He joined IFS in May 1961 in the sub-period of Mangla.

A clear picture emerges with progress nakshatra interpretation

Example: Queen Elizabeth II

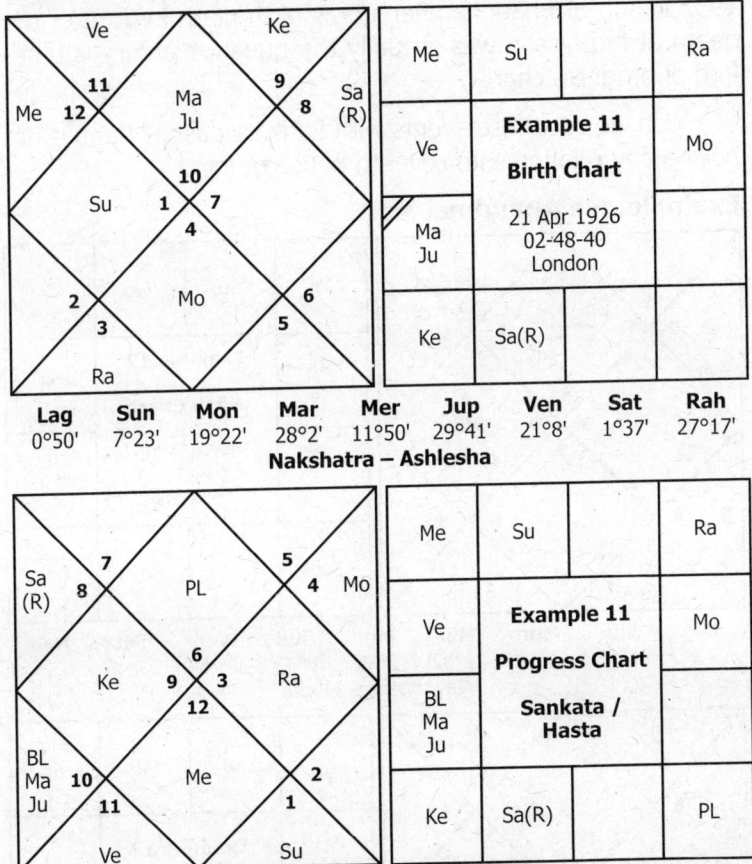

	Lag	Sun	Mon	Mar	Mer	Jup	Ven	Sat	Rah
	0°50'	7°23'	19°22'	28°2'	11°50'	29°41'	21°8'	1°37'	27°17'

Nakshatra – Ashlesha

Moon is the seventh lord of birth chart and is placed in seventh house. It is aspected by Mars and Jupiter. Jupiter is debilitated third lord and giver of yoga.

In the progress chart, Moon is in eleventh house. It is now aspected by progress seventh lord. Rahu acts as Mercury that is placed in seventh house. She married on 20 Nov., 1947. The aspect of Mars on this Moon gave controversies in this marriage.

For father we take ninth house. The maracas are Mercury and Mars. The eighth lord from ninth house is Jupiter. Moon is aspected by both Mars and Jupiter. Her father died on 6 Feb., 1952 in sub of Bhadrika. Mercury is birth ninth lord. After the death of father she was virtually the queen. Mercury is tenth lord of progress chart.

Can we see these events with Sankata dasha? Rahu is not having any relation with seventh house or lord.

Example: Ma Anandmai Ma

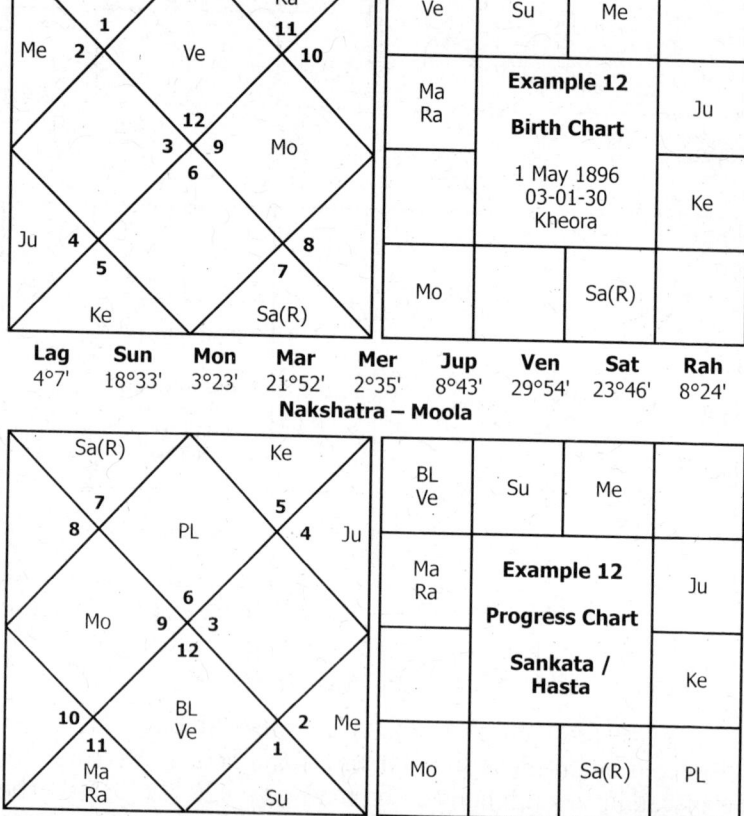

Lag	Sun	Mon	Mar	Mer	Jup	Ven	Sat	Rah
4°7'	18°33'	3°23'	21°52'	2°35'	8°43'	29°54'	23°46'	8°24'

Nakshatra – Moola

Moon is in tenth house of birth chart. Moon has Mercury and Jupiter is sixth and eighth from it. It is aspected by exalted Saturn from eighth house. This Moon gives eternal Samadhi.

In the progress chart Moon is in fourth house. It is aspected by Saturn from second house. Saturn also aspects Jupiter who is seventh lord of progress chart.

She took eternal Samadhi on 28 August 1982 in the sub period of Jupiter.

Sankata / U.Ashadha

Sun is the nakshatra lord. In the progress chart with Sagittarius progress lagna, Sun is the lord of ninth house. When Sun is related to tenth house in birth chart or in progress chart, it can give yoga karaka results of tenth house.

For Sagittarius lagna, Venus is not a good planet. When ill disposed in birth chart, it is not good for its significations.

The position is not good generally for the Capricorn progress lagna. Sun is now the eighth lord. Even now if Sun is exalted or debilitated it can give favorable results. Venus now becomes a yoga karaka and can give very good result if it is favorable in birth chart.

The progress lagna changes to Capricorn with the start of Pingla Sub period.

Example: Joined service

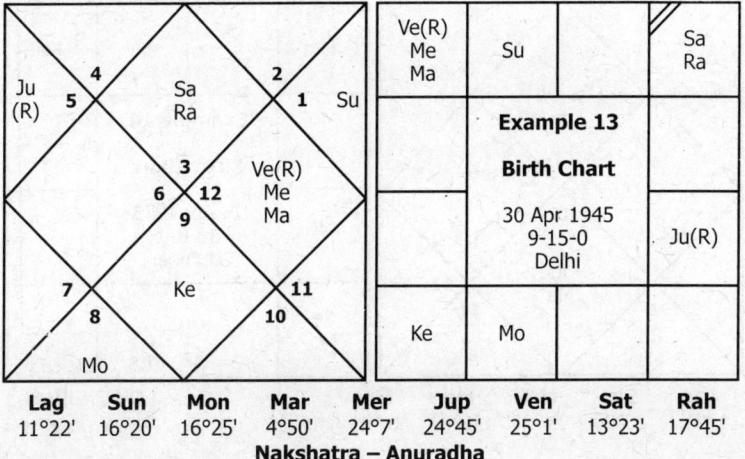

Lag	Sun	Mon	Mar	Mer	Jup	Ven	Sat	Rah
11°22'	16°20'	16°25'	4°50'	24°7'	24°45'	25°1'	13°23'	17°45'

Nakshatra – Anuradha

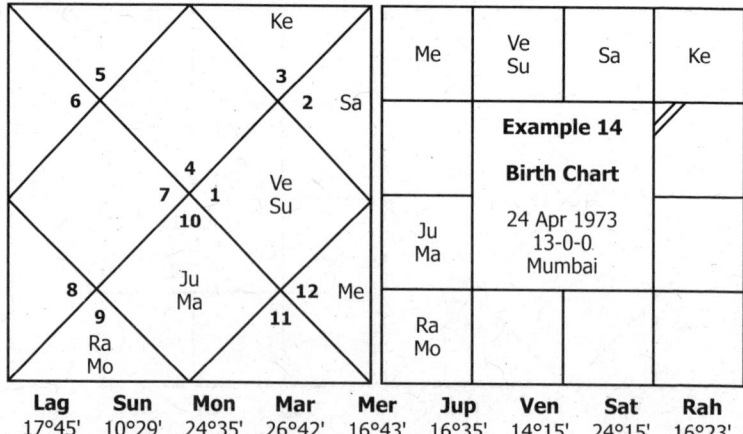

Ve(R) Me Ma	Su		BL Sa Ra
	Example 13		
	Progress Chart		
PL	**Sankata / U. Ashadha**		Ju(R)
Ke	Mo		

He joined class I service in November 1969.

In the birth chart, Sun is exalted in eleventh house. It is aspected by Jupiter who is tenth lord. Sun promises good events regarding profession.

In the progress chart, Sun is now in fourth house an aspects tenth house. The lord of tenth house is exalted in third house. The relation of Sun is again established with tenth house in progress chart.

He joined when the Siddha sub period started.

Example : Sachin Tandulkar

Me	Ve Su	Sa	Ke
	Example 14		
	Birth Chart		
Ju Ma	24 Apr 1973 13-0-0 Mumbai		
Ra Mo			

Lag	Sun	Mon	Mar	Mer	Jup	Ven	Sat	Rah
17°45'	10°29'	24°35'	26°42'	16°43'	16°35'	14°15'	24°15'	16°23'

Me	Su Ve	Sa	Ke
	Example 14 **Progress Chart**		BL
PL Ju Ma	**Sankata /** **U. Ashadha**		
Mo Ra			

In the birth chart Sun is exalted in eighth house. It is placed with Venus. Venus is the ninth and second lord. It can give much wealth.

In the progress chart Sun is in fourth house with tenth lord Venus.

In Sankata Siddha he was introduced to his coach Achrekar. He changed his school and started his coaching. This was a big stepping stone for his professional career.

Example: S.L.Shakdhar

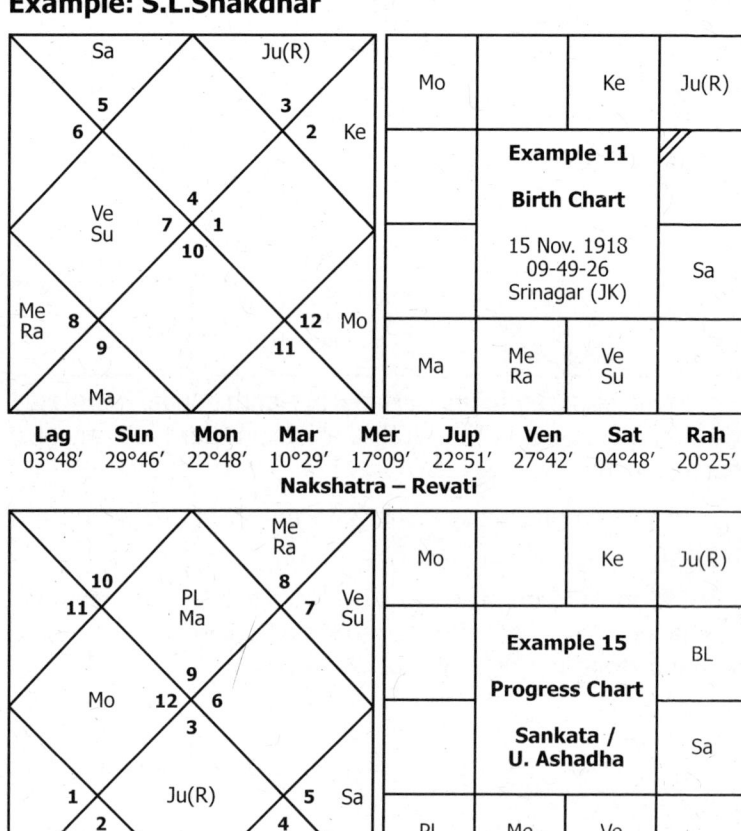

Lag	Sun	Mon	Mar	Mer	Jup	Ven	Sat	Rah
03°48′	29°46′	22°48′	10°29′	17°09′	22°51′	27°42′	04°48′	20°25′

Nakshatra – Revati

In the birth chart, Sun is the maraca lord of second house. It is aspected by the other maraca Saturn from second house. Saturn is the lord of eighth also. Saturn influences Ketu also.

In the progress chart, Saturn is again a maraca along with Mercury. Mercury is in Rahu Ketu axis. Sun is now badly afflicted. It is with Venus and aspected by Saturn.

He died on 18 May, 2002 in the sub of Sankata and sub sub of Ulka.

Example: Benazir Bhutto

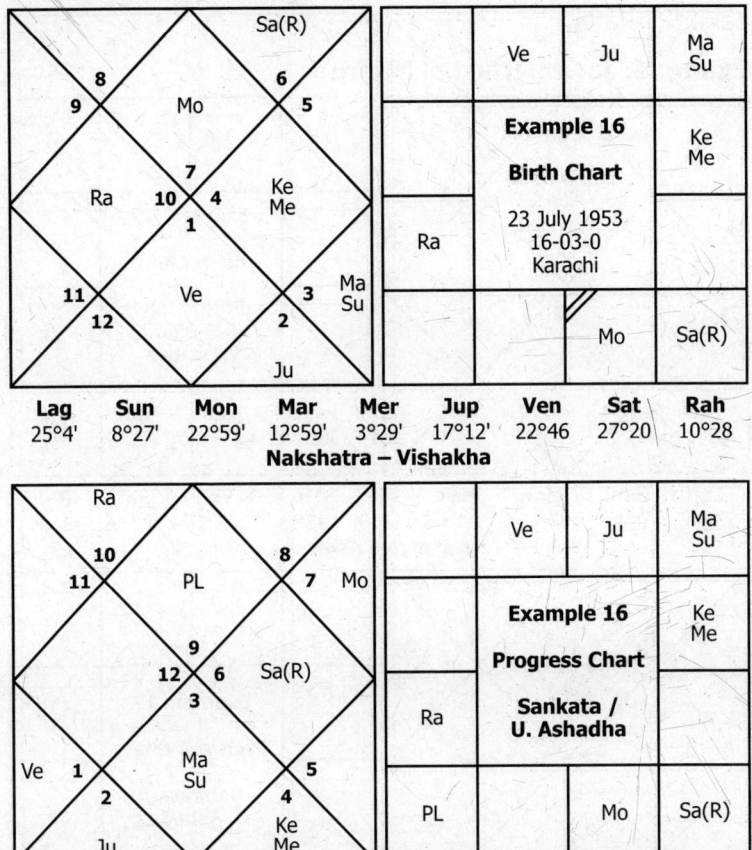

Lag	Sun	Mon	Mar	Mer	Jup	Ven	Sat	Rah
25°4'	8°27'	22°59'	12°59'	3°29'	17°12'	22°46'	27°20	10°28

Nakshatra – Vishakha

In the birth chart, Sun is the eleventh lord and placed in ninth house. Sun is with Mars and aspected by Saturn. Not a happy position of Sun. The ninth house is fully represented by Sun.

With Sagittarius progress lagna, Sun becomes the ninth lord. So Sun is again connected to ninth and is badly afflicted.

For father, the maraca is Saturn and that too very strong maraca as it is placed in second from ninth house. Jupiter is the eighth lord from ninth. Jupiter is aspecting Saturn and Rahu. Rahu acts as Saturn.

Her father was hanged to death on 4 April 1975 in sub period of Rahu.

Example: Jawaharlal Lal Nehru

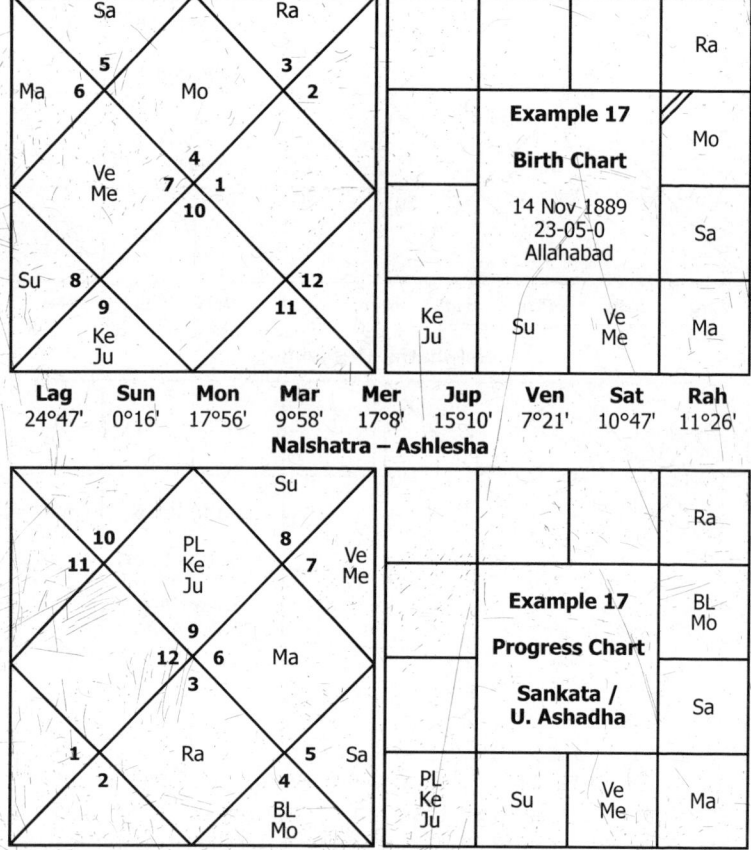

Lag	Sun	Mon	Mar	Mer	Jup	Ven	Sat	Rah
24°47'	0°16'	17°56'	9°58'	17°8'	15°10'	7°21'	10°47'	11°26'

Nalshatra – Ashlesha

Sun is the second lord of birth chart. It is placed in fifth house and is not aspected by any planet. Sun is in subh Kartari. It can give good results.

In the progress chart, Sun has moved to twelfth house. The tenth lord of birth chart is now in tenth house. The birth lagna lord is in eighth and the self and mind is scheming. Rahu acts as Mercury and Mercury is in eleventh house.

He became PM in Sankata sub itself.

Example: Queen Victoria

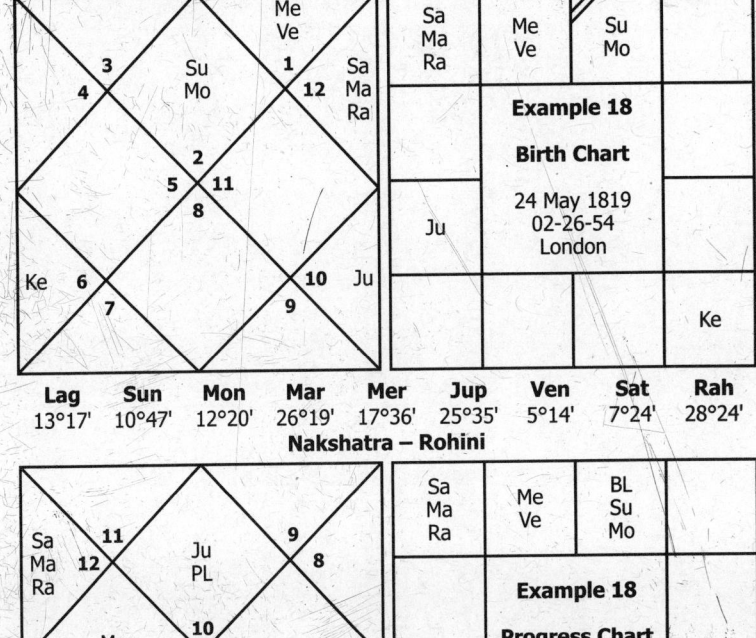

		Me Ve			Sa Ma Ra	Me Ve		Su Mo

Lag | Sun | Mon | Mar | Mer | Jup | Ven | Sat | Rah
13°17' | 10°47' | 12°20' | 26°19' | 17°36' | 25°35' | 5°14' | 7°24' | 28°24'

Nakshatra – Rohini

Sun is the fourth lord of birth chart and is in lagna with exalted third lord Moon. It is aspected by eighth lord Jupiter. Sun can give longevity related events. It is also aspected by Saturn.

In progress chart, Saturn and Moon are the maracas. Moon is with Sun and is aspected by Saturn. For this progress lagna, Sun is the eighth lord, connected with birth eighth lord.

She died on 22 Jan. 1901 in the sub of Mars. Mars is the birth maraca.